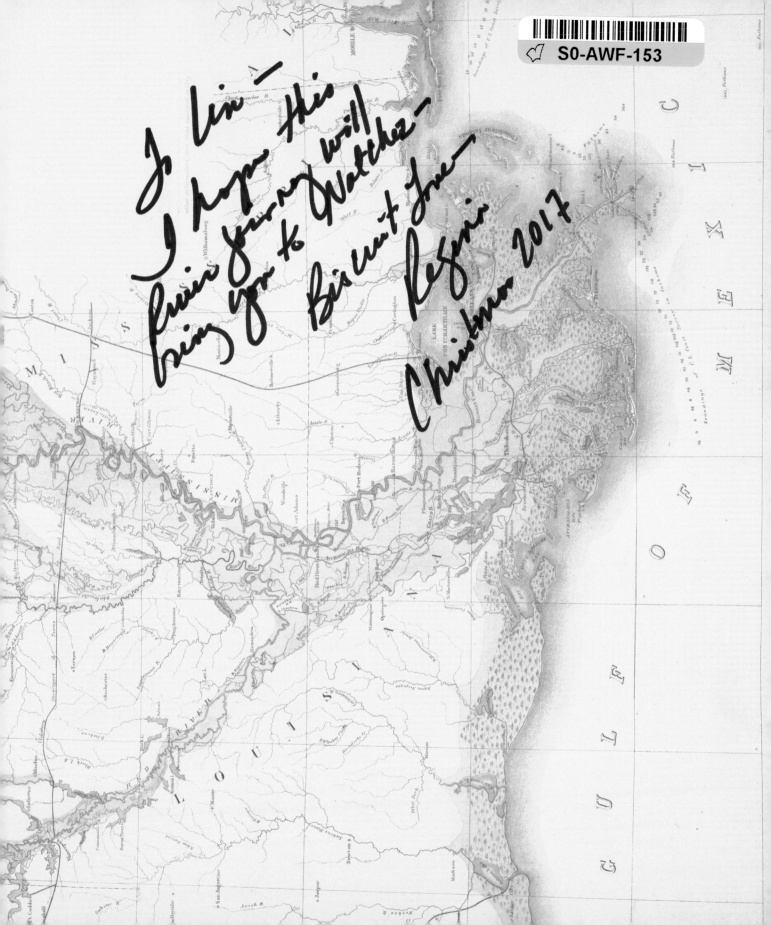

To Lin —
I hope this
business journey will
bring you to Natchez —
Biscuit Love —
Regina
Christmas 2017

Mississippi Current
COOKBOOK
A CULINARY JOURNEY DOWN AMERICA'S GREATEST RIVER

REGINA CHARBONEAU

Photographs by Ben Fink
Foreword by Julia Reed

LP

LYONS PRESS
Guilford, Connecticut

An imprint of Globe Pequot Press

Project editor: Meredith Dias
Text design: Sheryl Kober
Layout artist: Nancy Freeborn

Library of Congress Cataloging-in-Publication Data is available on file.
ISBN 978-0-7627-9374-7

Printed in the United States of America
10 9 8 7 6 5 4 3 2 1

Contents

Part I: The Headwaters: The Upper Mississippi River Region

Part II: Twain Country: The Middle Mississippi River Region

Biscuit Love

The first time I met Regina Charboneau was in her kitchen at Twin Oaks, the 1832 plantation house in Natchez she and her husband bought and lovingly restored in 2000. It could not have been a more fitting and (for me, at least) delightful introduction. She was making biscuits, a fairly routine task that in Regina's hands becomes a tour de force. Drawing from the croissant-making skills she learned as a culinary student in Paris, she rolls and folds and rolls and folds until the dough is streaked with gorgeous buttery ribbons. The end products are the flakiest, most meltingly delicious biscuits I've ever tasted, in a long and active life of tasting them.

Since then, I've returned to Twin Oaks many times for infusions of what those of us lucky enough to be in Regina's orbit all refer to as "Biscuit Love"—which is also a metaphor for her great company, innate graciousness, and bottomless generosity. I would happily follow Regina up and down the Mississippi for an extended dose of her hospitality and more examples of her inventive and always superb cooking. But now in *Mississippi Current* she has brought the River and its bounty home to me and all her lucky readers instead.

Like Regina, I was born on the Mississippi, about two hours north of Natchez in the Delta town of Greenville. My father's family's roots go back many generations in Caruthersville, Missouri, where there's a waterfront statue of my great-grandfather, a river engineer. Growing up, some of the most exciting social events I attended were the christenings of towboats at our once busy downtown port. In this book, I learned that the *J.M. White*, a riverboat so opulent that it was known as "the floating palace," traveled the river between New Orleans and Greenville from 1868 to 1886.

So I know what Regina, a seventh-generation Natchezian, means when she says she has Mississippi River water running through her veins. But what I didn't know about was the richness of the culinary traditions along the River from Minnesota to its mouth. While I've tasted Kentucky Burgoo and know well the pleasures of New Orleans's Eggs Sardou, gin fizzes, and Sazeracs, I had no idea of the crawfish parties hosted by Minnesota's sizable Swedish population or the Oktoberfest gatherings introduced by the German settlers in La Crosse, Wisconsin. I grew up eating the cultural phenomenon known as the Delta hot tamale (and can't wait to make and taste Regina's ingenious version made with smoked catfish), but now I'm equally fascinated by the toasted ravioli that St. Louis's Italian citizenry has made a local tradition.

Mississippi Current is a cultural and culinary treasure. Anyone interested in our country's vivid history or native foodways should make this fascinating journey with the ever fabulous Regina.

—Julia Reed

Introduction

The Mississippi River is America's greatest. At 2,340 miles in length, the River has provided our nation with an essential waterway for transporting goods and people, played an important role in wars and territorial disputes, and even become part of the American vernacular. How often have you heard someone ask, "Is that east or west of the Mississippi?" Popular food brands have different names east and west of the River: Edy's ice cream is west and Dreyer's ice cream east; Hellmann's mayonnaise west and Best Foods east. Call letters assigned to radio stations east of the Mississippi begin with the letter *W*, while those west of the River start with the letter *K*.

The Mississippi River also has an extraordinarily rich culinary history influenced by those who have inhabited its shores and waters, making it one of the most significant foodways in America. While many people are familiar with food from the lower stretch of the River—Memphis barbecue, Louisiana's Cajun cooking, and New Orleans's Creole traditions—few are aware of Minnesota's fish fries, Wisconsin's Oktoberfest celebrations, and Arkansas's farm suppers.

Join me on a culinary journey with menus and recipes from up and down the Mississippi, from the headwaters in Minnesota to the mouth at the Gulf of Mexico. You'll discover the foods and flavors as we visit in the cities and towns, farms, and historical homes on the River.

I am of the seventh generation of my family to be born in Natchez on the River. Food and entertaining have always been at the center of my life.

My mother was known for hosting endless dinners and parties with what seemed like no effort at all. People in town still talk about my father's cooking skills that came from his deep Louisiana roots. When I decided to travel away from the River, I really traveled away—Anchorage, Paris, San Francisco, Minneapolis, and New York. But no matter how many miles I traveled or the number of years I stayed away, none of those places really felt like home. Home was and always will be Natchez. And just like my parents', my life has always centered around food and entertaining. On my return, my husband Doug and I purchased Twin Oaks, primarily to raise our sons Jean-Luc and Martin as eighth-generations on the River. This historic house was perfect for my love of entertaining. Its six guest rooms allow people to come and partake in my culinary weekends, with cooking classes and tours of historic homes in Natchez, ours and others. Having learned so much about historic preservation with our 1832 home, we were hooked enough to find one of the oldest buildings in the Mississippi Territory and the oldest building in Natchez—the 1789 King's Tavern—to restore. It's now a restaurant offering wood-fired flatbreads and craft cocktails featuring many of the liquors made along the River, including the Charboneau Rum created by Doug and our son Jean-Luc in a distillery on the King's Tavern property. I would say I am home to stay.

Before my return, my Natchezian cooking roots went with me wherever I lived. After attending cooking school in Paris, I began to combine southern cooking and many of the ingredients that were native to the Lower Mississippi region—pecans, catfish, crawfish, oysters, and collard and mustard greens—with classic French influences. No matter where I lived or cooked, the foods of my River were woven into my dishes.

In my years away, Minneapolis held me for a while for two reasons—its location on the Mississippi and because it's my husband Doug's hometown. From the first day we met in Anchorage many years ago, it was the River that connected us, even though our culinary vocabularies were foreign to each other. For the first time I heard words like pierogi, spaetzle, brats, Polish sausage, and White Castle. My culinary lexicon likewise held new words for him: gumbo, oysters, mustard greens, jambalaya, and muffalettos. Through the years, our glossaries blended and expanded along with the cultural changes along the Mississippi.

In early 2011, when the new owners of the *American Queen* were planning the return of this original paddle-wheel steamboat to the River the following spring, they asked me to create the culinary direction for the opulent vessel. In doing so I embraced the entire River, not just my familiar ground. I learned about food from the Chippewa Native Americans, Scandinavians, Poles and other Eastern Europeans, and Hmong settlers along the Upper Mississippi; Germans, Italians, French, and Serbians in the middle region; and French, Spanish, English, Irish, Creole, African, and Vietnamese in the lower region. The indigenous foods and unique traditions in these three regions inspired me to expand my culinary boundaries. For the *American Queen* I created recipes using the cultural and agricultural influences of the cities and towns that lined the River, while adding my personal style to create contemporary versions of many dishes.

My travels along this majestic waterway have made me aware of how much America's greatest river and its shores have to offer. My hope is that you will take away menus for every season and occasion rich with recipes and ideas for entertaining, Mississippi River style. Let me introduce you to *Mississippi Current*.

HOW TO USE THE BOOK

Although *Mississippi Current* is divided into three regions with specific menus and recipes, you are certainly welcome to mix and match them as you see fit and depending on the availability of seasonal ingredients. I couldn't help but be enthusiastic about all that each region has to offer. While many menus contain multiple courses, feel free to serve as many or as few as you wish. It is fine to trim menus down if you choose, as well as to borrow recipes from other stops along the mighty River.

Part I
The Headwaters: The Upper Mississippi River Region

ST. PAUL, MINNESOTA, TO QUINCY, ILLINOIS

amuel Clemens's love for the Upper Mississippi rivals my love of the Lower Mississippi. In an interview with the *Chicago Tribune* in July 1886 he said, "Along the Upper Mississippi every hour brings something new. There are crowds of odd islands, bluffs, prairies, hills, woods, and villages—everything one could desire to amuse the children. Few people ever think of going there; however, Dickens, Corbett, Mother Trollope, and the other discriminating English people who 'wrote up' the country before 1842 had hardly an idea that such a stretch of river scenery existed. Their successors have followed in their footsteps; and as we form our opinions of our country from what other people say of us, of course we ignore the finest part of the Mississippi."

The Dakota, Chippewa, and Hopewell tribes were the region's first known inhabitants. Many of their culinary traditions and local ingredients—such as wild rice, pumpkin, corn, and pawpaws—are still in use. French and Spanish explorers began paddling the River in the 1500s, and the Upper Mississippi subsequently became a refuge for immigrants from around the globe. This part of the River is a mosaic of cultures, with diverse influences from German, Polish, Czech, French, Swedish, Norwegian, Vietnamese, and Hmong peoples. Hundreds of years of this melting pot have left a culinary legacy as rich as the silt on the banks of the Mississippi.

The river towns of Minnesota all grew as riverboat ports, especially St. Paul, but also St.

Anthony and Minneapolis. The state's population reached 200,000 by 1860, and most of those arrived by riverboat. New immigrants from Sweden settled in the ravine of Phalen's Creek. A similar community just downstream called Connemara was the home of Irish immigrants. By the 1890s in Minnesota, foreign-language newspapers flourished, with local publications in German, French, Norwegian, Swedish, Danish, Polish, and Czech. There was also an African-American paper, the *Appeal*, and the *Jewish Weekly* for Jewish immigrants. By the turn of the nineteenth century, the earliest immigrants were accepted as part of the community, but new immigrants from Eastern Europe and Russia faced discrimination. Whether accepted or not, all of the settlers left behind a culinary influence and cultural legacy that remain today.

During the Vietnam War the Hmong people of northern Vietnam and Laos worked with pro-American forces. After the Communist takeover of Saigon and Laos in 1975, the Hmong were subject to violent retributions. Thus began a significant migration of Hmong to the St. Paul area, and the most recent changes to the Upper River's table. Today a visit to a farmers' market in Minneapolis or St. Paul finds many Hmong farmers providing ingredients such as specialty greens, herbs, lemongrass, sweet onions, and raspberries, all locally grown, as well as imported lychees and longans.

GREAT RIVER ROAD PICNIC (FOR 6)

River Wine Spritzers with Strawberry–Black Pepper Syrup

Strawberry Lemonade

Pork and Ginger Slaw Sandwiches

Wild Rice Salad with Dried Apricots and Walnuts

Baked Sweet Potato Chips

Mississippi Mud Cookies

Some of the most stunning scenery along the Mississippi River can be found near the headwaters. The Great River Road National Scenic Byway starts at Itasca State Park in northern Minnesota and rambles 575 miles to the end of the state on both sides of the River, passing through lush green forests and the central lakes region as well as the Twin Cities, St. Paul and Minneapolis. Along the full 3,000 miles of the ten-state river roadway are plenty of parks, waterfalls, and locks and dams to make an ideal setting for a leisurely picnic.

Many of the Upper Mississippi region's winemakers are experimenting with grapes such Vignoles and Seyval that flourish in colder climates. Wines from this area tend to be on the sweet side, making them ideal for flavored wine-based drinks such as coolers and spritzers. (For a list of regional wineries that ship to other states, go to greatriver

roadwinetrail.org.) Any Chablis or un-oaked Chardonnay can be used for the spritzers. A homemade infused syrup is composed of fresh berries, sugar, and vodka. Vodka quickly extracts the berries' flavor, and you can add a bit of black pepper to the infusion to give it a mysterious zip.

Whether picnicking in a park or your backyard, offer the kids strawberry lemonade and the adults these flavored wine spritzers. Both beverages can be stored and served in eight-ounce Mason jars for easy travel and stylish serving. Pork sandwiches with a ginger-flavored slaw and homemade sweet potato chips are also perfect picnic fare. A wild rice salad with dried fruit and nuts is a nice change from the usual mayonnaise-laden salads. And remember, the dough for the chocolate cookies can be made weeks ahead and frozen—just remove from the freezer and bake when needed.

River Wine Spritzers with Strawberry–Black Pepper Syrup

2 cups hulled and quartered
  strawberries

1 cup sugar

1 tablespoon cracked black pepper

¼ cup fresh lemon juice

¼ cup vodka

1 (750-ml) bottle dry white wine

6 lemon twists

Sparkling water

1. Place the strawberries, sugar, and pepper in a Mason jar. To avoid fruit flies, cover the jar and let it sit for 3 hours. Stir in the lemon juice and vodka and let sit overnight.

2. Using a wooden spoon, mash the fruit well. Drain the strawberry-vodka syrup though a fine mesh into a clean jar. Discard the sediment.

3. If serving immediately, put 2 tablespoons of the strawberry-vodka syrup in each of six 8-ounce Mason jars. Add ice, five ounces of the white wine, and a lemon twist to each jar. Cover and shake well before serving. Top off with sparkling water and ice to taste.

 ## Strawberry Lemonade

1½ cups sugar

1 pint fresh strawberries, hulled

1 cup fresh lemon juice

1 tablespoon lemon zest

Put the sugar, strawberries, and 1 cup boiling water in a blender and puree. Strain the mixture, discarding the sediment, into a plastic container for transporting. Stir in the lemon juice, zest, and 3 cups cold water. Refrigerate and pour over ice in glasses to serve.

If taking the drinks on a picnic, pack the ice and sparkling water separately, and add some to each jar just before serving.

Pork and Ginger Slaw Sandwiches

Pork Roast

2 tablespoons extra virgin olive oil

2 tablespoons low-sodium soy sauce

4 garlic cloves

2 teaspoons kosher salt

2 teaspoons coarse black pepper

2 pounds boneless pork loin roast, rinsed and patted dry

1. Preheat the oven to 375°F.

2. Put the olive oil, soy sauce, and garlic into a blender. Blend until the garlic is pureed. Add the salt and pepper and blend briefly to combine. Smear the mixture all over the pork. Place the pork, fat side up, in a roasting pan.

3. Roast for 30 minutes at 375°F, then turn down the oven to 325°F, and continue roasting until an instant-read thermometer inserted into the thickest part of the meat reads 145°F, about 30 minutes. Remove the pork from the oven and let it rest until the juices are reabsorbed into the meat, 15 to 20 minutes. If there's time, cover and refrigerate for 2 hours or overnight for easier slicing.

Ginger Slaw

3 tablespoons sesame oil

2 tablespoons rice wine vinegar

1 tablespoon packed light brown sugar

1 tablespoon peeled and grated fresh ginger

2 teaspoons fresh lime juice

1 teaspoon white vinegar

1 tablespoon thinly sliced fresh basil leaves

1 tablespoon thinly sliced fresh mint leaves

1 (1-pound) package coleslaw mix

½ cup diced green onions, tops only

6 6-inch French baguettes

1. Whisk together the sesame oil, rice wine vinegar, brown sugar, ginger, lime juice, and white vinegar in a large bowl until the sugar dissolves. Stir in the basil and mint.

2. Add the slaw mix and green onions and toss well before serving.

Assembly

Slice the baguettes in half lengthwise and toast. Slice the Pork Roast into ¼ inch slices and divide evenly for 6 sandwiches. Top pork with Ginger Slaw. Wrap the sandwiches in parchment paper. (*Note:* These can be made 2–3 hours in advance.)

Cook the pork roast and make the slaw dressing the day before the picnic. Meat is easier to slice for sandwiches once it has been chilled.

1 cup wild rice

3 teaspoons kosher salt, divided

3 tablespoons extra virgin olive oil

2 tablespoons fresh orange juice

2 tablespoons raspberry vinegar

*½ cup chopped walnuts, lightly
 toasted (page 311)*

½ cup diced dried apricots

¼ cup dried cranberries

¼ cup golden raisins

*2 tablespoons chopped green onions,
 white bottoms and green tops*

*½ teaspoon freshly ground black
 pepper*

*For best results, add the other
ingredients to the warm rice.
Make it a day ahead, but, as
with all grain salads, serve it
at room temperature.*

1. Combine 4 cups water, the wild rice, and 2 teaspoons of the salt in a saucepan. Bring to a boil, lower the heat to a simmer, and cook, uncovered, until the rice is tender, 50 to 60 minutes. Drain the rice in a colander and then return it to the saucepan. Cover and let steam, off the heat, for 10 minutes.

2. While the rice is still warm, add the remaining 1 teaspoon salt, the olive oil, orange juice, and vinegar and stir well to coat the rice. Add the walnuts, apricots, cranberries, raisins, green onions, and pepper and toss well.

3. Transfer to a bowl and serve at room temperature.

1. Preheat the oven to 400°F. Line two baking sheets with aluminum foil.

2. Slice the potatoes ⅛-inch thick using a handheld slicer.

3. Arrange the slices in single layers on the prepared baking sheets. Drizzle with the oil, tossing to coat.

4. Bake the potatoes until edges begin to crisp. Using a spatula, turn the chips, and bake until the centers are soft and the edges are crisp, 12 to 14 minutes.

5. Remove from the oven and sprinkle the hot chips with the sea salt. Let stand for 10 minutes before serving, or cool completely and store in an airtight container. The chips are best eaten within 2 days.

2 large sweet potatoes, peeled
1 tablespoon extra virgin olive oil
½ teaspoon sea salt

A mandoline is a handy tool to have for thinly slicing fruit and vegetables. Plastic handheld slicers are available for less than twenty dollars.

The Upper Mississippi River Valley is the largest wine region in America. In 2009 it was designated by the Bureau of Alcohol, Tobacco, and Firearms (ATF) as an American Viticultural Area, an "official" grape-growing region that owes its status to the geography of the area and its soils, subsoils, and microclimates. The Upper Mississippi River Valley Viticultural Area includes the protected Upper Mississippi River Bluff Lands Alliance, which covers 50,000 acres of prairies, wetlands, and woodlands in four states. It measures 120 miles east to west and 225 miles north to south in southeastern Minnesota, southwestern Wisconsin, northwestern Illinois, and northeastern Iowa.

Mississippi Mud Cookies

1. Preheat the oven to 350°F. Line two baking sheets with parchment paper.

2. Whisk the flour, baking powder, and salt together in a bowl.

3. Melt 1 cup of the chocolate chips in a small microwave-safe bowl.

4. Cream the butter and sugar in the bowl of a stand mixer until light and fluffy, about 3 minutes. Add the eggs one at a time, blending well after each addition, stopping the machine as necessary to scrape down the sides. Add the melted chocolate and vanilla and mix until blended. Gradually add the dry ingredients into the chocolate mixture, and mix until blended. Using a rubber spatula, fold in the pecans, ½ cup of the chocolate chips, and the miniature marshmallows.

5. Drop the dough by heaping tablespoons, about 2 inches apart, onto the lined baking sheets. Bake the cookies until set, 10 to 12 minutes. Transfer the cookies to wire racks.

6. Combine the remaining 1 cup chocolate chips and the heavy cream in a microwave-safe bowl. Melt until smooth. Stir well. Dip a fork into the chocolate sauce and, using a zigzag motion, drizzle the melted chocolate on top of the cooled cookies.

MAKES 2 DOZEN

1½ cups all-purpose flour

1 teaspoon baking powder

½ teaspoon table salt

2½ cups semisweet chocolate chips, divided

½ cup (1 stick) salted butter, at room temperature

1 cup sugar

2 large eggs

1 teaspoon pure vanilla extract

1 cup chopped pecans

1½ cups miniature marshmallows

1 tablespoon heavy cream

> Some say that the word "Mississippi" is derived from the Chippewa words *mici zibi*, which mean "great river" in that Algonquin language, and which entered French as "Messipi." The earliest written use of the name is found on an early 1680s map recording the explorations of René-Robert Cavelier, Sieur de La Salle.

WILD RICE HARVEST DINNER (FOR 4)

Radish and Apple Salad

Split Pea–Smoked Tomato Soup

Chicken Breasts Stuffed with Wild Rice, Roasted Squash, and Walnut-Sage Pesto

Fry Bread with Rosemary-Garlic Hot Pepper Oil

Apple-Molasses Pudding

This menu is influenced by the Mississippi Chippewa, an Ojibwa band who have inhabited the headwaters of the Mississippi River for more than 250 years. Wild rice grown on Minnesota state waters is regulated and must be harvested in keeping with Native American traditions. Minnesota wild rice, for example, must be harvested from canoe, using only a pole for power and two rice-beater sticks as flails to knock the mature seeds into the bottom of the boat.

Long before the arrival of Europeans in this region, the Native Americans of the Upper Mississippi used pumpkin and other squash roasted, boiled, and dried as a major food source. The pairing of two indigenous ingredients seemed like a natural combination of flavors, with the earthiness of the wild rice and the sweetness of roasted pumpkin to stuff a chicken breast or to serve as a meatless side dish. Apples are another regional favorite. More than two dozen apple growers sell their produce along the fertile bluffs of the Upper Mississippi River under the Mississippi Valley Fruit Company label. Favorites include Zestar, Honeycrisp, Haralson, Cortland, and Regent.

I find the best salads are often the simplest, like this combination of autumn radishes and thinly sliced tart apples. I wanted a light salad to complement the richness of the split pea soup, sparked by the addition of smoked tomatoes. As the main course, chicken breasts with wild rice and roasted pumpkin showcase the best ingredients from this region. Vegetarians in your party? Eliminate the chicken breasts and serve the wild rice and squash together. To impart a twist to traditional Indian fry bread, add hot pepper oil flavored with fresh rosemary and garlic. Fry bread can be made ahead and reheated. Indian pudding is possibly the precursor to upside-down cakes.

2 apples, cored and thinly sliced

½ small red onion, thinly sliced

4 red radishes, thinly sliced

1 tablespoon extra virgin olive oil

1 tablespoon fresh orange juice

1 teaspoon honey

¼ teaspoon kosher salt

¼ teaspoon freshly ground black
  pepper

1 sprig fresh rosemary

1 cup arugula

1. Combine the sliced apples, onions, radishes, olive oil, orange juice, and honey in a bowl. Toss well and season with salt and pepper. Add the rosemary sprig, cover, and refrigerate for 2 hours.

2. Remove the rosemary before spooning the salad onto a bed of arugula.

1. Melt the butter in a large pot over medium heat. Add the pureed onion and cook until golden brown, 3 to 4 minutes.

2. Add the split peas, 1 quart water, and any reserved juice from the smoked tomatoes. Bring to a boil. Lower the heat and simmer uncovered for 45 minutes, stirring every 10 to 15 minutes.

3. Add half of the smoked tomato pieces, the garlic, and the oregano and simmer for another 15 minutes.

4. Adjust the seasoning to taste. (I like to add a few dashes of hot sauce.)

5. Ladle the soup into four bowls and garnish with the remaining smoked tomatoes. Serve hot.

This soup may be prepared ahead. Let cool completely before refrigerating. It freezes well.

2 tablespoons salted butter

1 small white onion, peeled and pureed in a food processor

1 cup split peas, rinsed and picked over

1 recipe Oven-Smoked Tomatoes (page 313)

1 teaspoon minced garlic

½ teaspoon minced fresh oregano leaves

Tabasco, or other hot pepper sauce, optional

½ cup wild rice

2½ teaspoons kosher salt, divided

1 pound fresh butternut squash, halved and seeds removed (pumpkin can be substituted)

3 tablespoons extra virgin olive oil, divided

1 teaspoon freshly ground black pepper

½ cup diced white onions

¼ cup diced green onions, tops and white bottoms

1 garlic clove, minced

2 fresh sage leaves, thinly sliced

4 (6-ounce) boneless, skinless chicken breast halves, pounded to ¼-inch thickness

¼ cup dry white wine

½ cup Walnut-Sage Pesto (page 19)

The pesto can be made 2 days ahead. Bring to room temperature before using. Leftover pesto is excellent on Bacon-Sweet Potato Pierogi (page 39) or tossed with Spinach Spaetzle (page 78).

1. Place the rice, 2 cups water, and 1 teaspoon of the salt in a saucepan. Bring to a boil, then lower the heat and simmer, uncovered, until the rice is tender, 50 to 60 minutes. Drain the rice in a colander and return it to the saucepan. Cover and let steam, off the heat, for 10 minutes.

2. Preheat the oven to 400°F. Arrange the butternut squash halves in a baking dish in a single layer. Toss the squash with 1 tablespoon of the olive oil, ½ teaspoon of the salt, and ½ teaspoon of the pepper. Bake cut side up until brown at the edges and easily pierced with a fork, about 30 to 45 minutes. Remove the squash from the oven. When cool enough to handle, peel off the skin with a knife. Cut the squash into ½-inch cubes. Lower the heat to 350°F.

3. Heat 1 tablespoon of the olive oil in a skillet over medium heat until almost smoking. Add the white onions and cook until soft, about 3 to 4 minutes. Add the green onions and garlic and sauté for 1 minute. Add the cooked wild rice and stir until all of the ingredients are well combined. Stir in the squash, being careful not to overmix.

4. Lay the chicken breasts, skin side down, on a work surface, and lightly season with the remaining 1 teaspoon salt and ½ teaspoon pepper. Spread ⅓ cup rice-squash mixture across the bottom of each breast. Roll up and secure with wooden toothpicks.

5. Heat the remaining 1 tablespoon olive oil over medium heat in an ovenproof skillet large enough to hold the chicken in a single layer. Add the chicken breasts to the pan and brown on both sides, about 2 minutes per side. Add the white wine to the skillet. Cover and bake until the chicken is cooked through, about 25 minutes. Spoon 2 tablespoons of the Walnut-Sage Pesto on top of each chicken breast and serve hot.

Walnut-Sage Pesto

1. Combine the parsley, olive oil, sage, and roasted garlic in a food processor. Process until pureed.

2. Add the walnuts and salt and pulse to finely chop the walnuts. (The pesto should be coarse, not smooth.)

3. If not using immediately, transfer to a covered container and refrigerate.

MAKES 2½ CUPS

¼ cup chopped fresh parsley

¼ cup extra virgin olive oil

6 fresh sage leaves

2 cloves Roasted Garlic (page 314)

2 cups walnuts, lightly toasted (page 311)

½ teaspoon kosher salt

Fry Bread with Rosemary-Garlic Hot Pepper Oil

**MAKES 4 (6-INCH) ROUND
FLATBREADS**

1½ cups all-purpose flour, divided

2 teaspoons nonfat dry milk

1 teaspoon baking powder

½ teaspoon kosher salt

2 teaspoons fresh rosemary

Vegetable oil, for frying

*1 recipe Rosemary-Garlic Hot
    Pepper Oil (below)*

1. Sift together 1 cup of the flour, the dry milk, baking powder and salt, into a large bowl. Then add rosemary. Add ½ cup water and stir with a fork until the mixture comes together into a tacky dough. Flour your hands well, using some of the remaining ½ cup flour. Using your hands, mix until the dough forms a soft and slightly sticky ball, being careful not to overwork the dough. Flour your hands generously and lightly flour a work surface with the remaining flour. Divide the dough into four pieces, and stretch and pat each piece into a 6-inch round. Let rest while oil heats.

2. Clip a deep-frying thermometer to the side of a dutch oven. Add oil to a depth of 2 inches and heat to 350°F. (Alternatively, an electric skillet or deep fryer set to 350°F can be used.) Preheat the oven to 175°F.

3. Using tongs, gently lower one of the rounds into the hot oil. Press down on the dough as it fries, so the top is submerged in the hot oil. Fry until golden brown, about 3 minutes, and then turn and fry the other side. Place the cooked fry bread on a paper towel or a brown paper bag to drain. Repeat with the remaining pieces of dough. To keep the fry bread warm, wrap in aluminum foil and place in the preheated oven for up to 1 hour.

4. Serve warm, with Rosemary-Garlic Hot Pepper Oil for dipping.

Rosemary-Garlic Hot Pepper Oil

MAKES ½ CUP

4 garlic cloves, peeled

½ cup extra virgin olive oil, divided

1 sprig fresh rosemary

½ teaspoon red pepper flakes

½ teaspoon kosher salt

1. Preheat the oven to 300°F. Place the garlic cloves in a small ovenproof skillet and drizzle with ½ teaspoon of the olive oil. Bake until the garlic is lightly browned and soft, about 15 minutes.

2. Remove the skillet from the oven and add the remaining olive oil, rosemary, red pepper flakes, and salt. Simmer over low heat for 5 minutes.

3. Pour the oil into a small bowl, discarding the rosemary, and serve as a dipping sauce for the fry bread.

Apple-Molasses Pudding

1. Preheat the oven to 350°F. Spray a 10 × 6-inch baking dish with vegetable oil spray.

2. Toss the sliced apples with ⅓ cup of the brown sugar in a bowl.

3. Combine the molasses, ¼ cup (½ stick) of the butter, the cornstarch, and 1 cup water in a saucepan and cook over low heat until thickened, about 4 minutes. Pour the mixture into the prepared baking dish.

4. Whisk together the flour, baking powder, salt, and remaining ⅔ cup brown sugar in a bowl. Add the remaining ¼ cup butter and the milk and mix until you have a smooth batter. Stir in the apples and pour the batter over the syrup in the baking dish.

5. Bake until the pudding is golden brown and firm around the edges, about 30 minutes. Let cool slightly before serving.

Vegetable oil spray

2½ cups peeled, cored, and sliced apples (about 3 medium apples)

1 cup packed light brown sugar, divided

1 cup molasses

½ cup (1 stick) salted butter, at room temperature, divided

1 tablespoon cornstarch

1⅓ cups sifted all-purpose flour

2½ teaspoons baking powder

½ teaspoon table salt

½ cup milk

MINNESOTA FISH FRY (FOR 6)

Watermelon, Feta, and Mint Salad

Broccoli and Red Cabbage Slaw with Lemon Dressing

Fried Walleye in Corn Flour Batter

Wild Rice and Corn Fritters

Cranberry Ketchup

Spicy Aïoli

Brown Sugar Custards and Brown Sugar–Toffee Cookies

Along the Upper Mississippi River during Lenten season, thousands of pounds of freshwater fish are fried to raise money for churches, fire brigades, and other local community groups in Minnesota and Wisconsin. Walleye, a delicate freshwater fish native to Canada and the northern United States, has always been the fish of choice in this area. But if you can't find walleye, look for yellow perch, lake trout, Pacific cod, or farm-raised catfish—they will be delicious.

When frying, I dust fish with corn flour instead of all-purpose flour, for a lighter coating. You can put the hot oil from frying the fish to more good use by cooking up some Wild Rice and Corn Fritters. (For information on deep-frying, see page 310.) The salads and sauces that accompany the fish and fritters in this menu are welcome changes from the usual slaw and cocktail and tartar sauces.

This is a perfect menu to pair with beer. Fill a large tub with ice and bottles of local craft beers, such as pale ale, cream ale, or British-style bitter beer. Local breweries are popping up everywhere, especially along the Mississippi River. In 2006, Surly Brewing opened a wave of edgy microbreweries; Brainerd Lakes Beer, Cold Spring, Canal Park, Flat Earth, and Great Waters are just a few. The fans who love them became known as the Surly Nation and pushed the so-called Surly Bill. Passed in 2011, it allows Minnesota breweries to sell their own beer on the premises.

1 small watermelon, about
  2 pounds

8 ounces feta, crumbled

4 fresh mint leaves, thinly sliced

1. Slice the watermelon in half lengthwise and then slice again horizontally to make 4 quarters. Using a fork, gently remove as many seeds as possible from the watermelon.

2. Lay one melon quarter flat on a work surface. Insert a melon baller into the center of the watermelon flesh and twist in a complete circular motion to form a ball. Put each ball in a serving bowl. When you get to the rind, don't dig into it; you want just the sweetest, red part of the melon.

3. Sprinkle the feta and mint over the melon balls and serve.

The melon balls can be prepared the day before and stored in a plastic container with a lid, but add the feta and mint no more than 1 hour before serving.

1. Whisk together the lemon juice, sugar, and vinegar in a small bowl. Add the mayonnaise and lemon zest and whisk until smooth.

2. Combine the cabbage, broccoli, and raisins in a serving bowl. Add the dressing and toss to coat. Cover and refrigerate for at least 2 and up to 6 hours before serving. Serve chilled.

The dressing can be made ahead and refrigerated for 3 to 4 days.

1 tablespoon fresh lemon juice

2 teaspoons sugar

1 teaspoon apple cider vinegar

3 tablespoons mayonnaise

1 teaspoon finely grated lemon zest

3 cups shredded red cabbage

2 cups broccoli florets

½ cup golden raisins

Stocks in the News
The Good News...
GameStop
$40.94
Finisar
$15.80
FNSR
Daily closes
65-day moving average

1. Whisk together the buttermilk, egg, and ½ cup water in a dish shallow enough to hold the fillets in a single layer. Add 2 teaspoons of the salt, ½ teaspoon garlic powder, and ¼ teaspoon cayenne, and whisk until well combined.

2. Arrange the fillets in the seasoned buttermilk in a single layer. Cover and refrigerate for 30 minutes to 1 hour before frying.

3. Clip a deep-frying thermometer to the side of a dutch oven. Half fill the pot with oil and heat to 350°F. (Alternatively, an electric skillet or deep fryer set to 350°F can be used.)

4. Preheat the oven to 175°F. While the oil is heating, whisk together the corn flour, remaining 1 teaspoon salt, 1 teaspoon black pepper, ½ teaspoon garlic powder, and ¼ teaspoon cayenne in a shallow dish.

5. Remove the fillets one at a time from the egg wash, shaking to remove any excess liquid, and dredge in the seasoned corn flour to coat both sides. Gently lower the fillets into the hot oil in batches, being careful not to overcrowd the pot. Fry the fish until golden brown, 3 to 4 minutes per side, turning once. Place the cooked fish on a paper-towel-lined baking sheet and place in the oven to keep warm while cooking the remaining fish fillets and Wild Rice and Corn Fritters (page 28). Do not cover or crowd the fillets, or the fish will become soggy. Keep the oil hot, replenishing as necessary, to fry the fritters. Serve hot.

1 cup buttermilk

1 large egg

3 teaspoons kosher salt, divided

1 teaspoon garlic powder, divided

½ teaspoon cayenne, divided

6 (6- to 7-ounce) firm white fish fillets, such as walleye, perch, trout, or cod, cut into 3-inch pieces

Vegetable oil, for frying

2 cups corn flour (see Source Guide, page 316)

1 teaspoon freshly ground black pepper

Corn flour is finely ground and gluten free. Although made from corn, it has more the consistency of flour. It is not cornstarch. (What we know as cornstarch is often called corn flour in other countries.) Corn flour is not the same as masa harina, which is corn dried with lime and then ground, although they are both gluten free. Bob's Red Mill is a good source for certified organic and gluten free corn flour.

MAKES 1 DOZEN

¼ cup wild rice

1½ teaspoons kosher salt, divided

½ cup all-purpose flour

1½ teaspoons baking powder

½ teaspoon cayenne

1 cup fresh or frozen corn kernels,
   thawed and patted dry if frozen

1 large egg, separated

½ cup chopped green onions,
   tops and white bottoms

1 teaspoon minced garlic

If using frozen corn kernels instead of fresh, make sure they are thawed and patted dry before adding them to the batter. Wet or frozen corn will make the fritters soggy. Fry the fritters within an hour of shaping them.

1. Place the rice, 1 cup water, and ½ teaspoon of the salt in a saucepan. Bring to a boil, then lower the heat to a simmer and cook, uncovered, until the rice is tender, 50 to 60 minutes. Drain the rice in a colander and return it to the saucepan. Cover and let steam, off the heat, for 10 minutes. Let rice cool to room temperature, about 25 minutes.

2. Whisk together the flour, remaining 1 teaspoon salt, baking powder, and cayenne in a medium bowl. Stir the cooled rice, corn, egg yolk, green onions, and garlic into the flour mixture.

3. Using a handheld mixer, whip the egg white in a bowl until stiff enough to hold peaks, but not dry. With a rubber spatula, gently fold the whipped egg white into the rice-corn mixture, being careful not to overmix.

4. Using your hands, shape twelve 1-inch-round fritters, using about 2 tablespoons of the batter for each. Gently lower four fritters at a time into the 350°F oil left over from frying the fish. (Alternatively, clip a deep-frying thermometer to the side of a dutch oven. Half fill the pot with vegetable oil and heat to 350°F.) Fry the fritters until golden brown, 3 to 4 minutes per side, turning once. To test for doneness, insert a wooden skewer into the center of a fritter. If it comes out clean, the fritter is done. If there's batter on the skewer, return the fritter to the oil and cook for another minute.

5. Using tongs or a skimmer remove the fritters to paper towels or brown paper bags to drain. Serve hot.

Cranberry Ketchup

MAKES ABOUT 2½ CUPS

2 cups fresh or frozen cranberries, rinsed and picked over

½ cup white vinegar

¼ cup packed light brown sugar

1 tablespoon cane syrup, such as Steen's Pure Cane Syrup (see Source Guide, page 316)

1 tablespoon garlic powder

1 tablespoon onion powder

1 teaspoon kosher salt

¼ teaspoon ground allspice

1. Place the cranberries in a food processor and process until smooth.

2. Combine the cranberry puree, vinegar, brown sugar, cane syrup, garlic powder, onion powder, salt, and allspice in a saucepan and stir to blend.

3. Bring the mixture to a boil, then lower the heat to a simmer. Cook uncovered until the mixture is thick, about 10 minutes, stirring occasionally. Remove from the heat and let cool to room temperature.

4. Pour the ketchup into an airtight container, cover, and refrigerate until needed, or up to 2 weeks. The ketchup also can be frozen for up to 3 months.

Spicy Aïoli

MAKES 1½ CUPS

2 garlic cloves

2 large egg yolks

1 teaspoon Dijon mustard

1 teaspoon Tabasco, or other hot pepper sauce

1¼ cups extra virgin olive oil

1. Place the garlic and egg yolks in a food processor or blender. Process until the garlic is pureed and the yolks are pale yellow, 2 to 3 minutes.

2. Add the mustard and Tabasco to the egg yolk mixture and process to incorporate. With the motor running, slowly add the oil in a thin stream, processing until it is incorporated and the mixture is the consistency of mayonnaise.

The aïoli can be made in advance and refrigerated for up to 3 days.

Brown Sugar Custards

2 tablespoons salted butter

1½ cups packed light brown sugar, divided

1 quart heavy cream

2 teaspoons pure vanilla extract

7 large egg yolks

1. Preheat the oven to 325°F.

2. Melt the butter in a saucepan over low heat. Stir in ½ cup of the sugar and cook until sugar is dissolved, then divide the sugar among six 7-to-8-ounce ramekins or custard cups, swirling to coat the bottoms evenly. Arrange the ramekins in a large roasting pan.

3. Bring the cream and vanilla to a simmer in a medium saucepan over medium-high heat. Remove from the heat and let cool for about 10 minutes before adding to egg yolk mixture.

4. Whisk the remaining 1 cup brown sugar and the egg yolks in a bowl until well blended, about 2 minutes. Do not let the egg yolk mixture become frothy; overmixing will prevent the custards from setting well.

5. Gradually add the hot cream, whisking constantly.

6. Divide the custard among the prepared ramekins. Add enough hot water to the roasting pan to come halfway up the sides of the ramekins. Bake just until the custards are firm, yet jiggle slightly when shaken, 40 to 45 minutes. Remove from the water bath and let cool.

7. Cover with plastic wrap and refrigerate until chilled, at least 2 hours, or overnight.

The custards can be refrigerated for up to 3 days.

Brown Sugar–Toffee Cookies

1. Preheat the oven to 350°F. Lightly spray two baking sheets with vegetable oil spray or line with parchment paper.

2. Whisk together the flour, baking soda, and salt in a medium bowl.

3. Beat the butter, brown sugar, and granulated sugar in the bowl of a stand mixer until light and fluffy. Add the eggs one at a time, beating well after each addition. Stir in the vanilla. Add the flour mixture and beat until just combined, being careful not to overmix. Using a rubber spatula, fold in the toffee bits.

4. Using a tablespoon, drop the dough onto the prepared baking sheets, leaving 3 inches between the mounds. Bake until just golden brown around the edges, switching the baking sheets between oven racks halfway through the cooking time, about 10 minutes for a slightly chewy cookie. (For a crisper cookie, bake an additional 2 minutes.)

5. Remove from the oven and transfer the cookies to a wire rack to cool slightly before serving.

The cookies will keep in an airtight container at room temperature for up to 3 days.

MAKES 2 DOZEN COOKIES

Vegetable oil spray

2½ cups all-purpose flour

1 teaspoon baking soda

½ teaspoon table salt

1 cup (2 sticks) salted butter, at room temperature

1 cup packed light brown sugar

1 cup granulated sugar

2 large eggs

1 tablespoon pure vanilla extract

1 (8-ounce) bag Hershey's Heath Bits'O Brickle toffee bits

NORDEAST PIEROGI DINNER (FOR 6)

Smoked Turkey Cabbage Rolls with Tomato Gravy

Roasted Beets in Caraway Vinegar Sauce

Bacon–Sweet Potato Pierogi

Sautéed Chard and Beet Greens

Poppy-Seed Ice Cream Roll with Sour Cherry Sauce

The entire Upper Mississippi region is peppered with Northern and Eastern European immigrants. "Nordeast" Minneapolis for many years had a concentration of Polish, German, Russian, and Ukrainian residents. The neighborhoods remained true to native customs, languages, and, of course, the foods from the residents' countries. Now that Nordeast is known for indie bands, artists, art-filled cafés, farmers markets, and hip new restaurants, many contemporary chefs in the area are putting new twists on traditional recipes. But the culinary anchors of this neighborhood still stand strong, including the landmark Kramarczuk's. In the late 1940s the Kramarczuk family emigrated from the Ukraine to the United States where Wasyl, with his expertise in sausage making, and Anna, with her baking and cooking skills, started the butcher shop and deli. Their classic Eastern European fare remains in demand from the neighborhood old-timers to the new hipsters.

When my husband Doug, born and raised in this neighborhood, first introduced me to his part of the River and its food, I have to admit that the mysterious pierogi—the white dumplings with white potato filling topped with white sour cream—intrigued me enough to experiment. My favorite, featured in this menu, has become bacon–sweet potato topped with sautéed chard and beet greens instead of the traditional sour cream. We start with roasted beets served with a caraway-flavored vinegar sauce, followed by cabbage rolls filled with meat from smoked turkey wings and legs and seasoned rice dressing topped with a quick-to-make tomato gravy. Since poppy seeds are frequently used in Eastern European baked goods, dessert is a light poppy-seed sponge cake filled with vanilla ice cream that is rolled and then topped with sautéed sour cherries.

1 smoked turkey leg

1 smoked turkey wing

1 head cabbage (2 to 2½ pounds), tough outer leaves removed

¾ cup long-grain white rice

½ cup finely chopped yellow onions

1½ teaspoons kosher salt, divided

1 teaspoon minced garlic

1 teaspoon fresh thyme leaves

¼ teaspoon red pepper flakes

½ cup tomato sauce

½ cup heavy cream

½ teaspoon freshly ground black pepper

1. To make the stock, place the turkey leg and wing in a large saucepan, add 4 cups water, and bring to a boil. Lower the heat to a simmer and cook uncovered for 30 minutes. Using tongs, remove the leg and wing to a bowl, reserving the stock in the pot.

2. Meanwhile, invert the cabbage and, with a sharp knife, remove the hard core. Gently separate six large leaves from the head and place in a stainless steel bowl. Cover with boiling water, cover, and let stand until the leaves are limp, about 10 minutes. Drain well in a colander. (Wrap and refrigerate the remaining cabbage for another use.)

3. Place 1½ cups of the turkey stock in a clean saucepan. Add the rice, onions, 1 teaspoon of the salt, the garlic, thyme, and red pepper. Bring the mixture to a boil over medium-high heat. Reduce the heat to low, cover, and simmer undisturbed until the rice is tender and all the liquid has been absorbed, 15 to 20 minutes. Remove from the heat, fluff the rice with a fork, and let cool, uncovered, for 10 to 15 minutes.

4. When the turkey leg and wing are cool enough to handle, remove and discard the skin and bones. Chop the meat into ¼-inch pieces. Stir the diced turkey into the rice.

5. Preheat the oven to 350°F.

6. Place one cabbage leaf on a work surface. Spoon ⅓ cup of the turkey-rice mixture onto the center of the leaf. Fold the bottom stem end of the leaf over the filling, then fold over the sides, and roll up into a tight package. Place the cabbage roll, seam side down, in a baking dish large enough to hold the six rolls in one layer. Repeat with the remaining leaves and filling.

7. Pour ⅓ cup of the remaining turkey stock over the cabbage rolls, cover tightly with aluminum foil, and bake until the cabbage becomes almost translucent, about 30 minutes.

8. Lower the heat to 175°F. Transfer the cabbage rolls to an ovenproof serving dish, uncovered, and place in the oven to keep warm.

9. Strain the liquid from the baking dish through a mesh strainer into a saucepan. Add the tomato sauce, heavy cream, remaining ½ teaspoon salt, and the pepper, stir, and bring to a boil. Cook, stirring frequently, until the sauce is thick and reduced by one-third. Remove from the heat and adjust the seasoning to taste. Remove the platter of cabbage rolls from the oven. Pour the hot sauce over the cabbage rolls and serve.

Although you have to buy a whole head of cabbage for the six leaves needed, cabbage lasts weeks if well wrapped and refrigerated. You can double or triple the recipe and freeze the cabbage rolls, or use the cabbage in soups or slaws.

6 medium beets, trimmed with
   ½ inch stem remaining (greens
   and stems reserved for Sautéed
   Chard and Beet Greens, page 42)

1 tablespoon vegetable oil

2 teaspoons kosher salt, divided

1 teaspoon freshly ground black
   pepper

1 teaspoon caraway seeds

3 tablespoons malt vinegar

1 shallot, minced

1 tablespoon sugar

3 tablespoons sour cream

1. Preheat the oven to 400°F.

2. Lightly coat the beets with the oil and season with 1 teaspoon of the salt and the pepper. Place the beets in a baking dish and bake until they can easily be pierced with a fork, 45 to 55 minutes. Remove from the oven and let sit until cool enough to handle.

3. Slice and discard a thin sliver on the tops and bottoms of the beets. Using your fingers, rub off the beet skins. Quarter the beets and place in a serving dish. Let cool to room temperature, then cover and refrigerate if not using right away.

4. Place the caraway seeds in a small, dry skillet over medium heat. Cook until the seeds are fragrant and make a popping sound, shaking the skillet from side to side to keep the seeds from burning, about 1 minute. Lower the heat.

5. Add the vinegar, shallot, sugar, and remaining 1 teaspoon salt to the skillet and cook over low heat until the vinegar has almost evaporated, about 1 minute.

6. Remove the skillet from the heat and whisk in the sour cream. Like the beets, this dressing can be served at room temperature or chilled. When ready to serve, stir the dressing until smooth and drizzle over beets.

The beets can be roasted and refrigerated for a day or two. The dressing can be prepared ahead as well, but don't dress the beets until just before serving.

1. Preheat the oven to 350°F.

2. Place the sweet potato on a baking sheet and bake until it can be easily pierced with a fork, 35 to 40 minutes. When cool enough to handle, peel off the skin. Put the sweet potato in a bowl and mash thoroughly. You should have about 1 cup.

3. Add the cooked bacon, green onions, salt, and pepper to the bowl with the sweet potato and mix well. (The filling can be made ahead to this point, covered, and refrigerated for up to 3 days.)

4. Place 2 teaspoons of the bacon-sweet potato filling on one half of a pierogi dough circle. (You do not need to wet the dough; it is soft enough to hold together when the edges are pressed.) Fold the dough over the filling to make a half moon and press down on the dough edges with the tines of a fork to seal. Place on a baking sheet and cover with a clean dish towel or plastic wrap to keep from drying out. Continue with the remaining dough and filling. Let the pierogi rest, covered, for 20 minutes before cooking.

5. Line a baking sheet with paper towels. Bring a large pot of salted water to a boil. Add the pierogi, three or four at a time, to the boiling water and cook until they float to the surface, about 3 minutes. Transfer with a slotted spoon to the prepared baking sheet and let the pierogi dry for 15 to 20 minutes.

6. Heat 1 tablespoon of olive oil at a time in a skillet over medium-high heat. Add more oil as you cook the pierogi in batches. Being careful not to overcrowd, sauté the pierogi until lightly browned, about 2 minutes per side. Serve hot with Sauteed Chard and Beet Greens (page 42) on top.

---

1 medium sweet potato, skin left on

3 thick slices smoked bacon, diced and cooked until brown and crisp (page 310)

¼ cup chopped green onions, green tops only

½ teaspoon kosher salt

½ teaspoon freshly ground black pepper

1 recipe Pierogi Dough (page 40)

3 tablespoons extra virgin olive oil

The uncooked pierogi can be frozen on a baking sheet lined with parchment paper, then kept frozen in a ziplock plastic bag for up to 3 months.

Pierogi Dough

MAKES 12 (3½-INCH) PIEROGI

1 large egg

3 tablespoons sour cream

1⅓ cups all-purpose flour

½ teaspoon kosher salt

6 tablespoons salted butter, cold and cut into ½-inch pieces

1. Whisk together the egg and sour cream in a bowl until well blended.

2. Put the flour and salt in a food processor and blend to combine. Add the butter and pulse until the butter is the size of peas.

3. Add the egg–sour cream mixture to the processor and pulse until a ball forms, being careful not to overmix. Form the dough into a disk, wrap tightly in plastic, and refrigerate for at least 30 minutes.

4. On a lightly floured work surface, roll out the dough to ¼-inch thickness. Using a 3½-inch round cookie cutter, cut out twelve circles, rerolling the dough as necessary.

5. Proceed to fill the pierogi (page 39), keeping the unfilled circles covered to prevent drying out.

The dough circles can be made in advance, frozen on a baking sheet lined with parchment paper, and kept frozen in a ziplock plastic bag for up to 1 month.

2 tablespoons extra virgin olive oil, or 2 tablespoons bacon grease

1 small white onion, peeled and thinly sliced

5 ounces chard greens and stems (1 bunch), preferably rainbow chard, cut into 3-inch pieces

Greens and stems from 1 bunch of beets, about 4 ounces, rinsed, spun dry, and cut into 2-inch pieces

1 tablespoon aged balsamic vinegar

½ teaspoon kosher salt

⅛ teaspoon freshly ground black pepper

Heat the olive oil in a large skillet over medium heat. Add the onions and cook, stirring, until soft, about 4 minutes. Add the chard and beet greens and cook, stirring, until tender, 5 to 7 minutes. Add the vinegar, salt and pepper and stir well. Spoon the greens over the pierogi before serving.

1. Preheat the oven to 375°F. Line a 15½ × 10½ × 1-inch jellyroll pan with parchment paper. Generously dust a clean kitchen towel with confectioners' sugar and set aside.

2. Place the egg yolks in the bowl of a stand mixer fitted with a whisk attachment. Beat the eggs until they are light and lemon colored, 3 to 5 minutes. With the motor running, gradually add ⅓ cup of the sugar, the melted butter, lemon juice, and lemon zest, and beat until pale yellow. Transfer to a clean bowl.

3. Wash the machine bowl and whisk with warm, soapy water and dry completely. (The egg whites will not rise if there is any fat remaining in the bowl or on the whisk.) Place the egg whites in the clean bowl and beat until soft peaks form when the whisk is raised. Gradually beat in the remaining ⅓ cup of the extra fine sugar until stiff peaks form.

4. Sift the flour, baking soda, and salt into a large clean bowl; stir in the egg yolk mixture and poppy seeds. Gently fold one-quarter of the egg whites into the flour-yolk mixture to lighten it. Then gently fold in the remaining egg whites until no white streaks remain.

5. Pour the batter into the prepared pan, spreading evenly with a rubber spatula, and bake for 12 minutes. The cake should not brown, but should spring back when lightly pressed with a finger.

6. Remove the cake from the oven and invert it onto the prepared towel, leaving on the parchment paper. Allow the cake to cool.

7. Remove the parchment paper and spread the ice cream on the un-sugared side. Spread the the softened vanilla ice cream across the cake, leaving ½-inch border along the sides. Roll up the cake, using the towel for support and gently peeling it away as you go. Wrap the cake tightly

MAKES 1 (14-INCH) CAKE

Confectioners' sugar, for dusting

5 large eggs, separated

⅔ cup extra fine sugar, divided

3 tablespoons salted butter, melted

1 teaspoon fresh lemon juice

½ teaspoon finely grated lemon zest

⅔ cup cake flour, sifted

1 teaspoon baking soda

¼ teaspoon table salt

2 tablespoons poppy seeds

1 pint good-quality vanilla ice cream, softened in the refrigerator

1 recipe Sour Cherry Sauce (page 45)

with plastic wrap and aluminum foil, and then freeze until the ice cream hardens, at least 3 hours and up to 2 weeks.

8. To serve, place the cake on a clean cutting board and evenly trim the ends. Slice the cake into 1-inch-thick servings, spoon the warm cherry sauce over each, and serve.

Sour Cherry Sauce

1. Combine the sugar, orange juice, orange zest, and butter in a heavy saucepan with a candy thermometer clipped to the side. Cook over medium heat, stirring, until the sugar dissolves. Stop stirring and continue to cook until the mixture becomes a syrup and reaches the soft ball stage, registering 235°F to 240°F on the candy thermometer.

2. Remove the pan from the heat. Add the brandy (the mixture will bubble up). Return to medium heat and cook, stirring, for 1 minute. Add the cherries and cook until the mixture begins to thicken, about 5 minutes.

3. Remove the pan from the heat and let the sauce cool slightly before serving, so it does not melt the ice cream. Serve the sauce over slices of the ice cream cake roll.

This sauce can be made ahead and kept frozen for weeks if properly wrapped. I recommend wrapping in foil after first wrapping in plastic wrap.

MAKES ABOUT 2 CUPS

1 cup sugar

3 tablespoons fresh orange juice

1 tablespoon finely grated orange zest

1 tablespoon salted butter

3 tablespoons Christian Brothers Frost White Brandy, kirsch, or a neutral spirit such as vodka

1½ cups canned or bottled sour cherries, drained

KRÄFTSKIVA: SWEDISH CRAWFISH PARTY
(FOR 8)

Crawfish Boiled with Sea Salt and Dill Crowns

Stuffed Smoked Salmon Rounds with Rye Toasts

Herbed Potato Salad

Citrus-Caraway Aquavit and Pepper Aquavit

Lingonberry-Lemon Bars

Late summer crawfish parties, brought to the Upper River region by Swedish settlers, are becoming as popular as crawfish boils held in spring and early summer in the Lower Mississippi. At a traditional *kräftskiva*, there are *snapsvisor* (drinking songs), paper hats, and plenty of aquavit. *Kräftskiva* at the Bachelor Farmer restaurant in Minneapolis features contemporary bands, baseball caps, and piles of crawfish shipped in from Oregon. (Louisiana crawfish are banned in Minnesota because they're considered an invasive species that can thrive in the cold northern waters.)

Crawfish are boiled in salted water with fresh dill crowns—dill after it has flowered—rather than the Louisiana cayenne base. You'll notice that the dill flavor becomes more pronounced when the crawfish are served chilled. Since it's hard to fill up on crawfish, I also offer cream-cheese-and-caper-filled smoked salmon roll-ups with rye toasts and a Swedish-style potato salad. Aquavit is an herb-infused potato- or grain-based spirit similar to vodka but flavored with caraway, fennel, and other herbs and spices. This menu offers two recipes: one with citrus and caraway, the other with hot peppers. Be advised that these need to be prepared two weeks in advance, then kept in the freezer and served ice cold in chilled glasses. Finish the evening off with some lingonberry-lemon bars and hot coffee. *Skål!*

16 pounds live crawfish (see Source Guide, page 316)

2 cups kosher salt

1 cup sea salt

12 cloves garlic

1 tablespoon dried dill

8 fresh dill crowns (fresh dill that has flowered), or 1 additional tablespoon dried dill

2 tablespoons red pepper flakes

6 lemons, halved

1. Place the crawfish in a cooler or large plastic tub. Cover them with water. Discard any dead crawfish that rise to the surface.

2. Drain the water from the tub. Pour the kosher salt over the crawfish and cover with fresh water. Let the crawfish sit in the salted water for 5 minutes.

3. Stir gently with a large paddle or something similar to swish the crawfish around and rinse mud off the shells and gills. Drain the dirty water (this is where that drainage hole comes in handy). Run water over the crawfish until the water is clear. Drain the crawfish.

4. While the crawfish are purging, fill a large stockpot with 4 gallons of water and bring to a boil. Add the sea salt, garlic, dried dill, dill crowns, and red pepper. Squeeze the juice from the lemons into the water, and then add the lemon halves. Lower the heat, simmer for 10 minutes, then bring the water back to a full boil.

5. Add the crawfish and cook, uncovered, for 15 minutes. Turn off the heat, cover, and let stand for 15 minutes for the crawfish to absorb the flavors. Drain. Divide the crawfish into equal portions and serve hot.

Crawfish must be purged, or cleaned, before they are boiled, to rid them of impurities and mud. I clean them outdoors using an old ice chest with a drainage hole (specifically kept for this purpose) and a garden hose.

Stuffed Smoked Salmon Rounds with Rye Toasts

1. Combine the cream cheese, capers, lemon zest, and dill in a bowl. Beat with a handheld mixer until well blended.

2. Arrange 1 salmon slice on a work surface. Add 2 tablespoons of the cream cheese in the center, fold the edges to surround the filling and place on a decorative platter. Repeat with the remaining ingredients.

3. Lightly butter the rye bread on both sides and cut into quarters. Heat a skillet over medium heat. Add the quarters to the skillet and cook until lightly toasted on each side, about 1 minute. To serve, arrange the rye toasts on the platter around the salmon rounds.

The salmon rounds can be made up to 1 day in advance and kept tightly wrapped and refrigerated, or frozen for up to 2 weeks.

8 ounces cream cheese, at room temperature

1 tablespoon capers, drained

2 teaspoons finely grated lemon zest

1 teaspoon finely chopped fresh dill

8 thin slices smoked salmon (about 8 ounces), very cold

8 slices dark rye bread, crusts removed

1 tablespoon salted butter, at room temperature

Herbed Potato Salad

1. Place the potato cubes in a pot and add enough water to cover by 1 inch. Bring to a boil, lower the heat, and simmer until just fork tender, 8 to 10 minutes.

2. Drain the potatoes in a colander and let sit for 5 minutes. Place the warm potatoes in a bowl. Add the remaining ingredients and stir well with a rubber spatula to blend. Serve at room temperature.

The potato salad can be prepared and refrigerated 1 day in advance. Bring to room temperature before serving.

2 pounds fingerling potatoes, cut into 1-inch cubes

¼ cup apple cider vinegar

⅓ cup extra virgin olive oil

¼ cup chopped green onions, white parts only

¼ cup minced mixed fresh soft herbs, such as basil, mint, chervil, parsley, oregano, or dill

2 teaspoons kosher salt

1 teaspoon freshly ground black pepper

Citrus-Caraway Aquavit

1. Combine the vodka, anise, lemon and orange rinds, sugar, and caraway seeds in a Mason jar. Cover tightly, shake well, and let sit for 2 weeks at room temperature, lightly shaking the jar occasionally.

2. Strain the liquid into the reserved vodka bottle, replace the cap, and place in the freezer until very cold. Rinse eight shot glasses or vodka glasses with water and place in the freezer until frosty, about 15 minutes. Serve the aquavit in the chilled glasses.

Keep this aquavit in the freezer; it should be served ice cold and it will last for months.

1 pint potato vodka, empty bottle reserved

2 whole star anise

Zest of 1 lemon, cut into 1-inch strips

Zest of 1 orange, cut into 1-inch strips

1 tablespoon sugar

1 teaspoon caraway seeds

Pepper Aquavit

1. Combine the vodka, star anise, orange rind, sugar, and red pepper flakes in a Mason jar. Cover tightly, shake well, and let sit for 2 weeks at room temperature, lightly shaking the jar occasionally.

2. Strain the liquid into the reserved vodka bottle, replace the cap, and place in the freezer until very cold. Rinse eight shot glasses or vodka glasses with water and place in the freezer until frosty, about 15 minutes. Serve the aquavit in the chilled glasses.

Keep this aquavit in the freezer; it should be served ice cold and it will last for months.

MAKES 1 PINT

1 pint potato vodka, or your favorite unflavored vodka, empty bottle reserved

2 whole star anise

Zest of 1 orange, cut into 1-inch strips

1 tablespoon sugar

1 teaspoon red pepper flakes

Lingonberry-Lemon Bars

1. Position the rack in the middle of the oven and preheat the oven to 350°F. Line a rimmed 9- × 13-inch baking sheet with aluminum foil, leaving a 1-inch overhang at the sides. Spray the foil with vegetable oil spray and set aside.

2. To make the crust, combine the flour, 1 cup of the confectioners' sugar, and the butter in a food processor and process until the dough comes together, about 1 minute.

3. Press the dough into the bottom and ½ inch up the sides of the prepared pan, making sure there are no cracks. Bake until set and light golden brown, about 10 minutes. Remove from the oven and reduce the temperature to 300°F.

4. To make the filling, whisk together the eggs, egg yolks, granulated sugar, and flour in a bowl until well blended. Whisk in the lemon juice and zest.

5. Spread the lingonberry jam over the baked crust, taking care not to crack or damage the crust. Pour the lemon filling over the lingonberry jam, spreading to the edges with a rubber spatula. Bake until the filling is firm, 30 to 35 minutes.

6. Remove the pan to a wire rack and let cool completely. Refrigerate the pan until the filling is set, about 2 hours. Using the sides of the foil, lift out onto a large cutting board and slice into 12 equal bars. Dust with confectioners' sugar before serving.

These bars can be frozen, undusted, in an airtight container for 10 to 12 weeks. Once thawed, dust with confectioners' sugar before serving.

MAKES 1 DOZEN

Crust

Vegetable oil spray

2 cups all-purpose flour

1 cup confectioners' sugar, plus more for garnish

¾ cup (1½ sticks) cold salted butter, cut into ½-inch pieces

Filling

4 large eggs

2 large egg yolks

2 cups granulated sugar

⅓ cup all-purpose flour, sifted

1 cup fresh lemon juice

1 teaspoon finely grated lemon zest

6 ounces lingonberry jam

Confectioners' sugar

NEW YEAR'S EVE BUFFET (FOR 12)

Ginger-Lychee Martinis

Green Bean and Brussels Sprout Salad

Spicy Shrimp Salad in Lettuce Cups

Ginger Pork Sausage

Chicken Skewers with Sesame Sea Salt and Spicy Lime Dipping Sauce

Sugar and Spice Rice

Mini Banana Cakes with Basil-and-Mint-Infused Lemon Syrup

Like all settlers along the River, the Hmong have made a conscious effort to to retain their foods and their culture. Many families grow their own vegetables and herbs on small plots. As with other Asian cultures, rice is at the center of their meals along with vegetables, chiles, fish sauce, and small amounts of meat.

The Hmong New Year is celebrated in November or December, but a Hmong-inspired buffet is a festive way to celebrate any New Year or special event. Start the party with ginger-lychee-infused vodka martinis, or offer a crisp white wine such as a Sancerre or other Sauvignon Blanc. For those who prefer red, select something light, like a Pinot Noir.

This salad is dressed much like the green papaya salads served in Southeast Asia, but it uses quartered brussels sprouts with green beans and cherry tomatoes. Spicy shrimp salad is served in individual lettuce cups. The Asian pork sausage is fermented and usually takes several days to make, but I reproduce the same flavors by poking pinholes in pork sausages and soaking them in a vinegar-and-lime brine seasoned with fresh ginger and lemongrass. Another favorite included in this feast—chicken skewers—has just three ingredients: chicken tenders, toasted sesame seeds, and toasted sea salt. And to finish everything off, individual banana cakes drizzled with a mint-lemon syrup help ring in the New Year.

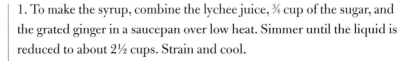

6 cups lychee juice, such as Jan's Lychee 100% Juice (see Source Guide, page 316)

1 cup sugar, divided

2 tablespoons peeled and grated fresh ginger

3 tablespoons candied ginger

2 cups vodka

1. To make the syrup, combine the lychee juice, ¾ cup of the sugar, and the grated ginger in a saucepan over low heat. Simmer until the liquid is reduced to about 2½ cups. Strain and cool.

2. To make the ginger sugar for the rims of the glasses, place the remaining ¼ cup sugar and the candied ginger in a food processor. Process until the ginger is the consistency of coarse salt. Pour the ginger sugar onto a plate. Fold a paper towel into quarters, soak with water, and place on another plate. Press the rims of martini glasses into the wet towel, and then press the rims into the ginger sugar.

3. To make the martinis, combine the lychee-ginger syrup, vodka, and 1 cup of ice in a pitcher. Stir vigorously and strain into the martini glasses. Serve cold.

1. Place the peanuts in a heavy plastic bag, seal, and, using a rolling pin, crush the peanuts to the consistency of brown rice.

2. Combine half of the crushed peanuts, the lime juice, sugar, lemon juice, Sriracha, and fish sauce in a bowl, and stir to dissolve the sugar. Stir in the cilantro.

3. Bring a large saucepan of lightly salted water to a boil. While waiting for the water to boil, fill a large bowl with ice and water. Cook the beans and brussels sprouts separately until they are just tender, 2 to 3 minutes. Drain in a colander and immediately transfer to the bowl of ice water to stop them from cooking. Drain the vegetables in a colander. Place the vegetables and tomatoes in a serving bowl. Add dressing onto the vegetables and toss to coat. Let marinate for 1 hour in the refrigerator. Garnish the salad with the remaining half of the peanuts and serve.

¾ cup lightly salted dry roasted peanuts, divided

¼ cup fresh lime juice

¼ cup sugar

2 tablespoons fresh lemon juice

2 tablespoons Sriracha

1 tablespoon fish sauce (Ka-Me preferred)

¼ cup chopped fresh cilantro leaves

1 pound brussels sprouts, bottoms trimmed, quartered

1 pound green beans, stem ends trimmed

2 cups (1 pound) halved cherry tomatoes

The vegetables and dressing can be prepared 1 day ahead and stored separately in the refrigerator. Dress the vegetables up to 1 hour before serving.

½ cup sesame oil

2 tablespoons Sriracha

3 pounds shrimp (21–25 count), peeled, deveined, thawed if frozen, and thoroughly dried

¾ cup chopped green onions, tops and bottoms

½ cup chopped fresh cilantro leaves

¼ cup chopped fresh mint leaves

¼ cup chopped fresh basil leaves

24 iceberg lettuce leaves, tender center leaves only

3 limes, each cut into 8 wedges, for garnish

1. Heat the oil in a skillet over medium-high heat. When the oil is almost smoking, add the Sriracha and shrimp and cook, stirring constantly, until the shrimp are cooked and firm, 3 to 4 minutes. Remove the shrimp to a bowl.

2. When the shrimp have cooled for 10 minutes, add the green onions, cilantro, mint, and basil, and toss.

3. Evenly distribute the shrimp salad among the lettuce leaves. Top each with a lime wedge.

The shrimp salad can be prepared 1 day ahead. Assemble in lettuce cups just before serving.

12 pork breakfast sausages, pierced all over with a toothpick

¼ cup fresh lime juice

¼ cup rice wine vinegar

1½ tablespoons peeled and grated fresh ginger

Vegetable oil spray

12 wooden or metal skewers

¼ cup chopped fresh cilantro leaves

1. Arrange the sausage links in a shallow baking dish.

2. Whisk the lime juice, vinegar, and ginger in a bowl. Pour over the sausages and cover tightly with plastic wrap. Refrigerate for 2 hours. Turn the sausages and refrigerate again until ready to cook.

3. Heat a skillet over medium heat. Lightly coat the bottom of skillet with the vegetable spray. Add the sausages in batches and cook, turning, until they are brown on all sides and an instant-read thermometer inserted into the middle of a sausage reaches 160°F. Once cooked, skewer each sausage lengthwise and arrange on a serving platter.

4. Add the cilantro to the pan and cook, stirring, until wilted. Garnish the sausages with the cilantro and serve with the Chicken Skewers with Sesame Sea Salt and Spicy Lime Dipping Sauce (page 59).

Chicken Skewers with Sesame Sea Salt and Spicy Lime Dipping Sauce

1. If using wooden skewers, arrange them in a shallow dish. Cover with water and soak for 15 minutes.

2. Preheat the oven to 400°F. Line a baking sheet with aluminum foil and set aside.

3. Using a mortar and pestle, lightly crush the sesame seeds, taking care not to make a paste. (Alternatively, place the seeds in a blender and pulse to crush, 15 to 20 seconds.)

4. Place a large cast-iron skillet over medium heat. Add the sea salt to the skillet and toast, stirring constantly, until the salt turns gray. Add the sesame seeds and toast, stirring constantly, until golden brown, about 30 seconds, being careful not to let them burn. Transfer the sesame-salt mixture to a plate.

5. Thread the chicken tenders lengthwise onto the skewers. In the same skillet, add just enough oil to coat the surface. Add the chicken skewers and cook, turning, until the chicken is brown. Place the skewers on the prepared baking sheet. Sprinkle some of the sesame-salt mixture onto each skewer. Bake until the chicken is cooked through, about 10 minutes. Serve hot with the Spicy Lime Dipping Sauce and Ginger Pork Sausage (page 58) on the side.

12 wooden or metal skewers

⅓ cup sesame seeds

3 teaspoons coarse sea salt

12 (2-ounce) chicken tenders

3 tablespoons vegetable oil

1 recipe Spicy Lime Dipping Sauce (below)

Spicy Lime Dipping Sauce

Combine all of the ingredients in a blender and process for 1 minute. Place in an airtight container and refrigerate until ready to serve.

The sauce will keep for up to 2 weeks refrigerated.

½ cup fresh lime juice

2 teaspoons sugar

2 tablespoons Sriracha

1 tablespoon fish sauce

3 tablespoons fresh cilantro leaves

3 cups sweet rice, well rinsed and
    drained in a colander

1 cup black rice, well rinsed and
    drained in a colander

2 cups sweet coconut milk

¼ cup Thai red curry paste

2 teaspoons kosher salt

1. Combine the sweet and black rice, coconut milk, and curry paste in a large saucepan. Stir well to coat the rice with all of the ingredients. Cover and refrigerate for at least 2 and up to 12 hours.

2. Add 5¾ cups water and the salt to the saucepan and stir well. Bring to a boil and cook for 2 minutes. Lower the heat, cover, and simmer undisturbed until all of the liquid has been absorbed, about 20 minutes.

3. Remove the pan from the heat. Fluff the rice with a fork, cover, and let sit for 10 minutes before serving.

Sticky rice, also known as sweet rice, is grown primarily in Southeast and East Asia. It is especially sticky when cooked and is called "glutinous rice" because of its gluey nature, not to be confused with "glutenous" (containing gluten). This is actually a good dish for people who must eat a gluten-free diet! Another glutinous rice is black rice, also called forbidden rice, grown in Indonesia and Thailand. Black rice is higher in nutritional value than other rices, much like brown rice.

If you have a rice cooker, follow the manufacturer's directions and cook the sweet and black rice together. Whether using a rice cooker or the stovetop method, the rice and other ingredients must marinate for at least two hours before cooking.

1. Preheat the oven to 350°F. Spray a 12-cup Bundt muffin pan with vegetable oil.

2. To make the cakes, place the flour, the baking powder, baking soda, and salt in a bowl and whisk to combine.

3. In the bowl of a stand mixer fitted with a paddle attachment, cream together the butter and sugar on medium speed until light and fluffy, 3 to 4 minutes. Add the buttermilk and then the eggs one at a time, blending well after each addition, stopping the machine as necessary to scrape down the sides. Add the bananas and vanilla and mix until just blended. With the mixer on low speed, gradually add the dry ingredients into the banana mixture, and mix until blended.

4. Divide the batter between the prepared Bundt pans. Each cup should be ¾ full. Bake until the cakes are golden and a tester inserted into the center comes out clean, about 20 minutes.

5. Remove the cakes to a wire rack and let cool in the pans for 10 minutes. Turn out the cakes onto the wire rack and let cool to room temperature.

The cakes can be made a day or two in advance to make party preparation easier. Cool the cakes completely and wrap each individually in plastic wrap to keep fresh.

Cakes
MAKES 12 MINI CAKES

Vegetable oil spray

2½ cups all-purpose flour

2 teaspoons baking powder

1 teaspoon baking soda

½ teaspoon table salt

1 cup salted butter, at room temperature

1½ cups sugar

2 large eggs

1½ cups mashed ripe bananas (about 2 bananas)

1 teaspoon pure vanilla extract

¼ cup plus 1 tablespoon buttermilk

6. To make the syrup, combine the sugar, lemon juice, and minced basil and mint leaves in a saucepan. Bring to a simmer over low heat and cook until it begins to thicken into a syrup, 8 to10 minutes.

7. If serving right away, keep the basil and mint in the syrup, and keep the syrup warm. If making in advance, it is best to strain the herbs out and put the syrup in a clean container for later use.

8. Place a baking sheet lined with aluminum foil under the wire rack holding the cakes, to catch the syrup. Drizzle a generous tablespoon of the syrup over each cake. Garnish each cake with 1 mint leaf and a pinch of the lemon zest and serve.

The syrup can be made up to 3 days in advance and kept in an airtight container in the refrigerator. Reheat the syrup gently before using to ice the cakes.

Syrup
MAKES ABOUT 1 CUP

1 cup sugar

3 tablespoons fresh lemon juice

10 fresh basil leaves, minced

10 fresh mint leaves, minced, plus 12 whole fresh mint leaves for garnish

1 teaspoon finely grated lemon zest

LAURA INGALLS WILDER SUNDAY SUPPER
(FOR 6)

Angel Biscuits

Wilted Chard Salad

Smoked Oyster Chowder

Veal Rib Roast with Root Vegetables

Blueberry Pie with Lemon Drop Candy Dust

Generations of Americans know Laura Ingalls Wilder for her autobiographical *Little House* books, which tell of her hardscrabble prairie childhood with her pioneer family. She was born near Pepin, Wisconsin, home to Lake Pepin, the widest naturally occurring part of the Mississippi River, about sixty miles from Saint Paul, Minnesota. Pepin celebrates its distinction as the birthplace of Wilder and the setting for her beloved books every September during Laura Ingalls Wilder Days. These are a festival of traditional music and crafts, quilts, pioneer games, even a Laura look-alike contest, as well as an old-fashioned small town parade. Other cities claim and celebrate her life and books, but not with the passion and commitment of Pepin.

In one of her books, *By the Shores of Silver Lake,* Wilder eloquently described a smoked oyster stew: "In all her life, Laura had never tasted anything so good as that savory, fragrant, sea-tasting hot milk, with golden dots of melted cream

and black specks of pepper on its top, and the little dark canned oysters at its bottom. She sipped slowly, slowly from her spoon, to keep that taste going over her tongue as long as she could."

Although oysters aren't indigenous to the Upper Mississippi, they were in great demand starting in the nineteenth century, when they were delivered along the River by steamboats and railroads. Thomas Kensett, the father of canned foods in the United States, acquired a patent to preserve oysters in tin cans in 1825, so they were readily available. When it comes to oyster chowder, I prefer a combination of smoked oysters for flavoring and fresh, briny oysters to finish off the stew.

Angel biscuits, made with yeast and baking powder, are a favorite along the length of the River. They're ideal for sopping up the juices from the roast, vegetables, and wilted chard. Wilder, who also had a fondness for candy, would have loved this blueberry pie dusted with powdered lemon drops.

Angel Biscuits

MAKES 1 DOZEN

Vegetable oil spray

*1 envelope (2¼ teaspoons)
  active dry*

*2 cups all-purpose flour, plus more
  for rolling out*

2 tablespoons sugar

2 teaspoons baking powder

*½ cup (1 stick) cold salted
  margarine, cut into 1-inch pieces*

*2 tablespoons cold salted butter, cut
  into ½-inch pieces*

*½ cup warm (about 110°F)
  buttermilk*

1 tablespoon melted salted butter

1. Preheat the oven to 375°F. Spray a baking sheet with vegetable oil spray.

2. Combine ¼ cup warm (about 110°F) water and the yeast in a small bowl and let sit until the yeast is dissolved, 5 minutes.

3. Combine the flour, sugar, and baking powder in a food processor and pulse 2 to 3 times. Add the margarine and butter and pulse 6 to 7 times. Add the yeast mixture and buttermilk and pulse just until blended, 7 to 8 times, being careful not to overmix.

4. Turn the dough out onto a lightly floured surface. Form the dough with floured hands to make a smooth round about ½ inch thick.

5. Using a 2-inch biscuit cutter that has been dusted with flour, cut the dough into rounds. Gather the scraps and reshape about ½ inch thick. Transfer the biscuits to the prepared baking sheet. Cover with a clean towel and let rise in a warm place for about 30 minutes.

6. Brush the tops of the biscuits with the melted butter and bake until risen almost double in size and golden brown, 18 to 20 minutes. Remove from the oven and serve warm.

Angel biscuits are lighter and fluffier than all other biscuits because of the combination of yeast and baking powder.

1. Cook the bacon in a skillet over medium heat, stirring frequently, until brown and nearly crisp, about 4 minutes. Add the shallots and cook until soft, 1 minute.

2. Add the mustard, sugar, and cider vinegar and cook, stirring, until the sugar is dissolved. Add the olive oil and stir well to incorporate.

3. Add the chard and cook, tossing well, until it begins to wilt, about 30 seconds. Remove from the heat and serve hot.

The dressing may be prepared in the skillet up to 2 hours in advance. Reheat the dressing before cooking the chard.

5 thick slices smoked bacon, diced

1 shallot, minced

3 tablespoons Dijon mustard

2 tablespoons packed light brown sugar

2 tablespoons apple cider vinegar

3 tablespoons extra virgin olive oil

1 pound Swiss chard leaves, with ½ inch of stems remaining, cut in 1-inch strips

Spinach, baby mustard greens, or a mixture of sturdy greens can be used in place of the chard.

WISCONSIN RIVER TOWNS

The Wisconsin Great River Road parallels the Mississippi River for 250 miles, from Prescott in the north to Kieler in the south. Here you find thirty-three unique communities, including some of the oldest in Wisconsin, as well as many that seem to replicate European cultures. Swedish immigrants settled in these communities, along with French and French-Canadian settlers and some Germans, who brought their dairy farming and cheese-making skills with them. A Swede named Erik Peterson, later joined by family and friends, first settled Stockholm, Wisconsin, on the shores of Lake Pepin. The next town, Pepin, is where Laura Ingalls Wilder, the renowned author of the popular *Little House* series, was born on a nearby farm in 1867. Heading farther south, the landscape begins to change, with some of the tallest bluffs along the Wisconsin Great River Road located near La Crosse, where Germans brought the art of beer making. Downstream is DeSoto, named for the Spanish explorer Hernando de Soto, who in 1541 was the first European to see the Mississippi River. Prairie du Chien, Wisconsin's second oldest community, was settled in 1817 by Father Marie Joseph Dunand, a French Jesuit missionary who came up the River from St. Louis. Although there were other French and Spanish discoverers, it was mostly the Swedish and German settlers who left their culinary imprint on these river towns.

Smoked Oyster Chowder

2 (3-ounce) cans smoked oysters, drained

1½ cups half-and-half

1½ cups heavy cream

¼ cup (½ stick) salted butter

½ cup minced green onions

⅓ cup diced celery

⅓ cup diced white onions

1½ teaspoons minced garlic

1½ tablespoons all-purpose flour

1 tablespoon chopped fresh basil leaves

1 teaspoon red pepper flakes

1 pint shucked fresh oysters, with oyster liquor strained and reserved

½ teaspoon salt, optional

½ teaspoon ground white pepper, optional

1. Combine the smoked oysters, half-and-half, and heavy cream in a saucepan and gently cook over low heat, stirring occasionally, 12 to 15 minutes. (This is to flavor the cream mixture with the essence of the smoked oysters.)

2. Melt the butter in a large pot over low heat. Add the green onions, celery, and white onions and cook, stirring, until the vegetables are beginning to soften, 3 to 4 minutes. Add the garlic and cook, stirring, until fragrant, 1 minute. Add the flour and cook, whisking, to make a light roux, about 2 minutes.

3. Drain the smoked oysters in a colander positioned over a bowl, reserving the liquid and discarding the oysters. Add the warm cream to the roux and vegetables and cook over medium heat, stirring with a wooden spoon, until the cream is absorbed and the mixture is thick. Add the basil and red pepper flakes and cook, stirring, for 5 minutes.

4. Add the oyster liquor and cook, stirring, until well incorporated and starting to reduce, 2 to 3 minutes. Add the fresh oysters and cook just until heated through and starting to curl, 3 to 5 minutes. Adjust the seasoning to taste with salt and white pepper. Serve hot in warmed bowls.

Add the fresh oysters just before finishing the chowder, so they do not become rubbery and overcooked.

the fire
Then he and Ma
wheels again, and Pa hitched up
The rising sun was shortening all the sha
Hundreds of meadow larks were rising from the
prairie, singing higher and higher in the air. Their
songs came down from the great, clear sky like
a rain of music. And all over the land, where the
grasses waved and murmured under the wind,
thousands of little dickie-birds clung with their

107

1 (5-pound) veal rib roast with 6 bones

3 teaspoons kosher salt, divided

1½ teaspoons freshly ground black pepper, divided

5 tablespoons extra virgin olive oil, divided

3 medium carrots, peeled and cut into 1-inch pieces

3 medium Yukon gold potatoes, peeled and cut into 1-inch pieces

2 medium parsnips, peeled and cut into 1-inch pieces

2 medium sweet potatoes, peeled and cut into 1-inch pieces

6 chopped plus 6 whole fresh sage leaves

3 garlic cloves, thinly sliced

1 tablespoon cornstarch

2 teaspoons fresh lemon juice

1. Preheat the oven to 325°F.

2. Season the roast on all sides with 2 teaspoons of the salt and 1 teaspoon of the pepper. Heat 3 tablespoons of the olive oil in a dutch oven over high heat. Add the veal and sear, turning, until well browned on all sides, about 5 minutes.

3. Combine the carrots, potatoes, parsnips, and sweet potatoes in a large bowl. Season with the remaining 2 tablespoons olive oil, 1 teaspoon salt, ½ teaspoon pepper, and chopped sage. Toss to coat.

4. Place the sliced garlic and 6 whole sage leaves on top of the seared roast. Surround the roast with the vegetables.

5. Roast the veal and vegetables until an instant-read thermometer inserted into the thickest part of the roast registers 145°F, about 45 minutes. The veal roast will continue to cook when removed. Veal is best served between 150°F and 155 °F. Remove the roast to a cutting board, cover with aluminum foil, and let rest for 15 minutes before carving.

6. Reduce the oven temperature to 175°F. Pour the pan juices from the dutch oven into a saucepan, leaving the vegetables in the roasting pan. Place the vegetables in the oven to stay warm.

7. Whisk together the cornstarch, lemon juice, and ¼ cup water in a small bowl. Add the cornstarch mixture to the pan juices, whisk, and cook over medium heat until slightly thickened, 4 to 5 minutes.

8. Carve the veal between the bones into 6 portions and arrange on a platter, surrounded by the vegetables. Pour the warm gravy over the veal just before serving.

1. Preheat the oven to 350°F.

2. To make the filling, whisk together the sugar and cornstarch in a bowl. Add the blueberries (if using fresh, add 3 tablespoons water), melted butter, and lemon juice and gently stir to combine.

3. Remove the dough from the refrigerator. On a lightly floured surface, roll out one piece of dough into an 11-inch round, about ⅛-inch thick. Transfer to a 9-inch pie pan. Spoon the filling evenly into the piecrust. Roll out the remaining dough into a 10-inch circle. Place on top of the filling, tucking the overlapping crusts into the pan, forming a thick edge. Crimp the edges with a fork to seal. Cut two steam vents down the center of the top crust and pierce once on each side with the tines of a fork.

4. To make the topping, place the lemon drop candies in a food processor and process until pulverized to the consistency of sugar.

5. With a pastry brush, brush the piecrust with the egg wash, and then sprinkle with half of the crushed candy. Bake until the crust is evenly browned and the juices are bubbling, 50 to 60 minutes. Place the pie on a wire rack and sprinkle the remaining lemon candy on top. Let cool for at least 1 hour before serving.

The pie may be assembled and frozen without egg wash and candy. If frozen, let the pie sit at room temperature for 1 hour before adding egg wash and candy and baking.

1½ cups sugar

¼ cup cornstarch

4 cups fresh or frozen blueberries (no need to thaw if frozen)

2 tablespoons salted butter, melted

1 tablespoon fresh lemon juice

1 recipe Sweet Pie Dough (page 315)

¼ cup lemon drop candies

1 large egg beaten with 1 tablespoon water to make an egg wash

OKTOBERFEST PARTY (FOR 6)

Braised Red Cabbage Soup with Homemade Crème Fraîche

Curry Sausage

Chicken Wiener Schnitzel with Lemon and Parsley

Spinach Spaetzle

Deconstructed Apple Strudel

The influence of the German settlers holds strong along the banks of the River. In the early 1800s, breweries prospered in La Crosse, an ideal location midway between Milwaukee and St. Paul. It helped to have the resources needed for the brewing of beer nearby—water from the Mississippi, cereal grains from local farmers. Hops were a new, thriving crop right after the Civil War and turned into a "cash" crop for returning soldiers. But these farmers of the nineteenth century did not know about sustainable crops and disease management. Blight, then aphids, killed this once thriving crop. The Pacific Northwest became the largest producer of hops.

In the early 1900s, several sawmills closed and the breweries rose to save the industrial development of La Crosse. Then came the Volstead Act of 1919, which prohibited the production and selling of beer and other alcoholic beverages and led to the demise of small town breweries. Today microbreweries and brewpubs such as Pearl Street Brewery and City Brewery have led the beer revival in many towns along the Upper River.

Oktoberfest along the Upper River is celebrated with as much enthusiasm and partying as Mardi Gras is along the Lower Mississippi. For more than fifty years, La Crosse's German heritage has made the city's celebration one of the finest Oktoberfests in the nation. The food at Oktoberfest includes German classics combined with local inspiration. A savory compote of onions and peppers flavored with tomato and curry accompanies curry sausage. My braised cabbage soup is likewise sweetened with apples and soured with a touch of vinegar; another favorite seasoning is caraway and cumin. The ingredient that sets it apart is a colorless liqueur flavored with caraway seed, cumin, and fennel called kümmel.

Chicken Wiener Schnitzel is lightly sautéed and then baked rather than fried. My apple strudel is deconstructed and made up with crème anglaise, sautéed cinnamon apples, and cinnamon-sugared pastry strips on top. Choose a variety of seasonal autumn beers to serve, and then chant, "Oans, zwoa, drei, Gsuffa!" One, two, three drink up!

2 tablespoons extra virgin olive oil or bacon grease

1 large white onion, finely chopped

4 cups shredded red cabbage

2 medium Granny Smith apples, peeled, cored, and diced

¼ cup kümmel

6 cups low-sodium beef or vegetable broth

1 cup full-bodied red wine, such as Cabernet or Malbec

1 tablespoon aged balsamic vinegar

6 tablespoons Homemade Crème Fraîche (page 75)

5 thick slices smoked bacon, diced and cooked until crisp (page 310)

1. Heat the oil in a dutch oven over medium heat. Add the onions and cook, stirring, until golden, about 6 minutes. Add the cabbage and cook, stirring, until lightly brown, 10 to 12 minutes. Add the apples and cook, stirring, until soft, 2 to 3 minutes. Add the kümmel and cook until nearly evaporated, about 1 minute. Add the broth and bring to a low boil.

2. Reduce the heat and add the wine and balsamic vinegar. Simmer uncovered, stirring occasionally, until the cabbage is soft and the liquid is slightly reduced, 20 to 25 minutes.

3. Ladle the hot soup into warmed bowls. Spoon 1 tablespoon of the crème fraîche into the center of each portion and garnish with crisp bacon.

Kümmel is a caraway-flavored liqueur favored by the Dutch and Germans. If you cannot find kümmel, simmer together 1 teaspoon toasted caraway seeds, oy cup water, and 2 tablespoons honey for 2 minutes. Strain the seeds from the liquid before adding to soup.

The soup can be made and refrigerated 1 to 2 days ahead.

Homemade Crème Fraîche

Pour the cream and buttermilk into a clean Mason jar or heavy plastic container with a tight-fitting lid. Cover with plastic wrap and let sit at room temperature for 24 hours. Refrigerate until ready to use.

2 cups heavy cream

3 tablespoons buttermilk

Crème fraîche is similar to sour cream but not as tart, and can be purchased in many supermarkets. It's also easy to make, but plan ahead, as it has to be made a day or two in advance. In addition to use in garnishing soup, spoon some over steamed vegetables, fresh fruit, or baked potatoes.

The crème fraîche can be refrigerated for up to 1 week.

6 bratwursts, pierced all over with
   a fork

1 medium white onion, thinly sliced

1 green pepper, halved, seeded, and
   thinly sliced

1 cup (about 2) diced tomatoes

3 tablespoons brown sugar

1 tablespoon curry powder

1 tablespoon Worcestershire sauce

1. Heat a large skillet over medium heat. Add the bratwursts and cook, turning, until browned on all sides, 7 to 8 minutes. Transfer the sausages to a plate and pat with a paper towel. Pour off and discard half the fat from the skillet.

2. Add the onions to the fat remaining in the skillet and cook, stirring, on low heat until caramelized, about 5 minutes. Add the peppers and cook, stirring, until soft, 3 to 4 minutes. Add the tomatoes, brown sugar, curry, and Worcestershire sauce, and cook, stirring, until the sauce begins to thicken, about 3 minutes.

3. Slice the cooked bratwursts into 1-inch pieces. Return the sausages to the skillet and cook, stirring, to reheat, 2 minutes. Arrange the sausages on a serving platter, spoon the curry sauce over the top, and serve.

1. Season the chicken breasts on both sides, using ¼ teaspoon of the salt and ⅛ teaspoon of the pepper per breast.

2. Preheat the oven to 350°F. Line a baking sheet with aluminum foil and set aside.

3. Heat half of the oil in a large skillet over medium-high heat. Add three of the chicken breasts and cook until golden brown, about 2 minutes per side. Place the browned chicken breasts on the prepared baking sheet. Add the remaining oil to the pan and cook the remaining three chicken breasts. Place on the baking sheet and drizzle the lemon juice over the chicken breasts.

4. Wipe out the skillet with paper towels. Add the butter to the skillet and melt over medium heat. Add the parsley, garlic, and the remaining ½ teaspoon salt and ½ teaspoon pepper and stir to combine. Add the bread crumbs, stir to combine, and cook until the bread crumbs are fragrant and lightly toasted, 2 to 3 minutes. Spoon the bread crumbs evenly over the tops of the chicken breasts, patting down the crumbs lightly with the back of a spoon to make them adhere.

5. Bake until the chicken is warmed through, about 5 minutes. Serve hot with the lemon wedges on the side.

6 (5-ounce) boneless, skinless chicken breasts, pounded to ¼-inch thickness

2 teaspoons kosher salt, divided

1¼ teaspoons freshly ground black pepper

3 tablespoons vegetable oil

¼ cup fresh lemon juice

3 tablespoons salted butter

3 tablespoons chopped fresh parsley leaves

1 teaspoon minced garlic

½ cup panko bread crumbs

6 lemon wedges, for garnish

1½ cups all-purpose flour, plus
    more for the board

1½ teaspoons kosher salt

½ teaspoon ground white pepper

½ teaspoon ground nutmeg

1 teaspoon extra virgin olive oil

1 cup fresh baby spinach

¼ cup milk

1 tablespoon chopped green onions,
    green tops only

2 large eggs

3 tablespoons salted butter

Freshly ground black pepper,
    to taste

Spaetzle are easy to make if you have a spaetzle maker, which in my opinion is worth the small investment. To perfect your technique, first practice extruding the dough over a plate before trying it over the water. Alternatively, you can use a large-hole flat grater and a rubber spatula for similar results.

1. Whisk together 1½ cups of the flour, the salt, white pepper, and nutmeg in the bowl of a stand mixer.

2. Heat a small skillet over medium heat. Add the olive oil and, when hot, add the spinach, stirring until the spinach has wilted, 1 to 2 minutes. Remove from the heat and let cool slightly, about 5 minutes, and strain off any excess liquid.

3. Place the spinach, milk, and green onions in a blender and process until smooth. Add the eggs and pulse just to combine, 10 to 12 times. (Do not overmix the eggs; the mixture should be smooth but not frothy.)

4. Make a well in the center of the dry ingredients and pour in the egg-milk mixture. Using the paddle attachment, mix on low speed until the dough is smooth. Turn the dough out onto a lightly floured work surface and shape into a ball. Cover with a clean kitchen towel and let rest for 10 to 15 minutes.

5. Bring 3 quarts of salted water to a simmer. To form the spaetzle, add one-third of the dough to a spaetzle maker. While holding the spaetzle maker over the simmering water, push the dough through the holes with the hand attachment, being careful not to overcrowd the pot. (Alternatively, use a medium colander positioned over the pot, pushing the dough through the holes with a rubber spatula.) Cook, stirring gently to prevent sticking, until the spaetzle float to the surface, 3 to 4 minutes. Using a wire mesh strainer or skimmer, lift the cooked spaetzle to a clean colander set over a plate and drain well. Repeat with the remaining dough.

6. Melt the butter in a large skillet over medium heat. Add the spaetzle and cook, tossing with a large wooden spoon, until golden brown, 1 to 2 minutes. Season to taste with pepper before serving hot.

Deconstructed Apple Strudel

1. First, make the cinnamon crisps. Preheat the oven to 350°F. Line a baking sheet with parchment paper. Combine the granulated sugar and cinnamon in a small bowl and stir to blend.

2. On a lightly floured board, roll out the pie dough into a rectangle about ¼ inch thick and 12 inches square. Cut the dough into twenty-four 1 × 6-inch strips (four for each dessert). Transfer the strips to the prepared baking sheet. With a pastry brush, lightly brush the top of each strip with the egg wash and then sprinkle with the cinnamon sugar. Bake until golden brown and crisp, 18 to 20 minutes.

3. To make the crème anglaise, in a stand mixer fitted with a whisk attachment, beat the egg yolks and sugar on medium speed until the mixture is pale yellow and thick, 2 to 3 minutes.

4. Combine the cream, milk, and orange zest in the top of a double boiler set over simmering water and bring to a simmer over medium heat. Slowly drizzle about ½ cup of the hot milk mixture into the eggs with the machine on low speed and beat to combine, about 30 seconds. Pour the egg mixture into the double boiler and cook over medium heat, whisking frequently, until the sauce thickens and coats the back of a spoon.

5. Remove from the heat and strain through a fine mesh strainer into a clean bowl, pressing against the strainer with a rubber spatula. Divide the mixture among six shallow dessert bowls.

6. Finally, sauté the apples. Melt the butter in a skillet over medium heat. Add the apple slices, and cook until beginning to soften, 1 to 2 minutes. Sprinkle the brown sugar and cinnamon onto the apples, stir well, and cook until the apples are soft and fragrant, 2 to 3 minutes. Spoon the warm apples onto the crème anglaise and top each serving with four cinnamon crisps. Serve immediately.

Cinnamon Crisps

⅓ cup granulated sugar

2 teaspoons ground cinnamon

1 recipe Sweet Pie Dough (page 315)

1 large egg beaten with 1 tablespoon water to make an egg wash

Crème Anglaise

5 large egg yolks

½ cup granulated sugar

½ cup heavy cream

½ cup milk

3 (1-inch-long) strips orange zest

Sautéed Apples

2 tablespoons salted butter

4 Granny Smith apples, peeled, cored, and sliced

¼ cup packed light brown sugar

¼ teaspoon ground cinnamon

QUAD CITIES COOKOUT (FOR 6)

Mint Limeade

Iceberg Lettuce Slaw with Bacon, Tomatoes, and Blue Cheese,
and Celery Seed Dressing

Tavern Sliders on Sun-Dried Tomato Buns

Cauliflower Mac 'n' Cheese

Oven-Roasted Corn with Jalapeño-Lime Butter

Hot Fudge Sundaes

Midway between Minneapolis and St. Louis, five river cities converge on the Mississippi at the Iowa-Illinois boundary. These cities, Davenport and Bettendorf in Iowa and Rock Island, Moline, and East Moline in Illinois, are the center of the Quad Cities Metropolitan Area.

Popular in taverns, fast-food places, and homes throughout the Quad Cities and other parts of the Midwest are tavern sandwiches—better known as loose meat sandwiches—which are similar to today's Sloppy Joe but without tomato sauce. They were invented by butcher Fred Angell of Muscatine, Iowa, in 1926 and franchised under the name Maid-Rite. Everyone has his or her own idea of what a true loose meat sandwich should be. Some say it should be topped only with mustard and pickles, others insist on ketchup and cheese. For our cookout, homemade sun-dried tomato buns update this Midwestern sandwich, and instead of iceberg wedges with blue cheese dressing, the lettuce is grated and turned into a slaw with celery seed dressing, giving a new twist to the expected bacon, tomatoes, and blue cheese. To round out the feast, mac 'n' cheese with cauliflower will become a new favorite, and everybody's summer treat—corn on the cob—is oven-roasted and drizzled with jalapeño-lime butter for a little kick. Dessert is the classic that's hard to improve on: hot fudge sundaes. Homemade hot fudge sauce is the secret!

Juice of 4 limes

1 cup sugar

12 mint leaves, plus 6 sprigs of mint

12 ounces Sprite

1. Put the lime juice and 3 cups water into a saucepan.

2. In small bowl combine the sugar and 12 mint leaves and crush leaves with a fork, then add to the saucepan of lime juice. Place the saucepan over medium heat and cook until sugar is dissolved, about 3 minutes. Let cool to room temperature, and strain out crushed mint leaves.

3. Pour the lime mixture into a pitcher. Just before serving add 12 ounces Sprite, or soda water if you prefer a less sweet flavor. Fill glasses three-quarters full with ice, add the mint limeade, and garnish with a mint sprig.

Iceberg Lettuce Slaw with Bacon, Tomatoes, and Blue Cheese, and Celery Seed Dressing

1. To make the salad, combine the lettuce, tomatoes, bacon, and blue cheese in a salad bowl.

2. To make the dressing, place the sugar, onions, vinegar, mustard powder, and salt in a blender. Process until smooth, about 30 seconds. With the machine running, slowly add the olive oil in a thin stream and process until emulsified. Add the celery seeds and pulse to combine.

3. Toss the salad with the dressing. Cover and chill until ready to serve.

The salad and dressing can be made ahead and refrigerated until ready to serve.

1 head iceberg lettuce, cored and shredded

4 plum tomatoes or 2 medium tomatoes, seeded and cut into ½-inch dice

3 thick slices smoked bacon, cut into ½-inch dice and cooked crisp (page 310)

3 tablespoons crumbled blue cheese

Celery Seed Dressing

3 tablespoons sugar

2 tablespoons chopped white onions

2 tablespoons white vinegar

1 teaspoon mustard powder

½ teaspoon kosher salt

¼ cup extra virgin olive oil

1½ teaspoons celery seeds

1 tablespoon vegetable oil

3 garlic cloves, minced

1 medium white onion, cut into ¼-inch dice

2 pounds ground chuck

1 cup low-sodium beef broth

3 tablespoons Worcestershire sauce

2 teaspoons Lawry's Seasoned Salt

12 Sun-Dried Tomato Buns, sliced in half horizontally (page 85)

Yellow mustard

Hamburger dill pickles

1. Heat the oil in a large skillet over medium heat. Add the garlic and cook, stirring, until golden brown, about 1½ minutes. Add the onions and cook, stirring, until soft, about 3 minutes. Add the meat, increase heat to medium-high, and cook, stirring, until well browned and broken into small crumbles, about 15 minutes.

2. Once the meat is browned, stir in the beef broth, Worcestershire sauce, and seasoned salt. Bring to a simmer and cook uncovered, stirring occasionally, until the juices evaporate and the sauce is thick, 15 to 20 minutes.

3. Divide the meat among the sliced buns and serve with mustard and pickles on the side.

Sun-Dried Tomato Buns

1. Spray a large bowl with vegetable oil spray. Line a baking sheet with parchment paper or aluminum foil and set aside. Position one oven rack in the middle of the oven and the other rack in the top position.

2. Combine the milk, ½ cup water, the sun-dried tomato, butter, sugar, and salt in a saucepan. Bring just to a simmer; do not boil. Remove from the heat and let cool to 110°F.

3. Combine the flour and yeast in the bowl of a stand mixer fitted with the dough hook. Add the warm milk mixture and, with the mixer on low speed, beat until combined. Increase the speed to high and mix until the dough comes together and climbs the side of the hook, 3 to 4 minutes. (Alternatively, the dough can be made by hand. Combine the ingredients in a large bowl and mix with a heavy wooden spoon until the dough comes away from the sides of the bowl and forms a ball. Turn the dough out onto a lightly floured board and knead by hand until smooth and very pliable, 6 to 10 minutes.) Put the dough in the prepared bowl, turning to coat with oil on all sides. Cover the bowl with a kitchen towel. Let stand in a warm, draft-free place until doubled in size, about 1 hour.

4. Turn the dough out onto a lightly floured surface and divide into 12 pieces. Cupping your hand and exerting gentle pressure, roll each piece of dough against the work surface to form a smooth ball. Arrange the rolls on the prepared baking sheet, leaving 2 inches between them. Let the rolls relax for 1 to 2 minutes.

5. Flatten each roll with the palm of your hand into a 2-inch-wide disk. Cover the pan with a kitchen towel. Let stand in a warm, draft-free place until doubled in size, about 20 minutes.

6. Preheat the oven to 400°F.

7. Brush the tops and sides of the rolls with the egg wash. Bake for 12 minutes on the middle rack, and then move the baking sheet to the top rack. Bake until the rolls are golden brown, about 15 minutes more. Transfer the rolls to a wire rack to cool.

MAKES 1 DOZEN

Vegetable oil spray

½ cup milk

1 tablespoon drained and finely chopped oil-packed sun-dried tomato

1 tablespoon salted butter

1½ teaspoons sugar

¾ teaspoon kosher salt

2¾ cups all-purpose flour, plus more for the board

½ envelope (1⅛ teaspoons) active dry yeast

1 large egg beaten with 1 tablespoon water to make an egg wash

4 tablespoons salted butter, melted, divided

2 cups elbow macaroni

2 cups cauliflower pieces (about 1-inch)

1 cup milk

¾ cup heavy cream

2 tablespoons all-purpose flour

1 teaspoon mustard powder

1 teaspoon kosher salt

1 teaspoon freshly ground black pepper

1 cup shredded sharp white cheddar

1 cup shredded sharp yellow cheddar

1 recipe Homemade Bread Crumbs (page 312)

1. Preheat the oven to 350°F. Grease a 9 × 9 × 2-inch square baking dish with 1 tablespoon of the butter, spreading with your fingers to evenly coat the bottom and sides.

2. Bring 2 quarts of salted water to a boil in a large pot. Add the pasta and cook until nearly al dente but still firm, about 8 minutes. Add the cauliflower and cook until the pasta is al dente and the cauliflower is tender, 3 to 4 minutes. Drain in a colander, but don't rinse out the pot. Stir the pasta and cauliflower frequently while they cool to prevent the pasta from sticking together.

3. Combine the milk and cream in a microwave-safe measuring cup. Microwave on high until hot but not boiling, about 40 seconds. Put 2 tablespoons of the melted butter in the pasta pot over medium heat. Whisk in the flour and cook, whisking, to make a light roux, about 2 minutes. Gradually add the milk and cook, whisking, until the mixture boils and thickens, 3 to 4 minutes. Whisk in the mustard powder, salt, and pepper. Remove from the heat and add the cheeses, stirring until melted.

4. Add the drained pasta and cauliflower to the sauce and stir well to combine. Pour the mixture into the prepared baking dish. Sprinkle the bread crumbs evenly over the top of the pasta mixture. Reheat the remaining 1 tablespoon butter and drizzle over the bread crumbs. Bake until the top is golden brown and the cheese sauce is bubbling, 20 to 30 minutes. Let sit for 5 to 10 minutes before serving.

1. Preheat the oven to 400°F.

2. Shuck the corn, leaving the husks attached at their bases. Remove the corn silk and pull the husks back over the corn to cover the kernels. Place the corn on a baking sheet and roast until tender, 20 to 30 minutes.

3. Whisk together the butter, lime zest, lime juice, and jalapeños in a bowl until smooth.

4. Remove the corn from the oven. Using oven mitts, pull the husks away from the corn and slather with the whipped butter. Pull the husks back up around the corn and serve.

6 ears corn in their husks, stems trimmed

½ cup (1 stick) salted butter, at room temperature

1 teaspoon finely grated lime zest

1 teaspoon fresh lime juice

2 teaspoons minced pickled jalapeños

1 (14-ounce) can sweetened
  condensed milk

14 ounces high-quality dark
  chocolate, chopped

2 tablespoons salted butter,
  cut into pieces

1 tablespoon Kahlúa or other
  coffee-flavored liqueur, or brewed
  and chilled espresso

6 scoops vanilla, coffee, or chocolate
  ice cream

Optional toppings

Sweetened whipped cream
  (page 315)

6 chocolate-covered cherries with
  stems, or plain maraschino
  cherries

¼ cup chopped toasted walnuts
  (page 311)

1. In the top of a double boiler set over medium-low heat, heat the condensed milk until warm (about 110°F). Add the chocolate and cook, stirring with a wooden spoon, until smooth. Add the butter and Kahlúa, and cook, whisking, until smooth.

2. Place 1 scoop of ice cream in each of six ice cream coupes or shallow bowls. Spoon the hot fudge over the ice cream and garnish as desired with optional toppings.

Hot fudge can be reheated in a microwave-safe bowl on high at 30-second intervals until warm. Stir to distribute heat before using.

IOWA SUMMER SUPPER (FOR 4)

Chilled Dutch Salad

Grilled Pork Chops with Green Tomato–Corn Relish

Cheddar Carrot Crisp

Pawpaw Ice Cream

This menu celebrates Iowa's bounty—pork, corn, tomatoes, and pawpaws. It begins with Dutch salad, a meal in itself: boiled potatoes and eggs tossed with warm bacon dressing and served over a bed of chilled greens. I prefer a warm mustard vinaigrette to cold sliced potatoes and eggs on crisp salad greens for a lighter start. For the main course, a brine of mustard and apple cider vinegar ensures that the pork chops remain moist when grilled. The accompanying green tomato–corn relish has a touch of jalapeño heat.

Native Americans in the Upper Mississippi revered pawpaws, the largest fruit native to North America. Sometimes called a custard apple or the Midwest banana, it is neither an apple nor a banana. Pawpaw trees produce fruits that are two to ten inches long. They start green, then turn yellow, and finally black when they ripen in the fall. Best eaten when yellow, pawpaw fruit can be used fresh in pies, jams, and ice cream, or scooped out and frozen. With their short shelf life, pawpaws are a local indulgence in twenty-five Midwestern states, especially those that hug both sides of the Mississippi River. They are available from mid-August in southern states to mid-October in the north. If you can't find this elusive fruit, look for its tropical cousin, the cherimoya, often found at better greengrocers. A combination of bananas and papaya works just as well to make this custard ice cream.

Dressing

¼ *cup extra virgin olive oil*

1 teaspoon minced shallots

2 tablespoons Dijon mustard

2 tablespoons honey

1 tablespoon apple cider vinegar

½ *teaspoon kosher salt*

Salad

8 small red potatoes, such as Red
  Bliss, skin on

1 heart of romaine, cored and
  quartered

4 large hard-boiled eggs (page 310),
  sliced into ¼-inch rounds

1. To make the dressing, heat the olive oil in a saucepan over medium-low heat. Add the shallots and cook until soft, 1 to 2 minutes. Add the remaining ingredients and cook, stirring, until well blended, about 1 minute. Remove from the heat.

2. To make the salad, place the potatoes in a pot of salted water to cover by 1 inch. Bring to a boil and cook until the potatoes are just fork tender, 10 to 12 minutes. Drain in a colander. When cool enough to handle, thinly slice.

3. Arrange the romaine quarters on four plates. Arrange the potato and egg slices, alternating, on top of the lettuces. Drizzle the warm dressing over the salad before serving.

½ cup whole grain mustard

¼ cup honey

¼ cup apple juice

2 tablespoons fresh lemon juice

1 tablespoon apple cider vinegar

2 garlic cloves, minced

1 teaspoon kosher salt

½ teaspoon freshly ground black pepper

¼ teaspoon Tabasco or other hot sauce

4 (10-ounce) bone-in pork chops, about 1½ inches thick

1. To make the marinade, combine the mustard, honey, apple juice, lemon juice, vinegar, garlic, salt, pepper, and hot sauce in shallow dish large enough to hold the pork chops in a single layer. Whisk well to combine.

2. Add the pork chops to the marinade, turning to coat on both sides. Cover and refrigerate for 1 hour. Turn the chops and let marinate for 1 hour more. Remove the chops from the marinade and pat dry before cooking.

3. Preheat an outdoor grill. (Alternatively, heat a grill pan or cast-iron skillet over medium-high heat.) Grill the pork chops until they are cooked through and an instant-read thermometer inserted into the center reaches 155°F, 8 to 10 minutes per side. Serve hot with the Green Tomato–Corn Relish (page 95) on the side.

While the marinade can be prepared and refrigerated up to 2 days in advance, don't marinate the pork chops for more than 2 hours, or the meat will become mushy.

Green Tomato–Corn Relish

1. Line a large colander with cheesecloth and place in the sink or over a large bowl.

2. Combine the tomatoes, onions, and bell peppers in a food processor. Pulse 5 or 6 times to coarsely chop. Pour the mixture into the prepared colander and let drain at room temperature for 1 hour.

3. Heat a large skillet over medium heat. Add the corn to the dry pan and cook, stirring, until fragrant and golden, 3 to 4 minutes. Add the tomato mixture, jalapeño, brown and granulated sugars, and vinegar to the pan. Reduce the heat and simmer, stirring occasionally, until thick, about 20 minutes. Serve warm or chilled.

2 green tomatoes, quartered

1 medium white onion, peeled and quartered

1 red bell pepper, cored, seeded, and quartered

1 cup yellow corn kernels, fresh or, if frozen, thawed

1 teaspoon sliced pickled jalapeño

¼ cup packed light brown sugar

¼ cup granulated sugar

2 tablespoons white wine vinegar

4 large carrots cut into quarters

1 small white onion, peeled and quartered

¼ cup mayonnaise

½ cup grated sharp cheddar

1 teaspoon chopped fresh tarragon leaves, or ½ teaspoon dried

¼ cup Homemade Bread Crumbs (page 312) or store-bought fine dry bread crumbs

1. Preheat the oven to 350°F.

2. Bring 2 quarts water to a boil in a large saucepan. Add the carrots and onion and boil until just fork tender, about 4 minutes. Transfer with a strainer to a food processor. Pulse the vegetables 5 or 6 times until coarsely chopped. Transfer to a bowl.

3. Add the mayonnaise, cheddar, and tarragon to the vegetables and stir well to combine. Pour the mixture into a 1-quart baking dish. Sprinkle the top evenly with the bread crumbs and bake until bubbly and browned on top, 20 to 25 minutes. Serve hot.

1. Fill a large bowl with ice and cold water. Set aside.

2. To make the custard base, combine the egg yolks and sugar in a food processor and blend until pale yellow and thick, 3 to 4 minutes Add the cream and buttermilk, blending until well combined, 1 minute.

3. Place the custard mixture in the top of a double boiler with simmering water set over medium heat. Lower the heat and cook, stirring, until the mixture is warm and slightly thickened. (Alternatively, fill a medium saucepan one-third full with water and bring to a simmer over medium heat. Pour the custard mixture into a metal bowl that will fit over the saucepan without touching the water. Lower the heat and cook, stirring, until the mixture is slightly thickened.)

4. Combine the milk and cornstarch in a small bowl and stir to make a smooth slurry. Add the cornstarch slurry to the custard. Bring to a simmer and, stirring constantly with a heavy wooden spoon, cook until the custard is thick and coats the spoon, about 5 minutes. Remove from the heat and stir in the vanilla. Strain through a fine mesh strainer into a clean bowl. Discard the sediment.

5. Place the bowl of custard in the prepared bowl of ice and stir occasionally to cool. Cover with plastic wrap, pressing it directly against the surface to keep a skin from forming. Refrigerate until well chilled, about 2 hours.

6. Sprinkle the pawpaw with the lemon juice. Pour the custard into an ice cream maker and freeze according to the manufacturer's directions. Add the fruit halfway through the machine's freezing time. Serve the ice cream immediately.

4 large egg yolks

2 cups sugar

2 cups heavy cream

1 cup buttermilk

½ cup milk

2 tablespoons cornstarch

1 teaspoon pure vanilla extract

2 cups pawpaw fruit, or
1 cup mashed bananas
and 1 cup mashed papaya

1 tablespoon fresh lemon juice

If frozen, the ice cream will keep for 1 week: Pour the ice cream into a plastic container, put a piece of wax paper or plastic wrap on the surface, and freeze.

Part II
Twain Country: The Middle Mississippi River Region

HANNIBAL, MISSOURI, TO THE CONFLUENCE WITH
THE ARKANSAS RIVER

The middle region of the Mississippi River has two main influences—its deep connection to Mark Twain through his hometown of Hannibal, Missouri, and the graceful sophistication of St. Louis. The Germans made an impact with their knowledge of viticulture and farming in the region, but there is quite a bit of French influence still prevalent as well. In this section I share my captain's menu served on the riverboat *American Queen,* inspired by Samuel Clemens's favorite foods. To celebrate St. Louis I offer a menu with a twist on the city's best-known dish, fried ravioli. This region of the River serves up some of the best America has to offer—Missouri wines, black walnuts, wild game, blended with Arkansas farm-to-table, and, of course, the icing-on-the-cake river stories by Mark Twain.

Hannibal, Missouri, founded by Moses D. Bates in 1819, was a major docking port for steamboats and flatboats. Because of its prominence and location on the River, the population had doubled by 1860. A city with the ability to constantly reinvent itself, Hannibal has been home to many industries, including pork packing, soap and candle making, and lumber mills that boomed along with the railroad. When the railroads began to diminish, the city produced everything from shoes to buttons to cement.

About thirty miles to the south lies Louisiana, Missouri. When settled in 1817 by John Bryson, this town was all riverfront property. As in my hometown of Natchez, many residents today are direct descendants of the original settlers. Who would want to leave these lovely antebellum homes? Missouri's Department of Natural Resources claims that this remains the most intact Victorian streetscape in the state. Then there is Clarksville, a notable halfway mark between Canada and the Gulf of Mexico as well as a halfway point between Hannibal and St. Louis. The River is so elevated here that you can enjoy an eight-hundred-square-mile view.

Farther south lies the charming town of St. Charles, founded in 1769 by French-Canadian fur trader Louis Blanchette. It grew as a trading post and is now known as the place from which Lewis and Clark began their westward expedition in 1804. Later came German and Irish immigrants, whose culinary impact remains today.

In the nineteenth century, Italians flocked to a neighborhood of St. Louis today known as The Hill. Nearly three-quarters of its residents are Italian Americans, and it is home to a large number of locally renowned Italian restaurants, bakeries, grocery stores, and two bocce courts and gardens. The most recent wave of immigrants to claim St. Louis as home are the Bosnians who left their war-torn country and took refuge here two decades ago. Every cafe and restaurant up and down Gravois Street offers *cevapi* (cheh-VAH-pee), small beef sausage links usually spiced very simply with salt, pepper, and garlic and then served on a flat, round bread with a crust and texture similar to an English muffin's.

West from the Mississippi, southern Missouri boasts four recognized wine-growing areas. Downriver, where Missouri meets Kentucky and Tennessee, lies a region that was struck by three large earthquakes in 1812. New Madrid, once the largest settlement on the Mississippi River between St. Louis and Natchez, was destroyed. Some of the most dramatic effects of the earthquakes occurred on the River itself. Entire islands disappeared, banks caved in, large cracks opened and closed in the riverbeds, and water spouting from these fissures produced ocean-size waves. New sections of the river channel were formed and old channels cut off as boats capsized and an unknown number of people drowned. The region, called the New Madrid Seismic Zone, remains the epicenter of earthquakes in the area.

Desha County, Arkansas, and Bolivar County, Mississippi, located at the confluence of the Arkansas and Mississippi Rivers, both had towns that were washed away in 1874. Ironically, the towns that met their Waterloo were named Wellington and Napoleon.

MARK TWAIN'S CAPTAIN'S DINNER (FOR 8)

Twain Tea

Oysters Rockefeller with Herbsaint Hollandaise

Smoked Trout Canapés

Mock Turtle Soup

Asparagus, Eggs, and Roasted Beets on Chilled Romaine Hearts
with Maytag-Gin Dressing

Braised Short Ribs with Horseradish Mashed Potatoes

Fig-Pecan Bread Pudding with Caramelized Sugar Sauce

The image of steamboats cruising the Mississippi was firmly planted in the American imagination by Samuel Clemens, best known as Mark Twain. Once I began to mirror his journey on the River, I soon became enthralled and inspired by his work and life. I could not resist his charms and talents. A gourmet if not a gourmand, Twain left copious references to his favorite foods in his notes, letters, and other writings. The menu for his seventieth birthday dinner at Delmonico's in New York is an example: Oysters—Consommé Souveraine, Green Turtle—Timbales Perigourdine—Filets of Kingfish Meunière, Cucumbers, Persillade Potatoes—Saddle of Lamb Colbert, Stuffed Tomatoes—Baltimore Terrapin, Mushrooms on Toast with Cream, Sherbet with Kirsch—Quail, Red Head Duck, Fried Hominy and Currant Jelly—Salad: Celery Mayonnaise—Fancy Ice Cream, Assorted Cakes, Bonbons.

Here is the menu I would serve Mr. Clemens, if I were lucky enough to have his company at my table. It is a big one, so feel free to choose just a few dishes for your dinner.

I would begin the evening with Twain Tea—a stiff bourbon cocktail with orange marmalade and black tea, served chilled over ice. The dinner starts with oysters Rockefeller and smoked trout canapés. Mr. Twain loved green turtle soup. In his day cooks found they could duplicate the soup's flavor by using beef instead of expensive turtle. For sustainable reasons, I continue the tradition of a beef substitute. With enough sherry you can hardly tell the difference. A touch of gin is whisked into the Maytag blue cheese that is drizzled on the salad. Braised beef ribs are slow-cooked with red wine and a dark roux. Fig-and-pecan-studded bread pudding with a caramelized sugar sauce finishes the meal.

1 cup sweet orange marmalade

¼ cup sugar

2 cups good-quality bourbon

1½ cups strongly brewed black tea

8 thin half-moon orange slices,
   for garnish

1. Bring 1 cup water, the marmalade, and sugar to a boil in a saucepan. Reduce the heat and simmer, stirring, until the sugar dissolves and the marmalade melts, about 5 minutes. Remove from the heat and let cool. Strain this syrup into a pitcher. Add the bourbon and tea and stir well.

2. Fill eight old-fashioned or martini glasses with crushed ice and Twain Tea. Garnish the rim of each glass with an orange slice.

1. Preheat the oven to 450°F. Arrange the shucked oysters on the half shell on a large baking sheet.

2. Bring 2 quarts of salted water to a boil. Add the spinach and romaine to the boiling water and cook until very tender, 4 minutes. Pour the cooked greens into a mesh strainer to drain, pressing with the back of a heavy spoon to get rid of the excess liquid. Mince the greens and set aside.

3. Melt the butter in a large skillet over medium heat. Add the onions, celery, and parsley and cook, stirring, until the vegetables are soft, 4 minutes. Add the anchovy paste, cream, and Herbsaint, stir, and cook until thick and reduced by about one-third, 1½ to 2 minutes. Add the spinach-romaine mixture and Parmesan and stir well. Slowly stir in the bread crumbs, 1 tablespoon at a time, until the mixture tightens but is more like wet sand, being careful not to make it too dry.

4. Top each oyster with 1 heaping tablespoon of the greens mixture. Bake the oysters until golden brown, 10 to 15 minutes.

5. Remove from the oven and arrange the oysters on a platter. Top each oyster with Herbsaint Hollandaise and serve.

If oysters in the shell are not available, you can prepare these in small ramekins. Reusable stainless steel oyster shells can be found at sosoystershells.com.

18 oysters, shucked and on the half shell

1 pound fresh baby spinach

4 ounces romaine lettuce, cored and chopped into 1-inch pieces

¼ cup (½ stick) salted butter

¼ cup minced white onions

3 tablespoons minced celery hearts

2 teaspoons chopped fresh parsley leaves

1 teaspoon anchovy paste

¼ cup heavy cream

2 tablespoons Herbsaint or Pernod

¼ cup freshly grated Parmigiano-Reggiano

¼ cup Homemade Bread Crumbs (page 312), or fine dry bread crumbs

1 cup Herbsaint Hollandaise (page 312)

MAKES 16

*8 small (about 1½ inches round)
red potatoes, halved*

*2 ounces cream cheese, at room
temperature*

2 teaspoons mayonnaise

2 teaspoons sour cream

*3 ounces smoked trout (see Source
Guide, page 316), bones and skin
removed, flaked*

½ teaspoon fresh lemon juice

*1 teaspoon minced green onions,
tops only, or chives, plus
additional 1 tablespoon for
garnish*

1. Slice a thin piece from the rounded side of each potato half so that they will sit flat when stuffed.

2. Place the potatoes in a pot of salted water to cover by 1 inch and bring to a boil. Cook until the potatoes are just fork tender, 10 to 12 minutes. Drain in a colander. When the potatoes are cool enough to handle, use a small melon baller or teaspoon to scoop out the centers of the potatoes, leaving a ⅛-inch shell of flesh on the potato skins. Reserve the remaining potatoes for making the filling.

3. Combine the scooped-out potato flesh, cream cheese, mayonnaise, and sour cream in the bowl of a stand mixer fitted with a paddle attachment. Beat the mixture on low speed until creamy and smooth. Using a rubber spatula, fold in the trout, lemon juice, and green onions, mixing until just combined.

4. Fill each hollowed-out potato half with 2 teaspoons of the potato-trout mixture. Garnish each potato with some minced green onion or chive.

These can be made and refrigerated 24 hours ahead, but return to room temperature before serving.

1. Heat the olive oil in a dutch oven over medium heat. Season the meat with the salt and pepper. Cook the meat, turning, until browned on all sides, about 5 minutes.

2. With the browned meat still in the pan, melt the butter in the dutch oven. Add the onions, celery, bell pepper, garlic, thyme, basil, clove, and bay leaves and cook over medium heat until the vegetables are soft, about 10 minutes.

3. Add the beef and chicken stocks and bring to a simmer. Stir in the tomatoes and their juices, the tomato paste, sherry, roux, Worcestershire sauce, lemon halves (without squeezing out the juice), and Cajun Seasoning. Bring the mixture to a boil. Reduce the heat and simmer, uncovered, stirring occasionally until the meat is falling apart, 45 minutes to 1 hour. Skim the surface of any foam, then add the spinach, stir to incorporate, and simmer for 10 minutes.

4. Remove the pot from the heat and adjust the seasoning to taste. Ladle the soup into soup bowls, and garnish the top of each with grated egg before serving.

Once cooked, the meat should fall apart in the soup. If necessary, remove the meat, chop it, and then return it to the soup. Remove the lemon halves without squeezing them and the bay leaves before serving.

3 tablespoons extra virgin olive oil

2 pounds beef chuck roast, trimmed and cut into ½-inch cubes

1 tablespoon kosher salt

2 teaspoons freshly ground black pepper

1 cup (2 sticks) salted butter

2 cups chopped yellow onions

1½ cups chopped celery

1 cup chopped green bell pepper

2 tablespoons minced garlic

1 tablespoon chopped fresh thyme leaves

1 tablespoon dried basil

2 teaspoons ground clove

4 bay leaves

1½ quarts low-sodium beef broth

1½ quarts low-sodium chicken broth

1 (10-ounce) can diced tomatoes and their juices

1 (6-ounce) can tomato paste

2 cups dry sherry

½ cup Dark Roux (page 311)

¼ cup Worcestershire sauce

1 lemon, halved

1 teaspoon Cajun Seasoning (page 311)

2 cups baby spinach, coarsely chopped

3 large hard-boiled eggs (page 310), finely grated

Asparagus, Eggs, and Roasted Beets on Chilled Romaine Hearts with Maytag-Gin Dressing

4 large beets, well scrubbed and trimmed with ½ inch stem remaining

2 teaspoons vegetable oil

24 thin asparagus spears, stems trimmed

4 large hard-boiled eggs (page 310), sliced into ¼-inch rounds

2 romaine hearts, ends trimmed and cut lengthwise into quarters

½ cup Maytag-Gin Dressing (page 104)

1. Preheat oven to 375°F. Rub ½ teaspoon of the oil onto each beet. Wrap the beets individually in aluminum foil and place on a baking sheet. Bake until they can easily be pierced with a fork, 45 minutes to 1 hour. Remove from the oven, unwrap, and let sit until cool enough to handle.

2. Slice and discard a thin sliver on the tops and bottoms of the beets. Using your fingers (preferably in rubber gloves, as beets stain), rub off the beet skins. Slice each beet into six ½-inch-thick slices and place on a large dish. The beets should be cooled and then refrigerated until well chilled before plating.

3. In a saucepan large enough for the asparagus to lie sideways, bring 1 quart of salted water to a boil. While waiting for the water to boil, fill a large bowl with ice and water. To keep the asparagus spears in a bunch, secure them with a rubber band or butcher's twine. Carefully place the asparagus in the pot standing upright and cook for 1 minute. Using tongs, gently lay the asparagus flat in the water so the spears are completely submerged, and cook until just tender, 1 to 2 minutes, depending upon the thickness of the spears. Transfer with tongs to the ice bath, cut the rubber band or twine, and let chill completely. Pat dry on kitchen towels.

4. On each of eight salad plates, fan three beet slices on the left side. On the right side of the plate, intersperse three asparagus spears with three egg slices. Place one romaine wedge in the center of each plate and lightly drizzle with the dressing before serving.

Maytag-Gin Dressing

1. Combine the garlic, mustard powder, onion salt, and white pepper in a bowl and stir to combine. Add the vinegar and Worcestershire sauce and whisk. Let sit for 5 minutes.

2. Whisk in mayonnaise, sour cream, and gin. Whisk until smooth, and then add the crumbled blue cheese.

MAKES 2½ CUPS

1 small garlic clove, minced

½ teaspoon mustard powder

¼ teaspoon onion salt

1 pinch ground white pepper

1 tablespoon red wine vinegar

½ teaspoon Worcestershire sauce

1 cup mayonnaise

½ cup sour cream

1½ ounces gin

4 ounces Maytag or other blue cheese, crumbled

The dressing can be made a day in advance and kept covered in the refrigerator.

Braised Short Ribs with Horseradish Mashed Potatoes

8 choice or prime beef short ribs,
   each 14 ounces

4 teaspoons kosher salt

4 teaspoons freshly ground black
   pepper

¼ teaspoon garlic powder

2½ cups red wine

¼ cup Dark Roux (page 311)

4 sprigs rosemary

4 garlic cloves

1 recipe Horseradish Mashed
   Potatoes (page 112)

1. Preheat the oven to 375°F.

2. Heat a large skillet over medium-high heat until very hot. Season the short ribs well with the salt, pepper, and garlic powder. The meat has enough fat that you do not need oil to brown these. Brown the ribs in the skillet on all sides. You may need to do this in batches. Place the seared ribs in a roasting pan.

3. Once meat is removed, deglaze the skillet with the red wine. Continue to cook over medium heat for 3 to 4 minutes, and then add 2 cups water and ¼ cup dark roux to the skillet over medium heat. Cook over medium heat, stirring to dissolve the roux. Strain out debris and pour mixture over the ribs in the roasting pan.

4. Roast for 30 minutes at 375°F uncovered. Then cover, lower to the oven heat to 325°F, and continue cooking the ribs for 60 minutes.

5. Pour the sauce into a bowl, leaving the ribs in the roasting pan. Allow to cool before refrigerating. Once the sauce is cooled, remove the chilled fat from the top of the sauce. Pour the defatted sauce over the ribs and reheat in a preheated 350°F oven for 25 minutes.

6. Serve with Horseradish Mashed Potatoes.

Have a butcher special cut your 14-ounce bone-in beef short ribs. You should request "choice"-or, if your budget and market availability allow, "prime" grade.

This dish is best made a day in advance.

Horseradish Mashed Potatoes

6 medium Yukon Gold potatoes
(about 3 pounds), washed and
peeled

3 teaspoons salt, divided

3 tablespoons butter

½ cup buttermilk

2 tablespoons prepared horseradish

1. In large saucepan combine potatoes, 2 teaspoons salt, and enough water to cover; heat to boiling on high. Reduce heat to low and simmer, covered, until fork tender, about 20 minutes.

2. In microwave-safe bowl heat butter and buttermilk for 30 to 40 seconds, until butter is melted.

3. Drain potatoes and let dry for 5 minutes, then transfer to a larger microwavable bowl. Using a hand mixer, whip potatoes with warmed butter and buttermilk until creamy, about 2 minutes. Stir in 1 teaspoon of salt and horseradish. Cover with plastic and microwave for 2 minutes to heat before serving.

1. Preheat the oven to 350°F. Lightly spray an 11 × 7-inch baking dish with the vegetable oil spray. (Alternatively, spray eight 1-cup ramekins or molds with the spray and place on a baking sheet.)

2. Combine the eggs, cream, and sugar in the bowl of a stand mixer fitted with a whisk attachment. Beat on medium speed until light and fluffy, 2 to 3 minutes. Add the cinnamon and orange zest and beat for 30 seconds.

3. Using a rubber spatula, fold in the bread cubes, pecans, and figs; stir well to incorporate and coat the bread. Pour the mixture into the prepared baking dish and bake until the custard is set and the top is golden brown, 50 minutes for the baking dish or 40 minutes for 1-cup ramekins. Let the bread pudding cool for 10 minutes before serving.

4. Spoon the bread pudding onto dessert plates and drizzle caramelized sugar sauce over each portion. Serve hot.

I have made my fair share of bread puddings, and this is my favorite. I use soft bread instead of the traditional stale bread. Bread pudding should be creamy, and this one is.

Vegetable oil spray

6 large eggs

2 cups heavy cream

1 cup packed light brown sugar

1 teaspoon ground cinnamon

1 teaspoon finely grated orange zest

3 cups cubed hotdog or hamburger buns (5 buns)

1 cup chopped pecans, toasted (page 311)

1 cup quartered dried figs

1 recipe Caramelized Sugar Sauce (page 115)

Caramelized Sugar Sauce

1. Place the sugar in a heavy saucepan over medium heat. Cook undisturbed until the sugar begins to caramelize. When the caramel begins to bubble and turn brown, stir gently with a long-handled wooden spoon. Cook, stirring, until the sugar becomes amber-brown syrup. Remove from the heat and slowly add 1 cup water, stirring constantly. (The mixture will bubble up and pop.) Return to medium-low heat and cook, stirring, until all the caramelized sugar is dissolved.

2. Once the water is completely incorporated, remove from the heat and slowly add the bourbon, stirring constantly with a wooden spoon.

3. Let cool to room temperature before serving with the Fig-Pecan Bread Pudding (page 113).

When I have guests for cooking class weekends at Twin Oaks, I like to take the fear out of cooking. When it comes to caramelizing sugar, however, I try to put a little fear into my students, because there is nothing worse than a burn from hot sugar. Have everything prepped and organized, so there are no distractions while you're making the sugar sauce.

MAKES ABOUT 2 CUPS

3 cups sugar

½ cup bourbon

American Queen Flower Fizz

Sugar-Crusted Blackberry Muffins

Beignets

Eggs Sardou with Artichoke-Potato Hash

Melon Balls with Mint and Peach Syrup

Crêpes Suzette

From 1868 to 1886 the *J. M. White,* an opulent riverboat known as "the floating palace," traveled the River between New Orleans and Greenville, Mississippi. It was noted for its magnificent curved staircase, luxury decks, gilded ballroom, and large staterooms for 250 guests. Many of those details are replicated on the new *American Queen* that made its debut voyage on April 22, 2012. When creating the menus and recipes for the *American Queen,* I knew that an elegant brunch had to be included as a symbol of the meals served on the grand paddle wheelers of yesterday.

Since the regions along the Mississippi River are the birthplaces of American music—gospel, blues, and jazz—a traditional jazz brunch on the *American Queen* sets a festive mood. Instead of the orange flower water typically used in a Ramos Fizz, a traditional brunch cocktail, I created the *American Queen* Flower Fizz, made with iris-scented gin and rose water.

The menu begins with a basket of warm blackberry muffins and sugar-dusted beignets, followed by melon balls with a syrup infused with mint and peach schnapps. The main course is an updated version of a classic Sardou, replacing the artichoke bottoms with an artichoke heart and potato hash and, of course, the creamed spinach and Herbsaint Hollandaise. On the *American Queen,* we finish with Crêpes Suzette, a classic that will jazz up any party!

MAKES 4 (6-OUNCE) COCKTAILS

1 cup Magellan gin (iris-flavored gin), or 6 ounces gin and 2 ounces Crème de Violette or violet liqueur

½ cup heavy cream

½ cup Simple Syrup (page 314)

4 teaspoons fresh lemon juice

4 teaspoons fresh lime juice

½ cup liquid (pasteurized) egg whites, or 4 large egg whites

6 dashes rose water

Classic Method

Combine all of the ingredients in a cocktail shaker without ice (it's called a dry shake), cover, and shake for at least 30 seconds. Add 4 to 5 small ice cubes to the shaker and shake hard until the ice dissolves. Divide the mixture among 4 tall glasses half filled with ice.

Easy Method

Combine all of the ingredients in a blender and blend for 1 minute. Add 4 to 5 small ice cubes and blend until the ice dissolves and the mixture is frothy. Divide the mixture among 4 tall glasses half filled with ice.

Note: Pasteurized egg whites, found in the egg section of supermarkets, are heated to 130°F to make them safe from bacterial contamination. Anyone with a compromised immune system should use these instead of raw egg whites.

To make a decent fizz, you'll need to work in batches. A standard cocktail shaker makes four drinks. Double prep the ingredients for ease in repeating the process for the other four guests. While purists prefer the "classic" method, the blender method is quicker.

MAGELLAN GIN

I just love Magellan gin. I am always looking for that "special something," and the floral notes of Magellan, enhanced by the rose water, give this cocktail an incredible aroma and flavor. And while gin fizzes are typically made with orange flower water, I prefer the notes of rose water in my cocktail.

MAKES 1 DOZEN

Vegetable oil spray

2 cups all-purpose flour

1 tablespoon baking powder

2 large eggs

1 cup sour cream

¾ cup sugar

½ cup (1 stick) salted butter,
  melted

1 tablespoon buttermilk

1½ cups fresh or frozen blackberries
  (if frozen, do not thaw)

Topping

½ cup sugar

¼ cup all-purpose flour

3 tablespoons cold salted butter,
  cut into ½-inch pieces

½ cup pecans

1. Preheat the oven to 350°F. Lightly spray a 12-cup muffin tin with the vegetable oil spray. (Alternatively, line the tin with paper muffin liners.)

2. To make the muffins, whisk together the flour and baking powder in a bowl. Combine the eggs, sour cream, sugar, melted butter, and buttermilk in another large bowl and mix well.

3. Slowly add the wet ingredients to the dry ingredients. Mix with a heavy wooden spoon until the batter is stiff. Stir in the blackberries, being careful not to overmix and break the berries.

4. To make the topping, combine the sugar and flour in a food processor and pulse to blend. Add the butter and pulse until the butter is the size of peas. Add the pecans and pulse until the mixture resembles large crumbs.

5. Evenly divide the batter among the cups of the prepared muffin tin. Sprinkle about 4 teaspoons of the topping on each muffin. Bake on the middle rack of the oven until a tester inserted into the center of a muffin comes out clean, about 25 minutes. Let cool in the pan on a wire rack for 5 minutes, then turn the muffins out onto a wire rack, top sides up, to finish cooling.

THE PADDLE WHEELERS AND
THE MISSISSIPPI RIVER

The Mississippi paddle-wheel boat tradition began in earnest in 1811 when the steamer *New Orleans,* built by inventor Robert Fulton and politician-industrialist Robert Livingstone, began service between Natchez and New Orleans. After much trial and error, the familiar stern-wheeler had won out over the side-wheeler, which was often difficult to dock.

The boats, which offered various degrees of luxury, ranged in length from about 50 feet to more than 300 feet and were 10 to 80 feet wide. What made them so successful on the Mississippi was their extremely shallow draft—often as little as one foot. It was often said that the paddle-wheel steamer could "navigate on a heavy dew."

When cooking beignets, do not overcrowd them in the oil. Just do a few at a time and let the oil come back up to temperature between batches by waiting a minute or two, or they will not cook properly.

1. In a microwavable bowl, combine the milk, ½ cup water microwave on low until the liquid is hot but not scalding. Remove and let sit until an instant-read thermometer registers 110°F. Stir in sugar and sprinkle yeast on top. Let begin to activate for 10 minutes. Add 2 cups flour to bowl in stand mixer.

2. Add the yeast mixture to the flour and mix on medium speed until blended, about 2 minutes. Add the melted butter, egg yolk, and vanilla and mix on medium speed until a soft dough forms that pulls away from the sides of the bowl, 1 to 2 minutes. If the dough is too soft, add the remaining flour, 1 tablespoon at a time, as needed to make pliable dough that is not too tacky.

3. Oil a large bowl with 1 teaspoon of the vegetable oil. Put the dough in the bowl, turning to coat with oil on all sides. Cover the bowl with a kitchen towel. Let stand in a warm, draft-free place until doubled in size, about 1 hour. (If you prefer to make your dough the day before, at this point the dough can be covered with plastic wrap and refrigerated overnight. Let warm to room temperature before proceeding to step 4.)

4. Turn the dough out onto a lightly floured surface. Roll to ¼-inch thickness with a floured rolling pin. Using a sharp knife or pizza cutter, cut the dough into twelve 2½ × 3-inch rectangles.

5. Line a baking sheet with paper towels. Clip a deep-frying thermometer to the side of a dutch oven, half fill it with oil, and heat to 350°F. (Alternatively, an electric skillet or deep fryer set to 350°F can be used.)

6. Working in batches and using a long-handled slotted spoon or strainer, gently lower the dough into the oil, being careful not to overcrowd. Cook until the beignets are golden brown, turning once, 1 to 2 minutes per side.

7. Transfer the beignets to the paper-lined baking sheet to drain. Dust with confectioners' sugar and serve hot.

MAKES 1½ DOZEN

2 tablespoons milk

4 tablespoons sugar

1 envelope (2¼ teaspoons) active dry yeast

2¼ cups all-purpose flour, divided

1 tablespoon salted butter, melted

1 large egg yolk

1 teaspoon pure vanilla extract

1 teaspoon vegetable oil, plus enough for frying

Confectioners' sugar, for dusting

2 cups diced red potato

2 cups diced frozen artichoke hearts

1 tablespoon salted butter

½ cup diced white onion

¾ cup heavy cream

½ teaspoon minced garlic

1 tablespoon Herbsaint or Pernod

1 pounds fresh spinach leaves, stemmed

2 tablespoons white vinegar

8 large eggs

Herbsaint Hollandise (page 312)

Artichoke-Potato Hash:

1. Place diced red potato in a saucepan, covered in water with ½ teaspoon of salt over medium heat. Bring to a boil, add diced artichoke hearts, and cook until potatoes are tender, 3 to 4 minutes. Drain well.

2. Place a sauté pan over medium heat, add butter and diced onion. Cook for 1 minute, and then add the cooked potatoes and artichokes. Cook until browned about 2 minutes. Set aside.

Creamed Spinach:

1. Place heavy cream in a saucepan and reduce in half.

2. Add the garlic, Herbsaint, and spinach leaves. Cook for 2 minutes until spinach is wilted.

Poached Eggs:

1. Pour 4 inches of water into a large, deep skillet. Bring to a simmer over high heat, and then reduce to a bare simmer. Add the vinegar.

2. Being careful not to break the yolks, crack four of the eggs into individual small saucers. Gently slide into the barely simmering water, lifting the whites over the yolks. Poach until the whites and yolks are just set yet still soft in the center, 2 to 3 minutes. Using a slotted spoon, remove the eggs to a plate, tilting the plate to let the water run off. With a paring knife, trim off any of the trailing white part. Repeat with the remaining eggs.

In the center of each plate, place creamed spinach topped with a poached egg. Surround with hash and spoon Herbsaint Hollandaise (page 312) over the egg. Serve.

¼ cup sugar

2 tablespoons peach schnapps

2 cups honeydew melon balls

2 cups cantaloupe balls

6 fresh mint leaves, julienned

1. Combine the sugar, peach schnapps, and ¼ cup water in a small sauce-pan. Cook over medium heat, stirring, until the sugar dissolves and the syrup is reduced by half, about 4 minutes. Remove from the heat and let cool completely, at least 30 minutes.

2. Place the honeydew and cantaloupe balls in a bowl. Add the syrup and toss well.

3. Add the mint and toss lightly to distribute evenly. Cover and refriger-ate until well chilled, at least 2 hours and up to 1 day. Serve chilled in an attractive serving bowl or individual stemmed glasses or pretty bowls.

MAKES 8

Crêpes

2 large eggs

½ cup milk

⅛ teaspoon salt

1 cup all-purpose flour

2 tablespoons salted butter, melted

Vegetable oil spray

Sauce

¾ cup sugar

1 tablespoon finely grated orange zest

¼ cup (½ stick) salted butter

¼ cup Grand Marnier, Cointreau, or other orange-flavored liqueur

1. Whisk the eggs in a bowl. Add the milk, ½ cup water, and the salt and whisk to combine. Slowly whisk in the flour and the butter to make a smooth, thin batter. Let batter rest for 10 minutes before using.

2. Heat a 6-inch crepe pan or nonstick skillet over medium-high heat. When the pan is hot, lightly coat with the vegetable spray. Ladle about ¼ cup of the batter into the pan, tilting it to coat evenly with batter. Cook until the crepe is golden brown on the bottom and the top is set, about 1 minute. Using a rubber spatula, flip the crepe. Cook on the second side until light brown and set, about 30 seconds. Transfer to a plate. Repeat with the remaining batter, separating the cooked crepes with sheets of wax paper. (The crepes can be made up to 2 hours ahead and kept at room temperature.)

3. To make the sauce, combine the sugar and orange zest in a bowl. Let sit for 1 hour so that the zest can impart an orange flavor to the sugar.

4. Melt the butter in a large skillet over low heat, being careful not to let it brown. Add the orange sugar and cook, stirring constantly with a wooden spoon, until the sugar dissolves completely, about 2 minutes.

5. Fold eight crepes (the best ones, if you've made more) into quarters and place them in the skillet over medium heat, stirring to coat each evenly with the sauce. Carefully add the Grand Marnier and, using a long-handled lighter, ignite the contents. Stand away from the stove for a few seconds and let the flames die down. Turn off the burner. Place one crepe on each of eight dessert plates and serve immediately.

FLAMBÉ

When liquor or liqueur is added to a dish and set on fire, the dramatic technique is called flambé. A couple of safety tips: Use a long-handled lighter for safety. Never remove the pan from the stove when lighting the contents. The liquor will burn off, so just stand back for a few seconds and be patient. More-over, as always with kitchen safety, the fewer distractions, the better.

ST. LOUIS TOASTED RAVIOLI DINNER (FOR 6)

Limoncello Martinis

Antipasto Platter (Marinated Mozzarella Balls, Roasted Peppers, and Marinated Tomato-Basil Crostini)

Pan-Roasted Eggplant with Basil Vinaigrette

Toasted Ravioli (Spinach-Ricotta with Lemon and Anchovy, Mushroom-Sage, and Turkey-Pesto) with Marinara Sauce

Tiramisu "Martinis"

The Middle Mississippi is anchored by St. Louis, known as the Gateway to the West. For more than two hundred years, explorers and adventurers looking to settle into a new life traveled through St. Louis on their way to towns, farms, and cities west of the River. Italians who arrived in the 1800s to work in the clay mines imprinted their culinary influence on the city. St. Louis's most popular dish is "toasted" (actually fried) ravioli. While veal is the preferred ravioli filling, I offer three new ones, spinach with lemon and anchovy, mushroom-sage, and turkey-pesto. Feel free to make all or just one filling. A rich, thick marinara sauce accompanies the toasted ravioli.

This menu can be served in courses or, if doubled, as part of a buffet party menu. Limoncello martinis are made by the pitcher, so guests can refill their glasses. The marinated mozzarella, roasted peppers, tomatoes and basil on crostini, and roasted eggplant can be served with cocktails or as a salad tray with dinner. You can substitute egg roll wrappers for the ravioli dough, or even buy ravioli if you prefer. For dessert, I suggest a tiramisu layered into individual glasses like parfaits.

2¼ cups vodka

¾ cup limoncello

½ cup Simple Syrup (page 314)

6 lemon twists, for garnish

1. Combine the vodka, limoncello, and simple syrup in a pitcher.

2. Add ice to the pitcher. Using a long-handled bar spoon or iced tea-spoon, chip at the ice with a vigorous up-and-down motion until well chilled with tiny ice crystals floating on top, 30 to 45 seconds. Strain the mixture into six martini glasses. Garnish each glass with a lemon twist and serve immediately.

I use a ratio of 1 part limoncello to 3 parts vodka and some simple syrup. These are served "up," which means chilled but not over ice. To do so, vigorously stir the ice with a long-handled cocktail spoon in the mixing glass so when you strain the cocktail into the glass, it has thin ice shavings floating on the top. That is a perfect cocktail.

1. Place the mozzarella balls into a 1-quart Mason jar with a tight-fitting lid. Add enough olive oil to cover the cheese by ¾ inch. Add the lemon juice, rosemary, basil, garlic, salt, and red pepper. Cover tightly and shake well to mix the ingredients, being careful not to break the cheese.

2. Refrigerate for 12 hours. Bring to room temperature before serving.

Small mozzarella balls are called bocconcini, meaning "little bites," and often are sold under this name.

The marinated mozzarella balls will keep refrigerated for 1 week.

1 pound small mozzarella balls, drained

Extra virgin olive oil

2 tablespoons fresh lemon juice

One 3-inch sprig fresh rosemary

1 teaspoon minced fresh basil leaves

1 teaspoon minced garlic

½ teaspoon kosher salt

¼ teaspoon crushed red pepper

4 green, red, or yellow bell peppers,
  or a combination
3 tablespoons extra virgin olive oil
½ teaspoon kosher salt

1. Turn the burner on a gas stove to medium-high. Using metal tongs or a long-handled toasting fork, hold the peppers one at a time over the open flame, turning, until completely charred and blackened on all sides. (Alternatively, preheat a broiler to high. Place the peppers on the broiler pan and cook, turning as needed, until charred.) Transfer to a bowl, cover with plastic wrap, and let steam until cool enough to handle, 15 to 20 minutes.

2. Uncover the peppers. Working over the bowl to retain the juices, use a paring knife to remove the skins, cores, and seeds. Slice the peppers lengthwise into ½-inch-thick strips and return to the bowl with their juices.

3. Add the olive oil and salt, stirring to coat the peppers evenly.

The peppers will keep tightly covered in the refrigerator for up to 1 week.

1. Preheat oven to 350F. Trim ends of French bread, cut into ½-inch rounds, rub them with the garlic clove, and toast lightly on both sides.

2. Place the tomatoes in a bowl. Add the basil, olive oil, vinegar, lemon juice, minced garlic, salt, and pepper and toss to combine.

3. Divide the tomatoes between the toasts and serve immediately.

During the summer months, a huge variety of heirloom tomatoes are available along the length of the River. Throughout the country, farmers' markets and roadside farm stands are the best outlets for these jewels.

The tomato mixture can be made in advance, but top the toasts at the last minute so they don't get soggy.

1 (12-inch) loaf fresh French bread

1 whole garlic clove, peeled

2 large ripe tomatoes, seeded and diced

6 fresh basil leaves, julienned

2 tablespoons extra virgin olive oil

1 teaspoon aged balsamic vinegar

1 teaspoon fresh lemon juice

½ teaspoon fresh minced garlic

½ teaspoon kosher salt

½ teaspoon freshly ground black pepper

Pan-Roasted Eggplant with Basil Vinaigrette

¼ cup extra virgin olive oil

1 teaspoon minced garlic

1 teaspoon kosher salt

½ teaspoon cracked black pepper

*1 large eggplant, trimmed and
  sliced into ¼-inch rounds*

1 recipe Basil Vinaigrette (below)

1. Whisk together the olive oil, garlic, salt, and pepper in a large bowl. Add the eggplant rounds to the oil mixture and toss until evenly coated.

2. Preheat a large skillet over medium-high heat. Add the eggplant slices in batches and cook, turning, until slightly blacked on both sides, about 2 minutes per side.

3. Transfer the cooked eggplant to a platter and drizzle lightly with the basil vinaigrette. Let sit for 15 minutes before serving, so the eggplant will absorb the dressing.

Basil Vinaigrette

MAKES ¼ CUP

2 teaspoons apple cider vinegar

*2 teaspoons minced fresh basil
  leaves*

1 teaspoon fresh lemon juice

1 teaspoon minced shallots

3 tablespoons extra virgin olive oil

Whisk together the vinegar, basil, lemon juice, and shallots in a bowl. Slowly whisk in the olive oil. Use as a dressing for the pan-roasted eggplant or for other cooked summer vegetables.

Toasted Ravioli with Marinara Sauce

1. Line two baking sheets with aluminum foil. Using a 2-inch cookie cutter, cut 3 rounds from each egg roll wrapper. Transfer the cut wrappers to the baking sheet and cover with a damp kitchen towel to prevent the edges from drying and cracking as you work.

2. To make an egg wash, whisk together the eggs and milk in a shallow bowl. Place the bread crumbs in a second shallow bowl.

3. Spoon 1 tablespoon of filling into the center of each of twelve rounds. With your finger, moisten the edge around the filling with the egg wash. Place a second wrapper on top, pressing the edges to adhere. Crimp the edges with a fork to seal. Lay the assembled ravioli on the foil-covered baking sheet and cover with a damp towel while assembling the remaining ravioli. Repeat with the remaining ingredients.

Note: The ravioli can be made ahead up to this point and frozen on the baking sheet. Transfer to a heavy plastic freezer bag and keep in the freezer for up to 6 weeks. Thaw, covered, before using.

4. One at a time, dip the ravioli in the egg wash and then into the bread crumbs to coat completely. Lightly dust with flour and place on the second baking sheet. Repeat with the remaining ravioli.

5. Clip a candy or deep-frying thermometer to the side of a large cast-iron skillet or dutch oven. Add oil to a depth of 3 inches and heat to 350°F over medium heat. Using a slotted spoon, add five ravioli at a time and cook, turning once, until they float to the top and are golden brown, about 1½ minutes per side. Drain on paper towels and repeat with the remaining ravioli.

6. Serve the ravioli hot with the marinara sauce, and sprinkle the tops with the cheese, if desired.

MAKES 36 PIECES

1 (1-pound) package egg roll wrappers (24 count)

2 large eggs

¼ cup milk

2 cups Italian-style fine dry bread crumbs

1 recipe Mushroom-Sage Filling (page 137)

1 recipe Spinach-Ricotta with Lemon and Anchovy Filling (page 136)

1 recipe Turkey-Pesto Filling (page 137)

All-purpose flour, for dusting

Vegetable oil, for frying

1 recipe Marinara Sauce (page 138)

Freshly grated Parmigiano-Reggiano, optional

Spinach-Ricotta with Lemon and Anchovy Filling

MAKES ¾ CUP, ENOUGH FILLING FOR 12 RAVIOLI

1 tablespoon salted butter

2 teaspoons fresh lemon juice

1 teaspoon finely grated lemon zest

1 teaspoon anchovy paste

1 teaspoon minced garlic

½ teaspoon kosher salt

½ teaspoon freshly ground black
   pepper

½ cup frozen chopped spinach or
   cooked and chopped fresh spinach,
   drain off excess liquid

¼ cup ricotta, drained through
   cheesecloth until excess liquid is
   drained

2 tablespoons freshly grated
   Parmigiano-Reggiano

1. Melt the butter in a skillet over medium heat. Add the lemon juice, lemon zest, anchovy paste, garlic, salt, and pepper, and cook, stirring, for 30 seconds. Add the spinach and cook, stirring, to reduce any excess liquid, 1 to 2 minutes. Transfer the mixture to a bowl and let cool completely, about 20 minutes.

2. Add the ricotta and Parmesan, stirring well to incorporate. Cover and refrigerate until ready to use.

Mushroom-Sage Filling

1. Melt the butter in a skillet over medium heat. Add the mushrooms, sage, garlic, salt, and pepper. Cook, stirring, until the mushrooms are soft and start to give off their liquid, about 3 minutes.

2. Add the ricotta and Parmesan, stirring well to incorporate. Cover and refrigerate until ready to use.

You can make one, two, or all three of the fillings. The mushroom-sage filling is rich and satisfying. Sautéed spinach with lemon and anchovy is one of my favorite sides, so I use that as inspiration for another filling. For a leaner alternative to beef, try the ground turkey and pesto filling. The filled ravioli can be frozen after assembly for cooking and enjoying later.

MAKES ¾ CUP, ENOUGH FILLING FOR 12 RAVIOLI

1 tablespoon salted butter

½ cup diced button mushrooms

1 teaspoon chopped fresh sage leaves

½ teaspoon minced garlic

½ teaspoon kosher salt

½ teaspoon freshly ground black pepper

¼ cup ricotta, drained through cheesecloth until excess liquid is drained

2 tablespoons freshly grated Parmigiano-Reggiano

Turkey-Pesto Filling

1. Heat the oil in a skillet over medium heat. Add the turkey and cook, stirring, until the meat is browned and cooked through. Drain any excess liquid from the pan and add the pesto, stirring well to incorporate. Transfer the mixture to a bowl and let cool completely, about 20 minutes.

2. Add the ricotta and Parmesan, stirring well to incorporate. Cover and refrigerate until ready to use.

There are many good brands of pesto on the market, but you can also use my Walnut-Sage Pesto (page 19).

MAKES ¾ CUP, ENOUGH FILLING FOR 12 RAVIOLI

1 tablespoon extra virgin olive oil

¼ pound ground turkey

¼ cup prepared pesto sauce or Walnut-Sage Pesto (page 19)

¼ cup ricotta, drained through cheesecloth until excess liquid is drained

2 tablespoons freshly grated Parmigiano-Reggiano

Marinara Sauce

MAKES 3½ CUPS

¼ cup extra virgin olive oil

1 medium white onion, finely
   chopped

1 large carrot, finely chopped

3 garlic cloves, finely chopped

1 (28-ounce) can crushed tomatoes
   and their liquid

2 teaspoons kosher salt

½ teaspoon freshly ground black
   pepper

1 tablespoon chopped fresh basil
   leaves

2 teaspoons chopped fresh oregano
   leaves

2 tablespoons salted butter, cut into
   ½-inch pieces

1. Heat the olive oil in a dutch oven over medium heat. Add the onions and carrots and cook, stirring, until soft, 5 to 7 minutes. Add the garlic and cook, stirring, until fragrant, 1 minute.

2. Add the tomatoes and their liquid and stir to incorporate. Lower the heat and simmer, stirring occasionally, for 20 minutes. Add the salt, pepper, basil, and oregano and simmer until the sauce is reduced by one-quarter, about 15 minutes.

3. Add the butter one piece at a time and cook, stirring, adding each new piece before the previous one has completely melted. Remove from the heat and cover to keep warm before serving hot with the ravioli.

My friend Kathy DeTello Culpepper, who comes from a long line of great Italian cooks, taught me that adding a bit of butter to this recipe takes away any tomato bitterness and gives the sauce a rich flavor and smooth texture.

This sauce can also be used as a pizza topping or with cooked pasta.

1. Place the egg yolks and sugar in the bowl of a stand mixer fitted with a whisk attachment and beat on medium speed until the mixture is pale yellow and thick, 2 to 3 minutes. Add the mascarpone, brandy, and vanilla and beat just until blended. In a clean bowl with clean beaters, beat the egg whites with a handheld or stand mixer until soft peaks form.

2. Using a rubber spatula, thoroughly fold the whipped egg whites into the mascarpone mixture.

3. Stir together the coffee and Kahlúa in a shallow bowl.

4. One at a time, dip the ladyfingers into the coffee mixture, bottom sides only. (The ladyfingers quickly soak up the coffee mixture; so do not dip them for too long.) Arrange four ladyfinger halves around the sides and on the bottom of each of six martini glasses, placing the unsoaked side of the ladyfingers against the glass.

5. Spoon about ¼ cup of mascarpone mixture over the ladyfingers in each glass, spreading with a rubber spatula or the back of a spoon to completely cover the ladyfingers. Top with 2 ladyfinger halves, coated sides down, and spread 2 tablespoons mascarpone mixture over the top. Using a fine sieve, lightly dust the tops of each glass with the cocoa.

6. Loosely cover the martini glasses with plastic wrap and chill for at least 6 hours and up to 12 hours. Serve cold.

Six-ounce martini glasses are perfect for this presentation, but if you don't have them, use wine glasses, or even custard cups.

3 large eggs, separated

¾ cup sugar

1 cup mascarpone

2 tablespoons brandy

1 teaspoon pure vanilla extract

½ cup strong brewed coffee or brewed espresso, cooled

½ cup Kahlúa or other coffee-flavored liqueur

18 ladyfingers (the cake ones, not dried) cut in half

2 tablespoons unsweetened cocoa powder

MISSOURI WINE DINNER (FOR 4)

Poached Quail Eggs and Smoked Salmon with Frisée and Mustard-Lemon Vinaigrette

Smoked Trout Soup

Beef Tenderloin with Port-Anise Reduction

Corn, Mushroom, and Onion Tart

Black Walnut Cake with Brandied Plum Sauce

Winemaking has been part of the Show Me state's landscape since the mid 1800s, when German and some French settlers developed a wine region. Today Augusta, Hermann, and the two Ozarks are official American Viticulture Areas, and all are distinct wine-producing regions. Many Missouri vineyards began with German immigrants from Philadelphia being sold plots of land in Missouri that looked flat on maps but were essentially rocky hillsides. The settlers planted vineyards, and within ten years, steamboats brought visitors from St. Louis to Hermann's first Weinfest, featuring sweet Catawba wine. By the turn of the century, Hermann's winemakers had become wildly successful. One, Stone Hill Winery, had grown to be the second largest winery in the country. As in other parts of the country, Prohibition hit Missouri wineries hard. Now, generations later, Missouri's winemakers and small farmers have banded together to produce and market items whose names become synonymous with the virtues of the local terroir, much as the French do, linking specific locations with the grapes that are grown and the wine that is made there.

Freshwater trout may not come to mind when thinking of the Mississippi River, but the Meramec River, one of the longest free-flowing waterways in Missouri, travels 218 miles from its headwaters near Salem to the Mississippi near St. Louis. Missouri trout fishing, long popular, inspired the smoked trout soup in this menu.

This dinner menu can be paired with wines from any country and any region. As a start, the soft poached quail eggs wrapped in smoked salmon shine with flutes of Champagne or other sparkling wine. The smoked trout soup with jicama and tomatoes is light but savory enough for a sweet white or light red wine, while the beef tenderloin with a port sauce needs a sturdy, bold red wine. To finish off, walnut cake with brandied plum sauce can handle my favorite, a good port.

Poached Quail Eggs and Smoked Salmon with Frisée and Mustard-Lemon Vinaigrette

8 quail eggs or 4 small chicken eggs

1 teaspoon white vinegar

4 cups frisée or mixed bitter greens

2–3 tablespoons Mustard-Lemon Vinaigrette (page 312)

4 ounces sliced smoked salmon

1 tablespoon minced chives, for garnish

1. Pour water to a depth of 2 inches into a large deep skillet. Bring to a simmer over high heat, and then reduce to a bare simmer. Add the vinegar.

2. Being careful not to break the yolks, crack 4 of the quail eggs or 2 of the chicken eggs into individual tablespoons or small saucers. Gently slide into the barely simmering water, lifting the whites over the yolks with the back of a spoon. Poach until the whites and yolks are just set yet still soft in the center, 44 seconds to 1 minute for the quail eggs, and 2 to 3 minutes for the small chicken eggs. Using a slotted spoon, remove the eggs to a plate, tilting the plate to let the water run off the eggs. Repeat with the remaining eggs.

3. Place the frisée in a bowl and toss with the vinaigrette to taste. Divide the greens among 4 plates.

4. Cut the smoked salmon into 8 slices for quail eggs or 4 slices for chicken eggs. Gently wrap each poached egg in a slice of the salmon. Place two wrapped quail eggs or one wrapped chicken egg in the center of each salad. Garnish each serving with chives and serve immediately.

For a different take on the classic French salade frisée aux lardons, I top the poached eggs with some smoked salmon. Double the amounts for a main course salad.

MISSOURI WINE GRAPES

Here are some of the wine grapes grown in Missouri:

Catawba: A pink grape found growing by the Catawba River in North Carolina. Used in the production of pink and American sparkling wines, Catawba grapes produce a medium-bodied, sweet, fragrant, strawberry-scented wine.

Cayuga: A hybrid grape brought from New York's Finger Lakes wine country. Described as "Germanic" in style, which means higher in sugar and from cooler climates, wines made from the Cayuga grape are fragrant, fruity, and light-bodied.

Chambourcin: A medium-bodied, fruity red wine with an earthy touch of soft tannins.

Chardonel: A hybrid of Chardonnay and Seyval grapes. Whether fermented in oak or stainless steel barrels, Chardonel results in a dry, full-bodied wine.

Concord: Deep purple grapes known for intense fruity flavor and candy-like sweetness.

Norton: A hardy American grape with vigorous vines. Missouri's official state grape, it produces a rich, full-bodied dry red wine with berry flavors and spicy overtones.

Seyval Blanc: A French-American hybrid grape that makes dry to semidry, clean, crisp medium-bodied wines with a fresh herbal flavor.

St. Vincent: A hybrid grape made into a dry red wine, often with a vaguely perceptible sweetness, that is similar to Beaujolais Nouveau.

Traminette: A grape in the Gewürztraminer family that yields dry/semidry to sweet white wines with hints of peach, apricot, and floral aromas. The natural acidity gives balance to its light sweetness.

Vidal Blanc: Another French-American hybrid used to make a dry to semidry, full-bodied wine with fruity characteristics. Vidal's clean citrus flavors of lemon and grapefruit create a nicely balanced wine.

Vignoles: One of Missouri's most versatile white grapes, a French-American hybrid that finds uses ranging from dry wines to sweet late-harvest dessert wines. It has a floral aroma and fruity flavors of pineapple and apricot.

1. Heat the oil in a large pot over medium heat. Add the onion and cook, stirring, until soft, 3 to 4 minutes. Add the corn and cook, stirring, until starting to turn golden brown, 2 minutes.

2. Add the chicken broth, tomato juice, and tomatoes and their juices and bring to a boil. Reduce the heat and simmer until slightly reduced, about 25 minutes. (This is a light, thin soup, not thick, so it does not need to be cooked long.)

3. Pick over the smoked trout fillets for pin bones and shred the trout with a fork into ½-inch pieces. Set aside.

4. Add the green onions, jicama, and cilantro to the soup and cook until the jicama is just tender, 3 to 5 minutes. Reduce the heat to low and add the smoked trout just 5 minutes before serving.

1 tablespoon vegetable oil

¼ cup diced white onion

¼ cup fresh corn kernels, or frozen kernels, thawed

2 cups low-sodium chicken broth

1 cup tomato juice

½ cup canned diced tomatoes and their juices

4 ounces smoked trout fillets (see Source Guide, page 316)

¼ cup chopped green onions, tops and bottoms

¼ cup peeled and julienned jicama

2 teaspoons chopped fresh cilantro leaves

Beef Tenderloin with Port-Anise Reduction

1. Preheat the oven to 375°F. Line a heavy roasting pan with foil.

2. Heat over high heat a cast-iron skillet large enough to hold the beef. (Alternatively, heat a heavy roasting pan over two burners set to high heat.) Rub the roast on all sides with olive oil. Season with the salt and pepper, rubbing them into the meat. Reduce the heat to medium. Add the meat and sear for 1 minute on each side.

3. Place the tenderloin in the prepared roasting pan and roast until an instant-read thermometer inserted into the thickest part of the meat reads 125°F for rare-to-medium-rare, 18 to 20 minutes. Remove the pan from the oven. Using the aluminum foil, lift the meat onto a cutting board. Wrap the meat loosely in the foil and let rest for 10 to 15 minutes.

4. Carve the meat into 1-inch-thick slices and arrange on a platter. Spoon the sauce over the meat or serve on the side. Serve immediately.

1 (4-pound) beef tenderloin, trimmed of silver skin, at room temperature

1 tablespoon extra virgin olive oil

1 tablespoon kosher salt

1 tablespoon freshly ground black pepper

1 recipe Port-Anise Reduction (below)

It's important to let the beef rest before slicing it; this allows the juices to redistribute throughout the whole roast.

Port-Anise Reduction

Place all the ingredients in a saucepan and bring to a boil over medium heat. Reduce the heat to low and simmer until the wine is reduced to a syrup thick enough to coat the back of a spoon but still of pourable consistency, 15 to 20 minutes. Serve warm with the tenderloin.

MAKES ½ CUP

1 large shallot, halved and thinly sliced lengthwise

2 cups ruby port

3 whole star anise

STEAK VS. ROAST

My cousin once called my father, who was a wonderful cook, to ask his advice on how to cook a roast. When he asked her how large the piece of meat was, she responded, "Two pounds." He quickly replied, "Throw it in a hot skillet! That's not a roast. Two pounds is a steak." I count on a pound per person, because there is some shrinkage and it needs to be large enough to roast and still be medium rare.

Vegetable oil spray

1 sheet frozen puff pastry (from a 17¾-ounce package), thawed

All-purpose flour, for dusting

2 medium white onions, thinly sliced

1 cup fresh corn kernels, or frozen kernels, thawed

1 tablespoon salted butter

2 cups button mushrooms, thinly sliced

½ teaspoon chopped garlic

½ teaspoon chopped fresh thyme leaves

1. Preheat the oven to 350°F. Spray a large baking sheet with vegetable oil spray.

2. On a lightly floured work surface, roll out the puff pastry into a 12 × 16-inch rectangle. Cut the pastry into four pieces. Place the squares on the prepared baking sheet, leaving 2 inches between them. Bake for 10 minutes. They should begin to puff and brown. Remove from the oven and let rest on the baking sheet. Leave the oven on.

3. Heat a skillet over medium heat until very hot. Add the onions and cook, stirring, until caramelized, 6 to 8 minutes. Transfer the onions to a plate. Place the corn in the same hot skillet. Cook, stirring, until golden brown, 1 to 2 minutes. Transfer the corn to a clean plate.

4. Wipe the skillet with a paper towel. Melt the butter in the skillet. Add the mushrooms, garlic, and thyme and cook, stirring, until the mushrooms are brown, 3 to 4 minutes.

5. Divide the cooled onions among the 4 pastry squares, spreading evenly out to the edge. Spread the mushrooms on top.

6. Bake the tarts until the pastry turns light brown, about 10 minutes. Remove the baking sheet from the oven. Spread the corn evenly over the tops of the tarts. Bake until the pastry is golden brown and puffed, about 7 minutes. Remove from the oven and serve immediately.

If you let the skillet get hot enough, there's no need to add oil when caramelizing onions. I use this technique when I want less liquid in the onions, as when topping pastry with them.

Black Walnut Cake with Brandied Plum Sauce

MAKES 1 (10-INCH) CAKE

*1 tablespoon plus ½ cup (1 stick)
salted butter*

*1 cup finely chopped black walnuts,
English walnuts, or pecans*

*3 cups cake flour, plus more to dust
the cake pan*

½ teaspoon table salt

¼ teaspoon baking soda

3 cups sugar

6 large eggs

1 teaspoon pure vanilla extract

*1 cup sour cream (not low-fat or
fat-free)*

1 recipe Plum Sauce (page 151)

1. Preheat the oven to 300°F. Lightly grease a 10-inch Bundt pan or tube pan with 1 tablespoon of the butter. Flour the inside and shake out the excess. Sprinkle the nuts on the bottom of the pan.

2. Sift together the 3 cups of flour, the salt, and baking soda into a bowl.

3. In the bowl of a stand mixer fitted with a paddle attachment, cream together the remaining ½ cup butter and the sugar on medium speed until light and fluffy, 3 to 4 minutes Add the eggs, one at a time, beating well after each addition and scraping down the sides of the bowl as needed. Mix in the vanilla. Add the flour mixture alternately with the sour cream, beginning and ending with the flour mixture, and beating the batter after each addition until just combined.

4. Pour and evenly spread the batter into the prepared pan. Bake until a tester inserted into the center of the cake comes out clean, 1 hour and 15 minutes to 1 hour and 30 minutes. Let cool in the pan on a wire rack for 20 minutes, then gently turn the cake out onto a wire rack to finish cooling.

5. To serve, cut the cake into wedges. Spoon the plum sauce onto dessert plates and stand one piece of cake in each pool of sauce.

Brandied Plum Sauce

1. Place the sugar, cornstarch, and ¼ cup water in a saucepan over medium heat. Cook, stirring, until the mixture comes to a boil. Lower the heat to a simmer.

2. Add the plums, orange juice, and orange zest and stir well. Add the brandy and cinnamon and stir to combine. Bring the sauce to a simmer. Cook until the sauce is thick and not cloudy, 4 to 5 minutes.

3. Remove from the heat and let cool slightly before use.

This sauce can be made 2 days ahead, refrigerated, and reheated.

MAKES 1 CUP

1 cup confectioners' sugar

2 tablespoons cornstarch

4 plums, pitted and sliced ½ inch thick

3 tablespoons fresh orange juice

1 teaspoon finely grated orange zest

2 tablespoons brandy

¼ teaspoon ground cinnamon

WINE PAIRING

When it comes to pairing wines with food, I look at three things in wines: acid, tannin, and sweetness.

Acid: When it comes to balance, acid plays the most significant role. If a wine is too low in acid, it will taste flat and dull. If a wine is too high in acid, it will be tart and sour. Salads, seafood, and chicken pair well with the citrus element of whites and rosés, but do not be afraid to try a lighter red such as a Pinot Noir. It is light, fruity, often acidic, and generally lacking in tannic structure. The light body of this varietal pairs well with the lighter mouthfeel of seafood. Furthermore, its broad range of flavors makes it an ideal food wine. Whether you choose a Côtes du Rhône rosé or slightly oaky Chardonnay or a crisper German-style Riesling from Missouri, or whether you want to venture out into the world of reds, you are looking for qualities to complement your dish.

Tannin: Astringent tannins, most commonly found in red wine, impart a dry, puckery taste in the mouth. As red wines age and mellow, the tannins usually disappear. Lightly tannic wines (such as the French Beaujolais and Pinot Noir and Italian Chianti) are lighter in color. Medium tannic wines (such as California Merlot, Zinfandel, and the Spanish Rioja) are always crowd-pleasers. The higher tannic wines (such as Bordeaux and Cabernet Sauvignons) are more suited for enjoying with food. All of these wines go well with steak, fatty fish such as tuna and swordfish. and even chocolate.

Sweetness: The sweetness of a wine is determined by several factors—the amount of sugar in the wine, but also the relative levels of alcohol, acids, and tannins. Sugars and alcohol enhance a wine's sweetness; acids and tannins counteract it. When I refer to sweet wines, I prefer the medium sweetness of Riesling and Chenin Blanc. Even a few Australian and California winemakers have increased the sugar level of their Chardonnays for a large section of the population that prefers sugar over tannin. For me, there are two rules when it comes to sweet wines: "Sweet works with heat" and "Sweet works with sweet."

GENERAL GRANT'S BREAKFAST (FOR 4)

The General's Coffee

Broiled Catfish with Fried Eggs and Smoked Bacon

Grant's Buckwheat-Buttermilk Pancakes with Fig Syrup

Although President Ulysses S. Grant was born on the Ohio River, the Mississippi seemed to be more a part of his life. His bride came from St. Louis, and he settled in Galena, Illinois, on the River, and was working as a clerk in his father's leather store when the Civil War broke out. In September 1861, Brigadier General Ulysses S. Grant established Union Army headquarters in Cairo, Illinois, again on the Mississippi. In just seven years he went from being a clerk to president of the United States.

I have read in places that the general was a big eater who liked steak and smoked mackerel for breakfast. Other statements say that he was a very sparing eater but was fond of pork and beans, fruit, and buckwheat cakes. He loved bacon and buckwheat pancakes and often he started his day with a big breakfast of grilled mackerel, steak with thick-cut bacon, buckwheat pancakes, and strong coffee. Since no one eats a three-course breakfast these days, consider this entire menu for brunch or dinner, or eliminate a course for a lighter brunch.

To me, the word "strong" coupled with "coffee" means there must be some bourbon in it. When properly made with just four ingredients—coffee, sugar, bourbon, and a float of heavy cream—The General's Coffee is a satisfying addition to anyone's meal.

8 sugar cubes

6 ounces good-quality bourbon

4 cups freshly brewed, strong, hot coffee

½ cup heavy cream, lightly whipped

1. Place 2 sugar cubes in each of four 12-ounce footed glass coffee mugs.

2. Add 1½ ounces (3 tablespoons) bourbon to each mug. Using a muddler or the end of a heavy long-handled spoon, muddle the sugar and whiskey to dissolve the sugar. Pour 1 cup hot coffee into each mug.

3. To add the whipped cream to the mugs, rest the back of a teaspoon against the inside of the glass. Slowly pour the thickened cream down the spoon and into the glass. (This way the cream will float on top of the coffee for a better presentation.) Serve immediately.

THE RIVER AND THE CIVIL WAR

Beginning in 1861, Union and Confederate forces began the fight for control over the Mississippi River, which was vital for accessing supply lines and winning the war. Union forces were trying to gain control from two directions. Moving south, the Union won victories at New Madrid, Missouri, and Memphis, Tennessee. Moving north from the Gulf, the Union battled for New Orleans and Baton Rouge in Louisiana. Union troops secured New Orleans in 1862, but the Confederacy still controlled the River from Baton Rouge to St. Louis. Baton Rouge was lost to Union forces in May 1862. General Ulysses S. Grant's major objective was to capture Vicksburg, the most strategic Confederate stronghold on the River. The Siege of Vicksburg began on May 18 and dragged on until July 4, 1863. With the capture of Vicksburg, the North now controlled the entire length of the Mississippi River.

Broiled Catfish with Fried Eggs and Smoked Bacon

1. Lay the bacon flat in a large cast-iron skillet over medium heat. Cook, turning, until the bacon is brown and crisp, 10 to 15 minutes. (The bacon grease is used to cook the fish and eggs, so don't burn the bacon.)

2. Using tongs, transfer the bacon to paper towels to drain. Pour off, leaving ¼ inch of the bacon grease in the pan. Return the pan with the remaining bacon grease to the stovetop to cook the fish.

3. Season both sides of the fish fillets with the Cajun Seasoning. Heat the bacon grease over medium heat. Add the fish, being careful not to overcrowd the skillet. Cook until golden brown, about 3 minutes per side. Remove the fish to a warm plate.

4. Place 4 teaspoons of the reserved bacon grease in a nonstick skillet. Heat over low heat. Break the eggs one at a time into a saucer. Gently slide the eggs into the skillet and cover with a lid. Cook the eggs to desired doneness, about 3 to 4 minutes for over easy. The beauty of using the lid is you do not have to flip your eggs and risk breaking the yolk.

5. To serve, place 1 catfish fillet on each of 4 large plates. Top each piece of fish with a fried egg and arrange 2 slices of bacon on the side.

8 thick slices smoked bacon

4 (5- to 6-ounce) catfish fillets (see Source Guide, page 316)

1 tablespoon Cajun Seasoning (page 311)

4 large eggs

My favorite bacon is the hickory-smoked country bacon that comes from Benton's Smoky Mountain Country Hams & Bacon in North Madisonville, Tennessee, just south of Knoxville. I order it online (see Source Guide, page 316) and keep it in my freezer. When I want smoked bacon, I want to be able to smell the smoke, and Mr. Benton's bacon delivers.

Grant's Buckwheat-Buttermilk Pancakes with Fig Syrup

1 cup buckwheat flour

½ cup all-purpose flour

3 tablespoons sugar

1 teaspoon baking soda

½ teaspoon kosher salt

1 large egg

2 cups buttermilk

3 tablespoons salted butter, melted

Vegetable oil spray or vegetable oil, for coating the pan

1 recipe Fig Syrup (below)

1. Heat a cast-iron griddle or skillet over medium heat. Preheat the oven to 200°F.

2. Whisk together the buckwheat flour, all-purpose flour, sugar, baking soda, and salt in a bowl. In a second bowl, whisk together the egg, 1 cup of the buttermilk, and the butter. Add the wet ingredients to the dry ingredients and stir to combine. Slowly stir in some or all of the remaining 1 cup buttermilk, adding just enough to make a thick, pourable batter. (It is important not to overwork the batter; stir just to combine.) Let the batter rest for 5 minutes.

3. Lightly coat the heated griddle with vegetable oil spray or brush with vegetable oil. Working in batches, pour ¼ cup of the batter for each pancake onto the griddle. Cook until bubbles form on the surface, 2 to 3 minutes. Flip the pancakes and cook until browned on the bottom, 1 to 2 minutes.

4. Transfer the cooked pancakes to a baking sheet and place in the oven to keep warm while cooking the remaining pancakes.

5. Serve with fig syrup.

Fig Syrup

1 cup packed light brown sugar

2 tablespoons salted butter

12 ounces (2 cups) fresh Mission figs, stemmed and quartered

¼ teaspoon ground cinnamon

1. Combine the brown sugar, butter, and ¼ cup water in a saucepan. Bring to a simmer, stirring occasionally, over low heat. Cook until the syrup begins to thicken, about 20 minutes. Add the figs and cinnamon, stir to combine, and cook until it reaches the syrup stage (234°F on a candy thermometer) and large bubbles appear, about 5 to 7 minutes.

2. Remove from the heat and cover to keep warm until ready to serve with the pancakes.

DUCK HUNTERS' DINNER (FOR 4)

Salad with Magret and Duck Cracklings

Duck Livers with Shallots and Butter on Toast

Confit of Duck with Jezebel Sauce

Bourbon Sweet Potatoes

Cast-Iron Collards

Blackberry-Orange Sorbet

The Mississippi River and its banks provide food, water, shelter, nesting spots, and safety from predators for more than eight million ducks, geese, swans, and wading birds. Migratory ducks along the River include black, wood, mallard, teal, widgeon, pintail, and ring-necked ducks. While I cook hearty stews and gumbos made with wild ducks caught by friends, I prefer the milder flavors of farm-raised ducks. These also have more fat for making cracklings and rendering fat—and there's no birdshot to clean out. Have your butcher cut up one four-to-five-pound duck into eight pieces, breast fat removed and reserved. When rendering duck fat—as you will when preparing these dishes—it is always smart to strain the extra duck fat through a cheesecloth-lined sieve, let it cool, pour it into a container, and freeze it for future use such as roasting potatoes or other vegetables.

This menu uses every part of the duck, from the skin for crisp cracklings to the liver for a quick, buttery pâté to spread on toast. Separating the legs and thighs from the breast allows you to cook each part of the duck to perfection. You may choose to serve the salad topped with sliced duck breast for a main course. The Jezebel Sauce, rumored to have gotten its name for its tart and spicy flavor, remains one of my favorite sauces for duck. The combination of sweet potatoes and collard greens never fails to please. After a meal like this, blackberry-orange sorbet is a welcome light dessert.

2 Magret duck breasts

1 teaspoon kosher salt

1 teaspoon vegetable oil

3 ounces (½ cup) stemmed and
thinly sliced oyster mushrooms

3 ounces (½ cup) thinly sliced
button mushrooms

3 ounces (½ cup) stemmed and
thinly sliced portobello or shiitake
mushrooms

4 cups mixed salad greens

2 cups torn frisée or other bitter
salad greens

3 tablespoons Mustard-Lemon
Vinaigrette (page 312)

¼ cup chopped green onions, green
tops only, for garnish

1. Remove all the skin from the duck breasts to make cracklings. Cut the skin into ¼-inch strips, place them in a bowl, and season with the salt.

2. Lightly coat a large skillet with the vegetable oil and heat over low heat. Lay the skin strips flat in the pan fat side down and slowly cook until the fat begins to render. Increase the heat to medium. Cook, turning halfway through, until the strips are crisp and brown, 20 to 25 minutes. Transfer the cracklings to paper towels to drain.

3. Pour off all but 3 tablespoons of the duck fat from the skillet. Place skillet back over medium heat. When the duck fat is hot, add the duck breasts and brown on both sides for 3 to 4 minutes on each side. Remove the breasts to a pie plate and let rest in a 175°F oven while you sauté the mushrooms.

4. Place the skillet back over medium heat. Add the mushrooms and cook, stirring, until browned but retaining their shape, 2 to 3 minutes.

5. Combine the mixed greens and frisée in a bowl. Add the vinaigrette and toss to coat evenly. Divide the greens among four salad plates. Arrange the mushrooms and cracklings on the greens.

6. Slice the duck breasts on the bias into ½-inch slices and place on top of the salads. Garnish each serving with 1 tablespoon of the green onions and serve.

Duck Livers with Shallots and Butter on Toast

3 tablespoons salted butter, at room
  temperature

2 slices sourdough bread, crusts
  removed, cut into quarters

4 duck or 6 chicken livers

1 teaspoon freshly ground black
  pepper

½ teaspoon kosher salt

2 medium shallots, thinly sliced

¼ teaspoon minced garlic

2 teaspoons chopped parsley

1. Melt 1 tablespoon of the butter in a skillet over medium heat. In batches, add the bread and cook until toasted and light brown, 1 to 2 minutes per side. Transfer to a wire rack to cool and harden.

2. Rinse and dry the livers, remove the sinews, and cut the livers lengthwise into ¼ × 1½-inch slices. Season them on both sides with the pepper and salt.

3. Wipe out the skillet. Melt 1 tablespoon of the butter in the skillet over medium heat. Add the shallots and cook, stirring, until soft, 2 minutes Add the livers and cook, stirring, until cooked through and no longer pink, about 4 minutes. Stir in the garlic, the remaining 1 tablespoon butter, and the parsley and cook for 1 minute.

4. Arrange the toasts on a platter and top with the duck livers. Serve warm.

Confit of Duck with Jezebel Sauce

1. Preheat the oven to 275°F.

2. Rinse the legs and thighs, wipe them dry, and lightly season on both sides with the salt and pepper. Arrange the duck legs and thighs in a single layer in a shallow baking dish. Cover with the vegetable oil and add the garlic, thyme, and bay leaves, then cover the dish tightly with foil. Bake the duck pieces for 90 minutes. They should register 140°F on an instant-read thermometer inserted into the thickest part of the thigh.

3. Remove the duck pieces from the baking dish and, if not using immediately, refrigerate.

4. For the final cooking, bring the duck pieces back to room temperature. In a skillet large enough to hold all the pieces, heat the 3 tablespoons rendered duck fat over medium heat. Add the legs and thighs to the skillet and cook until crisp. Place the duck legs and thighs on a serving platter and serve Jezebel Sauce (below) on the side.

2 duck legs

2 duck thighs

1 teaspoon kosher salt

1 teaspoon freshly ground black pepper

2 cups vegetable oil (duck fat is preferred but not always available and expensive)

3 garlic cloves

2 sprigs fresh thyme

2 bay leaves

3 tablespoons rendered duck fat (from the Salad with Magret or a previous duck)

Jezebel Sauce

Combine the jelly, jam, and mustard in a saucepan over medium heat. Cook, stirring frequently, until the jelly and jam melt and blend with mustard, 12 to 14 minutes. Serve warm or at room temperature.

Jezebel Sauce is served all along the River on duck, chicken, and pork. The sauce can be kept refrigerated for 2 weeks. Reheat before serving.

MAKES ¾ CUP

½ cup red currant jelly

½ cup pineapple jam

½ cup Dijon mustard

2 large sweet potatoes

¼ cup packed light brown sugar

3 tablespoons salted butter

¼ cup bourbon

⅛ teaspoon ground cinnamon

1. Preheat the oven to 425°F.

2. Pierce the sweet potatoes several times with a fork and place on a baking sheet. Bake until tender, 40 to 60 minutes. Remove from the oven and let sit until cool enough to handle.

3. Cut the sweet potatoes in half lengthwise and scoop the flesh into a bowl. Discard the skins. Mash the potatoes with a fork.

4. Combine the brown sugar and butter in a saucepan. Bring to a simmer over medium heat and stir to melt the sugar. Add the bourbon and cinnamon and stir well to combine. Add the sweet potato flesh and whisk until smooth. Cook until heated through, 4 to 5 minutes. Serve hot.

COOKING WITH BOURBON

I'm often asked why I use so much bourbon in my cooking. Like adding vanilla to cake batter or cookie dough, bourbon brings out the inherent flavors of certain foods. Bourbon brings some smokiness to sweet potatoes as well as dessert sauces. There is always a bottle of both Prichard's bourbon and Blanton's in my kitchen next to a bottle of ruby port and a good vanilla extract.

Cast-Iron Collards

1. Rinse the collard greens well and drain them. Remove the tough stems and cut the leaves into 1-inch pieces.

2. Cook the bacon in a cast-iron skillet over medium-high heat, stirring frequently, until browned and crisp, about 5 minutes. Using a slotted spoon, transfer to paper towels to drain, reserving the bacon grease in the skillet.

3. Return the skillet to medium-high heat. Add the greens and cook, stirring, until wilted, 3 to 4 minutes. Add the apple juice, salt, and red pepper. Reduce the heat to low and cook the greens until tender, 5 to 6 minutes. Remove from the heat, stir in the reserved bacon, and serve hot.

Flash-frying collards is a fresh alternative to the traditional method of cooking them for a long time until they are soft. Apple juice is the finishing touch to make them just tender enough.

1 pound collard greens

2 tablespoons smoked bacon, diced

¼ cup apple juice

1 teaspoon kosher salt

¼ teaspoon crushed red pepper

Blackberry-Orange Sorbet

MAKES 1 QUART

1¼ cups sugar

1 pound fresh blackberries, or frozen
  unsweetened blackberries, thawed

2 tablespoons fresh orange juice

2 teaspoons finely grated orange zest

2 tablespoons Cointreau, Grand
  Marnier, or other orange-flavored
  liqueur

1. Bring 1 cup water to a boil in a saucepan. Remove the saucepan from the heat and add the sugar, stirring until completely dissolved.

2. Put the blackberries in a blender or food processor and process until pureed. Pour the sugar syrup into the blender with the blackberry puree and blend for 30 seconds. Strain the mixture through a fine mesh strainer over a bowl, pressing with the back of a heavy spoon to extract the juice and remove the seeds. Discard the sediment. Stir the orange juice, orange zest, and liqueur into the blackberry mixture. Cover and refrigerate until the mixture is thoroughly chilled, at least 3 hours or overnight.

3. Once the mixture is chilled, follow the manufacturer's instructions on an ice cream machine for freezing the sorbet. Transfer the sorbet to a plastic container with a tight-fitting lid and store in the freezer until ready to serve.

This sorbet is best made the day before serving. It keeps well in the freezer up to 10 days.

KENTUCKY BURGOO DINNER (FOR 8)

Fig-Infused Bourbon, and Fig-Bourbon Sidecars with
Cinnamon Sugar–Rimmed Glasses

Skillet Cornbread

Green Bean Salad with Honey Mustard Vinaigrette and Smoked Almonds

Burgoo with Beef, Chicken, and Andouille

Hummingbird Parfaits with Cream Cheese Ice Cream

Kentucky is known for bourbon, bluegrass, and horseracing, but it is also the state of rivers, too many to mention by name. The Ohio, Tennessee, Cumberland, and Kentucky are most recognized names, but there are more than forty rivers and creeks that run from Kentucky into the Mississippi.

This dinner starts with a cocktail homage to bourbon, the whiskey first made in Bourbon County, Kentucky. The bourbon is combined with figs and spices and allowed to infuse for one week. Kentucky is also known for burgoo, a spicy hunters' stew that was originally made with wild game—squirrel,

opossum, birds—and whatever vegetables were on hand and was served at home or at community dinners. This burgoo is made with beef, chicken, and andouille, and accompanied by a skillet of cornbread to mop up every drop of gravy. Kentucky also lays claim to being the home of the hummingbird cake, a layer cake with pineapple, bananas, and spices iced with a cream cheese frosting and topped with pecans. Instead of cake after this hearty meal, I serve hummingbird parfaits—homemade cream cheese ice cream and crushed pineapple sauce layered in tall glasses and topped with pecans.

Fig-Infused Bourbon

1 cup packed light brown sugar

4 whole cloves

1 cinnamon stick

1 vanilla bean, split lengthwise and
  seeds scraped out

1 cup fresh black Mission figs (in the
  South, the common fig), quartered

3 cups good-quality bourbon

1. Combine the brown sugar, 1 cup boiling water, the cloves, cinnamon stick, and vanilla bean halves and seeds in a 1-quart Mason jar. Add the figs and bourbon to the jar. Cover tightly and turn the jar over and back several times to distribute the ingredients. Refrigerate undisturbed for at least 1 week and up to 2 weeks.

2. Pour the bourbon mixture through a cheesecloth-lined strainer into a pitcher, and from there into a clean glass pop-top serving jar (or any jar you choose). Transfer the figs to a clean jar with a tight-fitting lid to enjoy as an ice cream topping or other dessert component.

Refrigerated, the figs will keep for 2 weeks and the fig-flavored bourbon will last for 3 months.

 Fig-Bourbon Sidecars with Cinnamon Sugar–Rimmed Glasses

¼ cup superfine sugar

¼ teaspoon ground cinnamon

6 ounces Fig-Infused Bourbon

2 ounces Cointreau, Grand
  Marnier, or other orange-flavored
  liqueur

2 ounces fresh lemon juice

4 lemon twists, for garnish

1. To make the cinnamon sugar for the rims of the glasses, stir together the sugar and cinnamon on a plate. Fold a paper towel into quarters, soak with water, and place on second plate. One at a time, press the rims of four martini glasses onto the wet towel and then into the cinnamon sugar, pressing lightly for the sugar to adhere.

2. To make the cocktails, combine 3 ounces of the bourbon, 1 ounce of the Cointreau, and 2 tablespoons of the lemon juice in a cocktail shaker filled with ice. Shake well and pour into two of the rimmed martini glasses. Repeat with the remaining ingredients and glasses. Garnish each glass with a lemon twist and serve cold. Make another batch of drinks to serve 8 guests.

Transform this into a winter cocktail by putting the ingredients in mugs and stirring ax cup boiling water into each.

Skillet Cornbread

1. Preheat the oven to 425°F. Position the oven rack in the center of the oven. Preheat a 9- or 10-inch cast-iron skillet in the oven while preparing the batter. (Alternatively, a 9-inch round baking dish can be used.)

2. Whisk together the cornmeal, flour, sugar, baking powder, salt, and baking soda in a large bowl. Whisk together the buttermilk, milk, and eggs in a second bowl. Add the wet ingredients to the dry ingredients. Whisk in ¼ cup of the melted butter.

3. Remove the skillet from the oven. Pour the remaining ¼ cup melted butter into the skillet, swirling to coat the bottom and sides. Pour the batter into the skillet. Bake until a cake tester or toothpick inserted into the center comes out clean, 20 to 25 minutes. Remove the cornbread from the oven and let cool in the skillet on a wire rack for 10 minutes before serving.

Stone-ground cornmeal makes the best skillet cornbread. As it can be difficult to find in a supermarket, I recommend you order yours from Delta Grind in Water Valley, Mississippi, in the northern Delta, just south of Oxford (see Source Guide, page 316).

1¼ cups yellow cornmeal,
   stone-ground if possible
   (see Source Guide, page 316)

¾ cup all-purpose flour

¼ cup granulated sugar

2 teaspoons baking powder

1½ teaspoons kosher salt

1 teaspoon baking soda

1 cup buttermilk

⅓ cup milk

2 large eggs, lightly beaten

½ cup (1 stick) salted butter,
   melted and divided

2 pounds green beans, trimmed and cut into 2-inch pieces

¼ cup honey mustard

2 tablespoons apple cider vinegar

⅓ cup vegetable oil

1 red onion, thinly sliced

1 red bell pepper, cored, seeded and julienned

¼ cup chopped smoked almonds

1. Bring a pot of salted water to a boil. Add the beans; turn off the heat, cover, and let sit until tender, about 3 minutes. Drain in a colander and transfer to an ice bath to cool. Drain well.

2. Whisk together the mustard and vinegar in a small bowl. Slowly add the oil a bit at a time, whisking, until the dressing is emulsified and creamy.

3. Combine the drained green beans, onions, and red peppers in a salad bowl. Add the vinaigrette and toss to coat evenly. Immediately before serving, sprinkle the almonds on top.

FLATBOATS

The first record of a flatboat traveling down the Mississippi was in the early 1780s, when a Pennsylvania farmer built one to ship his flour to the port of New Orleans. By the 1830s, thousands of flatboats traveled downstream on the River. The difference between flatboats and rafts is that a flatboat floats in the water, while a raft floats on the water.

These easy-to-build wooden boats were used for transportation one way only. Once the boat reached its destination, the boatman dismantled the boat, sold the wood, and walked back north, on a footpath that became known as the Natchez Trace.

In 1838 there was an actual war pitting Vicksburg residents and local law enforcement against the flatboat owners and crews. Merchants thought it unfair that flatboat owners didn't have to pay the same taxes on goods as they did. Cannons and guns were fired, but the matter quickly ended up in a different kind of battle—in court. In the 1840s some flatboat owners started paying steamboat proprietors to pull their boats back upriver, enabling the flats to carry goods in both directions. In the end, both the flatboats and the steamboats lost out to faster transportation provided by the railroads.

Burgoo with Beef, Chicken, and Andouille

1. Season the beef cubes and chicken quarters all over with the salt, garlic powder, and black pepper.

2. Heat 2 tablespoons of the vegetable oil in a dutch oven over high heat. Add the beef and sear, turning, until browned on all sides. Transfer the cooked beef to a bowl. Heat the remaining 1 tablespoon of oil in the dutch oven. Add the chicken and cook, turning, until browned on all sides. Transfer the chicken to the bowl with the beef. Cut the andouille into 2-inch lengths; add to the dutch oven, and cook, turning, until browned on all sides. Return the beef and chicken to the pot with the andouille. Reduce the heat to medium-high.

3. Stir in the garlic, jalapeños, lima beans, okra, and curry and stir well. Add enough water to cover the ingredients by 2 inches. Bring to a boil, lower the heat, and simmer uncovered, stirring occasionally, until vegetables are tender and liquid thickens, about 40 minutes. Using tongs, transfer all of the meats to a bowl. Skim off any excess fat from the surface.

4. Add the potatoes, onions, carrots, bell peppers, tomatoes, corn, green onions, brown sugar, parsley, and bourbon to the dutch oven. Simmer until the potatoes are tender, about 20 minutes. While the burgoo is simmering, remove the skin and bones from the chicken and discard. Cut the chicken meat into 2-inch pieces. Return the chicken pieces, beef, and andouille to the dutch oven and simmer for 5 minutes. Serve immediately in large soup bowls. Hot cornbread is the perfect accompaniment to this savory stew.

Fresh vegetables are always best, but depending on where you live, finding fresh okra, lima beans, and corn may be a challenge, so frozen can be substituted. There's no need to thaw the vegetables before adding them to the stew.

2 pounds beef sirloin roast, cut into 2-inch cubes

4 skin-on chicken leg quarters

1 tablespoon kosher salt

2 teaspoons garlic powder

2 teaspoons freshly ground black pepper

3 tablespoons vegetable oil, divided

1 pound andouille (see Source Guide, page 316) or other spicy smoked sausage

4 garlic cloves

1 fresh jalapeño, stemmed, quartered, and seeded

2 cups fresh or frozen lima beans

2 cups fresh or frozen diced okra

¼ cup curry powder

3 cups peeled and diced russet potatoes (2 large)

1 cup chopped white onions

1 cup diced carrots

1 cup diced green bell peppers

1 large tomato, peeled, seeded, and chopped

1 cup fresh or frozen corn kernels

½ cup diced green onions, white bottoms and tops

2 tablespoons packed light brown sugar

1 tablespoon finely chopped fresh parsley

1 cup bourbon

½ cup chopped pecans, toasted
(page 311)

1 recipe Pineapple Sauce
(page 177)

1 recipe Cream Cheese Ice Cream
(below)

1 cup Sweetened Whipped Cream
(page 315), optional

To assemble the parfaits, sprinkle 1½ teaspoons chopped pecans in the bottom of each of eight ice cream coupes or other decorative footed glasses. Spoon 1 tablespoon of the pineapple sauce over the pecans, and top with a 2-ounce scoop of ice cream. Top with another layer each of pecans, pineapple, and ice cream, followed by 1 tablespoon whipped cream, as desired, and then additional pineapple sauce and chopped pecans. Serve immediately.

Cream Cheese Ice Cream

MAKES 1 QUART

1½ cups heavy cream, divided

2 large egg yolks

¾ cup sugar, divided

4 ounces cream cheese, cut into
pieces, at room temperature

13 ounces whole milk, divided

1½ teaspoons cornstarch

⅛ teaspoon sea salt

¼ cup corn syrup

1 teaspoon pure vanilla extract

1. Make an ice bath by filling a large bowl with ice and cold water.

2. Place ½ cup of the heavy cream in a microwave-proof measuring cup. Heat until just hot, 40 seconds to 1 minute. Combine the egg yolks and ¼ cup of the sugar in a food processor and blend until pale yellow, 3 to 4 minutes. With the machine running, slowly add the hot cream through the feed tube and process to temper the egg yolks. Add the cream cheese and process until smooth.

3. Whisk together 2 tablespoons of the milk and the cornstarch in a bowl to make a smooth slurry.

4. Combine the remaining 1½ cups milk, 1 cup cream, ½ cup sugar, and ⅛ teaspoon salt with the corn syrup in a saucepan. Bring to a low boil, stirring, over medium-high heat. Lower the heat and simmer the mixture for about 4 minutes and then whisk in the slurry. Bring the mixture to a simmer, stirring constantly with a heavy wooden spoon, and cook until thickened, 3 to 4 minutes. Remove the saucepan from the heat and let the contents cool, stirring occasionally, about 15 minutes. Whisking

constantly, add the cream cheese mixture and vanilla to the cooled cream mixture, and beat until smooth. Transfer to a stainless steel bowl and place in the ice bath until completely cool, stirring occasionally. Cover the bowl with plastic wrap, pressing down onto the surface to prevent a skin from forming. Refrigerate until well chilled, at least 3 hours or overnight.

5. Once the mixture is chilled, follow the manufacturer's instructions for freezing the ice cream. Transfer to a plastic container with a tight-fitting lid and store in the freezer until ready to serve.

I add a few egg yolks to the slurry to maintain some of the richness of traditional custard.

Pineapple Sauce

MAKES 2 CUPS

1 (14-ounce) can crushed pineapple in 100 percent pineapple juice

1 cup sugar

Place the pineapple with its juice and the sugar in a saucepan over medium heat. Cook until thickened, stirring, until the liquid is reduced and sauce is thick, about 15 minutes.

The pineapple sauce can be made ahead and kept refrigerated for up to 2 weeks. Bring to room temperature before serving.

AFTERNOON TEA ALONG THE RIVER
(FOR 12)

River Punch

Whiskey Sour Punch

Tea Sandwiches (Tomato-Bacon and Cucumber)

Italian Sausage Savories

Cheese Pennies

Lemon Meringue Tartlets

When hosting Entertaining Southern Style classes on the *American Queen* or at my house, Twin Oaks, I share my number one rule: "Opening your home is gift enough." While good food and drink are always appreciated, what you serve to your guests is not nearly as important as inviting people for a visit.

I have a fondness for afternoon parties, especially at teatime. The food is casual, lighter, and can be prepared ahead, so you can enjoy time with your guests. I serve two punches, both with an almond flavor, but from two different sources. The nonalcoholic punch is laced with almond extract, whereas the frozen whiskey sour punch is enhanced by maraschino liqueur, not to be confused with the bright red, too-sweet cherries often served in cocktails. Maraschino is a clear, relatively dry liqueur made from sour marasca cherries, which are found almost exclusively on the coast of Croatia. The liqueur is made not only with the sour fruit but also with the crushed cherry pits, which give it a subtle bitter-almond flavor. Processed and distilled much like brandy, it is combined with pure cane syrup before it has aged, and is then filtered. It is one of the very few liqueurs in the world produced by distillation, and it can completely transform a mediocre cocktail into the most memorable one.

Open-faced tea sandwiches are timeless. The sausage savories with sage and the classic cheese pennies can be frozen ahead and baked just the morning of your tea party. I keep these easy-to-prepare individual lemon meringue tartlets in my freezer, as these party favorites both keep well frozen and take just minutes to thaw to the right consistency. They come in handy when a friend stops by for an afternoon cup of coffee or tea, or to make any teatime special.

MAKES 3 QUARTS

5 cups cold lemonade, made from frozen concentrate, divided

Decorative garnish of choice

½ cup sugar

12 ounces frozen pineapple juice concentrate

12 ounces frozen pink lemonade concentrate

12 ounces frozen Bacardi Strawberry Daiquiri concentrate

2 tablespoons pure almond extract

1 (1-liter) bottle ginger ale

1. To make the ice ring, pour 2½ cups of the lemonade made from the concentrate into an 8-inch ring mold. (A small bowl can substitute for the ring mold.) Freeze until the lemonade is slushy but not firm, about 2 hours.

2. Remove from the freezer and arrange the decorative fruit, mint, or flowers on top of the slushy lemonade. Carefully pour the remaining 2 ½ cups lemonade over the fruit. Cover the mold tightly with plastic wrap. Return to the freezer until the lemonade is completely set, at least 8 hours and up to 2 weeks.

3. To make the punch, bring 1 cup water to a boil. Combine the sugar with the boiling water in a large stainless steel bowl and stir to dissolve. Add 2 quarts of cool water and stir to combine. Add the pineapple and pink lemonade concentrates, daiquiri mix, and almond extract. Stir until all the ingredients are dissolved.

4. Place the bowl in the freezer until slushy, at least 4 hours. If you don't have freezer space, you can eliminate the freezing and substitute the ice ring with crushed ice.

5. To serve, pour the punch into a large punch bowl, add the ginger ale, and stir to combine. (It should be slushy.) Remove the ring mold from the freezer. Run warm water over the bottom of the ring mold until the decorative mold releases easily, 30 seconds to 1 minute. Place the decorative ring in the middle of the punch bowl and serve.

Ice rings made with fruit juice impart flavor to punches as they slowly melt. Ice rings can include blueberries, raspberries, or sliced strawberries, oranges, or lemons as well as whole mint leaves or small edible flowers.

MAKES 2 QUARTS

*8 ounces frozen lemonade
concentrate, thawed*

*2 ounces frozen orange juice
concentrate, thawed*

½ cup maraschino liqueur

2 cups good-quality bourbon

1. Combine the lemonade and orange juice in a stainless steel or plastic bowl. Add 2 cups water and stir well. Add the maraschino liqueur and bourbon, and stir to mix.

2. Cover tightly with plastic wrap and freeze until slushy, at least 4 hours.

3. Remove the punch from the freezer. There is enough sugar and liquor in this punch that you do not have to worry about it over-freezing. It will remain slushy. Stir vigorously to even out the ice crystals, and pour into a serving pitcher.

THE TAFT FLOTILLA

In 1909 President William Howard Taft and an entourage of governors and members of Congress traveled from St. Louis to New Orleans on a flotilla of riverboats, stopping at river towns along the way. His mission was to promote the deepening of certain parts of the Mississippi River to create economic development and make it easier to transport goods along the River. After an extensive study by the US Army Corps of Engineers, Congress finally authorized in 1930 the nine-foot channel navigation project using twenty-five locks and dams on the Upper Mississippi River. A twenty-sixth was built between 1979 and the mid-1990s at Mile 201—Left Bank of the Mississippi and named for Melvin Price, a Democratic representative from Illinois.

MAKES 3 DOZEN 2-INCH OPEN-FACED
SANDWICHES

*4 ounces cream cheese, at room
temperature*

2 tablespoons mayonnaise

1 teaspoon finely grated lemon zest

1 teaspoon minced fresh basil leaves

*12 slices thin white sandwich
bread, such as Pepperidge Farm
sourdough*

*1 medium cucumber, ends trimmed,
peeled, thinly sliced into rounds*

*6 whole basil leaves, thinly sliced,
for garnish*

*4 plum tomatoes, sliced into
¼-inch-thick rounds*

*3 thick slices smoked bacon, diced
and cooked until crisp (page 310)*

1. Place the cream cheese in a bowl and beat until smooth with a hand-held mixer. Add the mayonnaise and beat until smooth. Transfer half of the cream cheese mixture to a clean bowl, add the lemon zest, and stir to combine. Add the minced basil to the remaining cream cheese mixture in the original bowl and stir to combine.

2. Place the bread on a large cutting board. Using a 2-inch biscuit or cookie cutter, cut three rounds from each slice of bread.

3. Spread the lemon cream cheese onto the tops of half of the bread rounds. Top each with a cucumber slice and some thinly sliced basil. Arrange on a platter and cover with plastic wrap until ready to serve.

4. Spread the basil cream cheese onto the remaining bread rounds. Top each with a tomato slice and garnish with bacon. Arrange the sandwiches on a platter and serve immediately. These hold up well, but the tomatoes can make the bread soggy after a period of time.

These can be prepared the day before serving. To keep the sandwiches from becoming soggy, line a baking sheet with paper towels. Place the sandwiches on the paper towels, then cover tightly with plastic wrap and refrigerate. I prefer Pullman bread, as it has a denser texture and holds up better than a plain white bread. A worthy substitute is Pepperidge Farm sourdough.

1. Preheat the oven to 350° F. Line a baking sheet with aluminum foil and spray with vegetable oil.

2. Place the sausage meat in a skillet over medium heat and cook, stirring to break up the pieces, until browned and cooked through, 5 to 6 minutes. Transfer the meat to a colander to drain well. Discard the fat in the pan.

3. Place the cooked sausage meat in a bowl. Add the remaining ingredients and mix well. Using your hands, shape the mixture into thirty 1-inch balls.

4. Place the sausage balls 1 inch apart on the prepared baking sheet and bake until golden brown, 18 to 20 minutes.

The uncooked sausage balls can be frozen on a baking sheet. Transfer to a heavy plastic storage bag and freeze for up to 1 month. Transfer the frozen sausage balls to a baking sheet and thaw for 20 minutes at room temperature before baking.

Where I come from, Sausage Savories are typically made with Jimmy Dean sausage, cheddar, and Bisquick. I change these up a bit with Italian sausage and grated mozzarella. The addition of the pecorino or Parmesan and the basil gives that extra touch of flavor.

MAKES 30

Vegetable oil spray

1 pound sweet Italian sausage, removed from casings

½ pound mozzarella, grated

½ pound Pecorino-Romano or Parmigiano-Reggiano, grated

2 cups Bisquick, or other dry baking mixture

1 teaspoon dry basil leaves

1 teaspoon red pepper flakes

Cheese Pennies

MAKES ABOUT 60

1 cup (2 sticks) salted butter, at room temperature

2 teaspoons Worcestershire sauce

2 teaspoons Tabasco or other hot pepper sauce

2 cups all-purpose flour

5 cups (about 1½ pounds) grated sharp cheddar

2 cups pecan halves

1. Place the butter in the bowl of a stand mixer fitted with a paddle attachment and beat on medium speed until smooth, about 2 minutes. Add the Worcestershire and hot sauce and blend for 30 seconds. Add the flour and cheddar in batches, scraping down the sides of the bowl and paddle as needed between additions, and mixing just until it comes together as dough. (The dough will hold together, but the grated cheese will remain visible.)

2. Transfer the dough onto a lightly floured work surface. Divide the dough into four balls. With your hands, shape each ball into a log about 2 inches in diameter. Wrap each log separately in plastic wrap and chill for at least 1 hour or overnight.

3. Preheat the oven to 350°F. Line two baking sheets with parchment paper.

4. Place the logs on a work surface, unwrap, and slice each into ¼-inch-thick rounds. Place the rounds on the prepared baking sheets, ½ inch apart. Press a pecan half into the center of each round. Bake one baking sheet at a time on the middle rack of the oven. (If you bake both baking sheets at the same time, swap racks halfway through the cooking time.)

5. Bake until the edges are golden brown, about 12 minutes. (The pennies may seem soft in the center, but they will firm up when they cool.) Transfer the pennies to a wire rack to cool. Serve warm or at room temperature.

The cooled pennies can be stored in an airtight container for up to 1 week at room temperature.

Lemon Meringue Tartlets

1. Preheat the oven to 350°F. Lightly spray a 24-count mini-muffin pan lightly with vegetable oil spray.

2. Put the vanilla wafers in a food processor and process into crumbs, measuring about 2 cups. Add the melted butter and pulse until the dough holds together. Divide the cookie mixture among the mini-muffin sections. Press the mixture evenly into the bottoms and up the sides of the muffin wells. Bake until the crusts are golden brown, about 5 minutes.

3. For the custard, place the cream cheese in the bowl of a stand mixer fitted with a paddle attachment and beat on medium until creamy, about 2 minutes. Add the condensed milk and beat for 1 minute. Add the lemon juice, sugar, vanilla, and salt and beat until smooth, about 1 minute.

4. Divide the custard mixture among the prepared crusts. Bake until the edges are set but the centers are still a bit loose, 8 to 10 minutes. Remove from the oven and let cool completely on a wire rack, at least 1 hour.

5. Cover the pan with aluminum foil and freeze the tartlets until firm, at least 4 hours or overnight. Once they are frozen, run a paring knife dipped in hot water around the edge of each tartlet and remove them from the muffin tins. Put the tartlets on a baking sheet and keep in the freezer while making the meringue.

6. Preheat the oven to 450°F.

7. To prepare the meringue, put the egg whites in the bowl of a stand mixer fitted with a whisk attachment or a bowl with a hand mixer. Beat on medium speed until soft peaks form. Add the sugar and beat until the egg whites are shiny and stiff peaks form.

8. Spoon a teaspoon of the meringue on top of each tart, swirling the spoon to create peaks. Bake the tartlets until the meringue is lightly browned, 2 minutes. The tartlets can be served immediately.

MAKES 2 DOZEN

Crust

Vegetable oil spray

2 dozen vanilla wafer cookies

3 tablespoons salted butter, melted

Custard

8 ounces cream cheese, at room temperature

1 (14-ounce) can sweetened condensed milk

1 cup fresh lemon juice

¼ cup sugar

1½ teaspoons pure vanilla extract

⅛ teaspoon table salt

Meringue

3 large egg whites

1 cup sugar

The tartlets can be made and frozen up to 2 weeks in advance. Store in a plastic container with a layer of plastic wrap that doesn't touch the meringue.

ARKANSAS FARM-TO-TABLE SUPPER (FOR 6)

Grilled Peach Salad with Chipotle-Raspberry Vinaigrette

Chicken Potpie with Regina's Bacon-Thyme Biscuit Crust

Buttermilk Custards with Berries

From the central region of the state, the Arkansas River flows southward through the rich farmlands of the Arkansas delta to its confluence with the Mississippi River. The Great River Road and the Mississippi River run through ten Arkansas counties, which are some of the most productive agricultural areas in the United States. Rice, soybeans, and cotton still reign here. Peaches are number ten on the list of most productive Arkansas crops, making them worth including in this menu.

Farming in Arkansas is more than a way of life; it is at the heart of Arkansas's heritage. When the area was still a territory, more than 90 percent of Arkansans were farmers. Today, at least 45 to 50 percent of the state's population still make a living from the land. I spend a lot of time at my friend P. Allen Smith's farm overlooking the Arkansas River where it runs into the Mississippi, as I often do cooking segments for his syndicated shows. Allen, an award-winning designer, gardener, and lifestyle expert, and I share a love of food, flowers, fowl, and entertaining. No one (other than my father) has had more of an influence on my personal commitment to farm-to-table dining than Allen. At his farm, Moss Mountain, Allen has taught me about raising heritage poultry and always answers my questions about growing herbs, fruits, and vegetables. He can take credit for everything lovely on the grounds of my home, Twin Oaks, as well as many of the touches inside the house. We are always at home in each other's kitchens and company. We seem to be the confluence of farm and table.

At every meal we've cooked together, we have gathered most of the ingredients at Moss Mountain. This farm-to-table supper is an example of many that Allen and I have cooked together for friends and family. The grilled peach salad is a summer must. The chicken potpie knows no season. The buttermilk custard is a recipe that I created with Allen and his plentiful berry patches in mind.

Grilled Peach Salad with Chipotle-Raspberry Vinaigrette

*6 ripe small-to-medium peaches,
    peeled, halved, and pitted*

2 tablespoons extra virgin olive oil

1 teaspoon kosher salt

*1 teaspoon freshly ground black
    pepper*

3 cups mixed greens

*½ recipe Chipotle-Raspberry
    Vinaigrette (below)*

6 ounces fresh goat cheese, crumbled

1. Place the peaches in a large bowl and toss with the olive oil, salt, and pepper.

2. Preheat the grill to medium-high or 400°F. (Alternatively, preheat a grill pan over medium-high heat.) Place the peach halves flat side down, and cook to make grill marks, about 2 minutes. Turn and cook on the other sides, about 1 minute. (The peaches should remain firm enough to hold their shape.) Remove to a plate.

3. Place the greens in a large bowl and toss with 2 tablespoons of the vinaigrette. Arrange the greens on a decorative platter and place the peach halves on top, pit sides up. Divide the goat cheese among the peach halves, filling the centers, and drizzle with the remaining 2 tablespoons of dressing before serving.

Chipotle-Raspberry Vinaigrette

MAKES ½ CUP

1 chipotle pepper in adobo

2 tablespoons honey

1 tablespoon apple cider vinegar

1 tablespoon fresh lime juice

1 tablespoon seedless raspberry jam

½ teaspoon minced fresh garlic

½ teaspoon kosher salt

¼ cup vegetable oil

1. Remove the stem from the chipotle pepper and discard; remove seeds. Place the pepper and adobo in a blender or food processor and puree on medium speed.

2. Add the honey, vinegar, lime juice, jam, garlic, and salt to the blender and process until smooth. With the motor running, slowly add the oil in a thin, steady stream and process until the vinaigrette thickens.

3. Transfer to a clean container, cover, and refrigerate until ready to serve.

The vinaigrette will keep refrigerated for up to 5 days.

MAKES 2 (12-INCH) OR 3 (THREE 8-INCH) PIES

¼ cup extra virgin olive oil

3 tablespoons freshly ground black pepper

1 tablespoon kosher salt

1 tablespoon minced garlic

2 teaspoons dried tarragon

3 pounds boneless, skinless chicken breasts, cut into 1-inch cubes

Vegetable oil spray

2 cups trimmed and quartered brussels sprouts or chopped broccoli flowerets

2 cups diced, skin-on, small red potatoes, such as Red Bliss

1 cup sliced carrots in ¼-inch rounds

1 cup sliced celery in ¼-inch rounds

1 cup frozen green peas

¾ cup (1½ sticks) salted butter

1 cup chopped yellow onions

½ cup all-purpose flour

1 quart low-sodium chicken broth

2 cups heavy cream

2 teaspoons chopped fresh rosemary leaves

1 recipe Regina's Bacon-Thyme Biscuit Dough (page 195)

1. Combine the olive oil, black pepper, salt, garlic, and tarragon in a large bowl. Add the diced chicken to the olive oil mixture and stir to coat completely.

2. Spray a large skillet with vegetable oil spray and heat over medium-high heat. Add the chicken cubes and cook them just until browned, about 3 minutes. Transfer to a bowl.

3. Bring a large pot of salted water to a boil. While waiting for the water to boil, fill a large bowl with ice and water. Cook the vegetables separately until they are just tender, from 3 to 5 minutes each. The potatoes take the most time at 5 to 6 minutes, carrots and celery 4 to 5 minutes, and brussels sprouts 3 to 4 minutes. I don't blanch the peas.

4. As each vegetable is cooked, using a mesh strainer, transfer it to a colander and drain briefly. Immediately put the vegetable in the cold water to stop the cooking, replenishing the ice as needed to keep the water cold. Drain all of the vegetables in a colander.

5. Preheat the oven to 350°F. Melt the butter in a dutch oven over low heat. Add the onions, increase the heat to medium, and cook, stirring, until the onions are translucent, about 4 minutes. Slowly add the flour and cook, stirring constantly, to make a light roux, 3 to 4 minutes. Add the chicken broth and cream and increase the heat to medium high, stirring frequently, until the sauce begins to thicken. Add the browned chicken and drained vegetables, stirring well to incorporate. Remove from heat and adjust the seasoning to taste.

6. Divide the chicken filling between two 12-inch cast-iron skillets. (Alternatively, the filling can be divided between one skillet to cook and one 2-quart baking dish to freeze for a future meal.)

7. On a lightly floured surface, roll out the bacon-thyme biscuit dough into two 13-inch circles, ¼ inch thick. Transfer one dough circle to each of the filled cast-iron skillets, leaving a ½-inch overhang around all sides and pressing down to have the dough adhere. Place the skillets in the oven and bake until the top is browned, 35 to 40 minutes.

Regina's Bacon-Thyme Biscuit Dough

1. Put the flour, baking powder, sugar, and thyme in the bowl of a stand mixer fitted with the paddle attachment. Blend the dry ingredients on low for 15 seconds.

2. Add the margarine to the bowl. Turn the mixer on medium speed and count to ten. There should be visible chunks of margarine the size of quarters in the dough. Add the buttermilk and stir until dough is moist but pulled together, being careful not to overmix.

3. Generously flour a work surface and roll out the dough into a rectangle about 1 inch thick. Fold the dough in half, bringing the two short ends together, turn a half turn, and roll it out again. Spread half of the cooked bacon over the dough, and fold, turn, and roll out more two times. Add the remaining bacon and repeat for an additional two times, finishing with a ¼-inch-thick dough. Use the dough as directed in the potpie recipe.

These can be made ahead and frozen for later use, wrapped in plastic wrap and then in foil. Thaw in the refrigerator overnight and bake as directed.

MAKES 2 (12-INCH) OR 3 (8-INCH) PIECRUSTS

4 cups all-purpose flour, plus more for the board

¼ cup baking powder

¼ cup sugar

2 tablespoons minced fresh thyme leaves

1½ cups (3 sticks) cold margarine, cut into 2-inch cubes

1¾ cups cold buttermilk

8 thick slices smoked bacon, diced and cooked until crisp (page 310)

2 (¼-ounce) envelopes (2 table-
    spoons) unflavored gelatin

1 cup heavy cream

¾ cup sugar

1 teaspoon finely grated lemon zest

2 cups buttermilk

2 teaspoons pure vanilla extract

1½ cups fresh blackberries

1½ cups fresh raspberries

1. Place 2 tablespoons cool water and the gelatin in a small bowl and stir to blend. Let stand until the gelatin softens, about 5 minutes.

2. Combine the cream, sugar, and lemon zest in a saucepan and bring to a simmer over medium heat. Remove from the heat, add the gelatin, and stir to dissolve. Stir in the buttermilk and vanilla, and pour into six ½-cup glasses or bowls. Cover and refrigerate until set and firm to the touch, about 4 hours or overnight.

3. Combine the berries in a large bowl. Divide the berries evenly among the six custards and serve immediately.

Once you hit Memphis, the flavor and feel of the River changes once again. The Lower Mississippi region includes the length of the River and land on both sides that epitomizes southern hospitality and entertaining. In this section, the focus is on Mississippi River–style traditions and parties. Memphis is about beginnings: Long before he became president, Andrew Jackson began his career by settling the city of Memphis with General James Winchester and Judge John Overton. That city has always been a key travel and transportation center on the River, as well as a center of culture and music in the South since the early 1800s. The birth of the blues is as much a part of Memphis as of anywhere in the South. The city's music traditions include everything from the blues to the beginning of rock 'n' roll, rockabilly, and soul.

Traveling downriver, the charming river town of Helena, Arkansas, is home to the King Biscuit Blues Festival every October. To the south, Arkansas City is the gateway to ten thousand public acres of lakes and wooded areas, known for hunting, fishing, and bird-watching. When you get to the Mississippi Delta, you arrive in a world like no other with the Tamale Trail and the Blues Highway. Why is there a Tamale Trail along the River's Delta region? The most popular theory is that tamales made their way to the Mississippi Delta in the early twentieth century when Mexican migrant laborers were brought in to work the cotton harvests. The African Americans sharing the fields with the migrant workers learned how to make the tamales, an ideal field worker's lunch.

Natchez sits high on the bluffs of the River and was established by French colonists in 1716. One of the oldest and most important European settlements in the Lower Mississippi River Valley, Natchez once served as the capital of the Mississippi Territory and the state of Mississippi. A pivotal center of trade and commerce, Natchez was a melting pot of Native American, European, and African-American cultures for the first two centuries of its existence. With its wealth and European influence, it has always been the host of elegant parties. It is the southern terminus of the historic Natchez Trace, which once served many pilots of flatboats and keelboats as a road back to their homes in the Ohio River Valley after unloading their cargo in Natchez.

In the middle of the nineteenth century, vast tracts of land in the Mississippi and Louisiana lowlands were used to raise cotton and sugarcane with slave labor. Natchez became the principal port from which these crops were transported, both upriver to northern cities and downriver to New Orleans, from where much of the cargo was exported to Europe. The planters' fortunes allowed them to build majestic mansions before 1860, many of which survive to this day. These homes have become the center of tourism and form a major part of the city's architecture and identity.

When you leave the high bluffs of Natchez and head toward St. Francisville, the landscape changes. Sugarcane has an even richer history than cotton in this Lower River region. Louisiana's Great Mississippi River Road is a corridor almost seventy miles long located on both sides of the River between Baton Rouge and New Orleans. The area includes the River, levees, and Louisiana's best-known plantation houses built in the Greek revival style by wealthy sugar planters. This is the land of the Creole and Cajun people and their cuisine. This southern region of the River offers the simplicity of genuine soulful cooking as well as the grand style of gracious entertaining that has existed from Natchez to New Orleans for more than two hundred years.

From Baton Rouge to the Gulf of Mexico, the River is part of the deepwater port area where ships and freighters travel to and from the Gulf. If you were going by mile makers, it would appear I have written this book in the wrong order. All charts of the River begin with mile 0 at the "Head of the Passes" at the mouth of the Mississippi. These last, or first, miles are as culturally diverse as other regions on the River. The Acadians have lived and worked here for centuries, followed by immigrants from Croatia, Mexico, and Central America. In the 1980s many Vietnamese relocated here after the Vietnam War so they could continue their traditions as fishermen. Southeast Asian immigrants are now the majority of shrimp fishermen in this area.

AMERICAN QUEEN CHRISTENING LUNCHEON
(FOR 6)

Sweet Potato Soup with Orange and Ginger

Curried Chicken Salad with Cranberries and Pecans

Crab and Avocado Tower

Strawberries with Brown Sugar–Sour Cream Sauce

Naming ships is a four-thousand-year-old tradition. Beginning in the nineteenth century, the breaking of a bottle with liquid on the bow became the preferred ceremony for bringing luck to a boat. During the same century, it became a tradition that women would christen and become godmother of the ship. Champagne has been the beverage of choice ever since.

As Memphis is the home port of the *American Queen,* it seemed only fitting that Priscilla Presley, Elvis's wife, would be chosen as its godmother. When Priscilla christened the *American Queen* on April 22, 2012, I started the celebratory luncheon with a sweet potato soup flavored with orange and ginger. The next course was two salads—a tower of crab and avocado with a fresh salsa and a savory curried chicken salad—plated together. Fresh spring strawberries were in season, and they needed nothing more than a topping of brown sugar and sour cream.

3 tablespoons extra virgin olive oil

1 medium white onion, diced

1 tablespoon minced fresh ginger

1 teaspoon minced garlic

2 cups peeled and diced sweet
potatoes

½ cup peeled and diced Yukon Gold
or russet potatoes

½ cup fresh orange juice

1 tablespoon finely grated orange
zest

1 teaspoon kosher salt

1 cup heavy cream

1. Heat the olive oil in a dutch oven over medium heat. Add the onions and cook, stirring, until soft, about 5 minutes. Add the ginger and garlic and cook, stirring, for 1 minute. Add the sweet potatoes and Yukon Gold potatoes, cover with 3 cups water, the orange juice, zest, and salt and bring to a boil. Reduce the heat, cover, and simmer until the potatoes are tender and can be pierced with a fork, about 30 minutes.

2. Remove from the heat. Using an immersion blender, purée the soup until smooth. (Alternatively, the soup can be pureed in a blender in batches, and then returned to the pot.) Return the soup to medium heat. Add the cream and cook, stirring, until heated through, about 5 minutes.

3. Remove from the heat, ladle the soup into bowls, and serve.

This soup is just as good cold as it is hot. If served cold, add fresh lime wedges or a dollop of sour cream to liven it up a bit.

1. Preheat the oven to 350°F.

2. Place the chicken breasts in a baking dish and rub the skin with olive oil. Season on both sides with the salt and pepper. Bake until cooked through and an instant-read thermometer inserted into the thickest part of the chicken registers 155°F, 25 to 30 minutes. Remove from the oven and let sit until cool enough to handle. Discard the skin. Remove the meat from the bones and cut into ½-inch dice. Place the chicken in a large bowl.

3. Make a dressing by whisking together the mayonnaise, chutney, curry powder, wine, and salt in a small bowl.

4. Add half of the dressing to the chicken and stir well to combine. Add the celery, green onions, and cranberries, and stir well, adding more dressing to taste. Cover and refrigerate for at least 2 hours or overnight to allow the flavors to blend. Remove from the refrigerator and stir in the pecans.

5. Place a plate on a work surface. Using a 3-inch ring mold, arrange ½ cup of the greens in the bottom of the mold and top with a heaping ⅔ cup of the chicken salad. Press the chicken with the back of a spoon and remove the mold. Repeat with the remaining ingredients on the five remaining plates. Serve immediately.

1½ pounds bone-in, skin-on chicken breasts

3 tablespoons extra virgin olive oil

1 tablespoon kosher salt

1 tablespoon freshly ground black pepper

3 tablespoons mayonnaise

2 tablespoons Major Grey's mango chutney

1 tablespoon curry powder

1 tablespoon dry white wine

½ teaspoon kosher salt

1 stalk celery, trimmed and cut into ⅛-inch dice

2 tablespoons chopped green onions, white bottoms and green tops

2 tablespoons dried cranberries or Craisins

2 tablespoons chopped pecans, toasted (page 311)

3 cups mixed salad greens or arugula

Avocado Salsa

1½ cups (2 large) avocados, peeled,
    pitted, and cut into ¼-inch dice

¼ cup fresh lime juice

1 teaspoon kosher salt

1 teaspoon freshly ground black
    pepper

Vegetable Salsa

¼ cup bell pepper, cored, seeded,
    and cut into ⅛-inch dice

½ cup cucumber, peeled, seeded,
    and cut into ⅛-inch dice

½ cup Roma tomatoes, cored,
    seeded, and cut into ⅛ inch dice

¼ cup celery, cut into ⅛-inch dice

¼ cup minced red onion

¼ cup extra virgin olive oil

2 tablespoons sherry vinegar

1 tablespoon minced fresh cilantro
    leaves

1 teaspoon minced pickled jalapeños

1 teaspoon kosher salt

½ teaspoon freshly ground black
    pepper

1. To make the avocado salsa, combine all the ingredients in a bowl and stir.

2. To make the vegetable salsa, combine all the ingredients in a bowl and stir.

3. To make the crabmeat mixture, gently combine the ingredients, being careful not to break the lumps of crabmeat.

4. Place six large plates on a work surface. To make the towers, place a 3-inch ring mold in the center of one plate. Spoon ¼ cup of the avocado salsa in the bottom of the mold, pressing lightly with the back of a spoon to evenly distribute. Top with ¼ cup of the vegetable salsa and spread it out with the back of the spoon. Top with 2 tablespoons of the crabmeat mixture, spreading with the back of a spoon out to the edges. Remove the mold. Repeat with the remaining ingredients on the five remaining plates, and serve.

Crabmeat Mixture

1 pound lump crabmeat, picked over for shells and cartilage

2 tablespoons extra virgin olive oil

2 tablespoons fresh lemon juice

1 tablespoon minced fresh chives

½ teaspoon kosher salt

Strawberries with Brown Sugar–Sour Cream Sauce

1. Whisk the sour cream and sugar in a bowl until the sugar dissolves.

2. Divide the berries among six stemmed glasses. Pour 2 tablespoons of the sauce over each portion and serve.

1 cup sour cream

½ cup packed light brown sugar

4 cups (2 pints) strawberries, hulled and quartered

MEMPHIS-STYLE SUNDAY LUNCH (FOR 8)

Tennessee Coffee Punch

Shrimp Salad with Horseradish Sauce

Corn Muffins Filled with Barbecued Pulled Pork and Mustard Greens

Roasted Corn and Tomato Salad with Lime Vinaigrette

Chocolate–Peanut Butter Pies

Memphis is known for its music, art, and food. It's the birthplace of rock 'n' roll, soul music, and that famous Memphis sound. The Memphis College of Art has produced many creative forces, including two of the most creative people I know: Ben Fink, who made my food come alive with the stunning photographs that he shot for this book, and Pat Kerr Tigrett, a world-renowned Memphis-based wedding gown designer for thirty years, who is known for embellishing her amazing creations with vintage and one-of-a-kind pieces of lace. When it comes to entertaining, Pat also has her own style, which reflects her Tennessee farm roots.

This menu is modeled after one such party, when Pat offered guests a morning eye-opener—coffee milk punch flavored with Jack Daniel's Tennessee whiskey. Memphis is known for its slow-cooked pulled pork, mustard greens, and cornbread. All three are combined here with pulled pork made in a slow cooker and greens baked in individual corn muffins. There are also two side salads—shrimp with a touch of horseradish, and roasted corn with tomatoes and a lime-cilantro dressing.

No Memphis menu would be complete without a tribute to Elvis, the King of rock 'n' roll, who was known for his love of peanut butter. These frozen peanut butter pies make a smooth finish.

Tennessee Coffee Punch

¾ cup sugar

1 (500-ml) bottle Cool Brew Fresh
   Coffee Concentrate (see Source
   Guide, page 316), or 2 cups brewed
   strong coffee plus 1 tablespoon of
   espresso powder, chilled

2 cups half-and-half

2 cups heavy cream

1 cup Jack Daniel's

1 tablespoon pure vanilla extract

1. Place the sugar in a small bowl. Add ½ cup boiling water and stir to dissolve. Let cool completely.

2. Combine the cooled sugar water and the remaining ingredients in a pitcher filled with ice. Stir to mix well and then divide between eight footed glass coffee mugs or other glasses.

This can be made 1 day in advance and kept refrigerated. Add the ice just before serving.

Shrimp Salad with Horseradish Sauce

1. Whisk together the mayonnaise, ketchup, and horseradish in a bowl. Add the lemon juice and stir well.

2. Add the shrimp, celery, and green onion to the sauce and stir to coat. Refrigerate for 1 hour before serving. Divide the shrimp salad among eight salad plates, garnish with lemon slices, and serve.

¼ cup mayonnaise

2 tablespoons ketchup

1 tablespoon prepared horseradish

2 teaspoons fresh lemon juice

1½ pounds boiled large shrimp, peeled and deveined

1 cup diced celery

2 tablespoons diced green onion

1 lemon, sliced into 8 wedges, for garnish

Pulled Pork with Barbecue Sauce

1 medium white onion, finely chopped

2 cloves garlic, minced

2 cups ketchup

⅓ cup apple cider vinegar

¼ cup bourbon

¼ cup tomato paste

¾ cup packed dark brown sugar

¼ cup Worcestershire sauce

1 tablespoon liquid smoke

2 teaspooons kosher salt

1 teaspoon Tabasco or other hot pepper sauce

1 teaspoon freshly ground black pepper

4 pound boneless pork butt

1. Put the onions, garlic, ketchup, vinegar, bourbon, and tomato paste in a 4-quart slow cooker. Cook on medium, stirring, until the tomato paste is dissolved, about 3 minutes. Add the sugar, Worcestershire sauce, liquid smoke, salt, Tabasco, and black pepper. Stir until well blended. Place the pork in the slow cooker and turn to coat well with the wet ingredients.

2. Cover the slow cooker and set the termperature to high. Cook for 1 hour. Turn the temperature to low and cook undisturbed until the meat is tender and will pull apart when you pierce it with a fork, about 6 hours. Turn off the machine. Transfer the pork to a large bowl and let sit until just cool enough to handle. Use two forks to shred the meat. Cover and refrigerate until ready to use.

3. Pour the sauce from the slow cooker into a bowl and let cool to room temperature. Refrigerate the sauce until the fat congeals on the top, about 2 hours. Skim off the congealed fat with a spoon and discard. Pour the remaining sauce into the bowl with the pulled pork. Toss well to coat the meat evenly.

Corn Muffins

1. Preheat the oven to 350°F. Spray a 12-cup muffin tin with vegetable oil spray.

2. Combine the flour, cornmeal, baking powder, baking soda, and salt in a bowl. Whisk to combine.

3. Whisk the egg lightly in a large bowl. Add the sour cream, buttermilk, butter, and sugar. Whisk to combine. Stir in the creamed corn.

4. Add the wet ingredients to the dry ingredients. Stir to mix, being careful not to overmix.

5. Fill each cup halfway with the batter. Add 1 tablespoon of the pulled pork and evenly distribute the mustard greens in the muffin tin. Divide the remaining batter among the muffin cups, covering the filling.

6. Bake on the middle rack of the oven until the muffins are firm to the touch and lightly browned, 30 to 35 minutes. Remove from oven and let sit for 3 to 4 minutes before turning out. Serve warm.

I make these in square muffin pans, but feel free to use round ones if that's what you have.

MAKES 1 DOZEN

Vegetable oil spray

¾ cup all-purpose flour

¾ cup yellow cornmeal, stone-ground if possible (see Source Guide, page 316)

1 tablespoon baking powder

½ teaspoon baking soda

½ teaspoon table salt

1 large egg

¼ cup sour cream

¼ cup buttermilk

2 tablespoons salted butter, melted

1 tablespoon sugar

½ cup creamed corn

1 cup Old Glory canned cooked mustard greens, drained

3 tablespoons extra virgin olive oil

1 tablespoon fresh lime juice

1 teaspoon finely grated lime zest

1 teaspoon kosher salt

2 teaspoons sugar

Kernels from 2 ears corn

3 cups (2 large) tomatoes, seeded and diced

2 tablespoons coarsely chopped fresh cilantro leaves

1. Whisk together the olive oil, lime juice, zest, salt, and sugar in a bowl.

2. Heat a cast-iron skillet over medium heat until very hot. Place the corn kernels in the skillet and roast, stirring, until the kernels are browned on all sides. Transfer the corn to a bowl and add the dressing.

3. Add the tomatoes and cilantro and toss well to coat. Cover and refrigerate for 1 hour before serving.

Chocolate–Peanut Butter Pies

1. Preheat the oven to 350° F.

2. Place the chocolate cookies in a food processor and process to crumbs. Add the butter and pulse to make a dough. Divide the cookie mixture equally among the cups of a 12-cup muffin tin. Press the mixture evenly in the bottoms and halfway up the sides. Bake until the cookie shells are set, about 10 minutes. Remove from the oven and cool completely on a wire rack.

3. Pour the hot fudge sauce into a microwave-safe bowl. Microwave on high until the sauce is melted, stirring once, 30 to 45 seconds. Spoon 1 tablespoon of the sauce onto the crust in each muffin cup. Top each portion with 2 teaspoons chopped roasted peanuts.

4. Put the cream cheese in the bowl of a stand mixer fitted with a whisk attachment and beat until smooth, about 2 minutes. Add the peanut butter and beat until smooth, about 1 minute. Add the marshmallow creme and confectioners' sugar and beat for 2 minutes, scraping down the sides as needed. Divide the filling among the muffin tins. Cover and freeze until firm, at least 4 hours and up to 2 weeks.

5. When ready to plate, run a paring knife dipped in hot water around the outside of each pie to release from the muffin tin. Transfer the pies to dessert plates or a platter and let sit at room temperature for 5 to 10 minutes before serving.

20 Oreos (do not remove cream)

3 tablespoons salted butter, melted

1 (12.8-ounce) jar hot fudge sauce

½ cup chopped dry roasted salted peanuts

8 ounces cream cheese, at room temperature

1 cup creamy peanut butter

1 cup marshmallow creme

1 cup confectioners' sugar

DELTA TAMALE PARTY (FOR 12)

Deviled Eggs with Crabmeat and Wasabi Caviar

Peppadew Pimento Cheese on Fried Green Tomatoes

Smoked Catfish Tamales with Jalapeño Green Salsa

Coconut Cupcakes with Seven-Minute Icing

David L. Cohn, author of the memoir *Where I Lived and Was Raised,* best described the Delta's location when he wrote, "The Delta begins in the lobby of the Peabody Hotel in Memphis and ends on Catfish Row in Vicksburg." The Mississippi Delta is an alluvial plain, a landform of rich soil formed from sediments laid down during repeated floodings of a river. In Mississippi, this rich farmland was once home to a thriving cotton plantation economy. The Delta is the home of the blues and produced its share of well-known writers, including William Faulkner, John Grisham, Eudora Welty, and Richard Wright. (My husband Doug said that he used to have such respect for southern writers, but then, after getting to know my family, he realized that they just write what they see.)

One of my favorite southern authors is my friend Julia Reed. Julia is 100 percent Delta and the best of what I love about Mississippi people. She is elegant, tenacious, and has a wicked sense of humor. She knows about food and telling a story. This menu includes some favorite Delta dishes that I have updated, perfect for sharing with Julia and friends.

These deviled eggs, a Delta staple, are made with lump crabmeat and wasabi-spiced caviar. Every southern cook serves pimento cheese with crackers at just about every gathering. Instead of pimentos, I add Peppadew peppers—tangy pickled peppers from South America—and spoon it on slices of fried green tomatoes.

Many visitors to Mississippi are surprised to learn that spicy tamales have long been a Delta favorite on both sides of the River. Much has been written about their origin, but the consensus seems to be that Mexican migrant workers introduced tamales to African-American workers in the cotton fields. Delta tamales are traditionally made with cornmeal instead of the traditional masa. They're sold in restaurants, gas stations, and corner groceries. In place of the usual pork filling, I fill mine with smoked catfish.

While coconut layer cake with seven-minute frosting is the ultimate southern dessert, individual cupcakes are easier to make and serve. And finally, no southern meal would be complete without pitchers of sweet tea.

4 ounces cream cheese, at room
temperature

2 tablespoons mayonnaise

1 tablespoon Dijon mustard

½ teaspoon Tabasco or other hot
pepper sauce

½ teaspoon kosher salt

1 dozen large eggs, hard-boiled and
peeled (page 310)

½ cup (about 4 ounces) lump
crabmeat, picked over for shells
and cartilage

2 ounces wasabi caviar or
lumpfish roe

1. Whisk together the cream cheese and mayonnaise in a bowl until smooth. Whisk in the mustard, Tabasco, and salt.

2. Slice the eggs in half lengthwise. Remove the yolks and add them to the cream cheese mixture, whisking until smooth. Place the egg whites, hollow centers up, on a serving plate.

3. Spoon the yolk filling into the whites. Or, for a more elegant presentation, transfer the egg yolk mixture to a piping bag fitted with a small tip and pipe it into the egg whites.

4. Spoon the crabmeat on top of the yolk mixture, and top each egg with wasabi caviar. Wrap the plate of eggs with plastic wrap, refrigerate, and served chilled.

These eggs can be made 1 day ahead.

2 cups grated sharp cheddar

¼ cup mayonnaise

2 tablespoons diced Peppadew (see Source Guide, page 316)

1 tablespoon diced pimento pepper

1 teaspoon freshly ground black pepper, divided

1½ cups all-purpose flour, divided

1½ teaspoons kosher salt, divided

2 large eggs

1 cup buttermilk

2 cups cornmeal, stone-ground if possible (see Source Guide, page 316), or masa cornmeal

½ teaspoon garlic powder

¼ teaspoon cayenne

Vegetable oil, for frying

3 large green tomatoes, sliced into ½-inch-thick rounds

1. Combine the cheddar, mayonnaise, Peppadews, pimentos, and ½ teaspoon of the black pepper in a bowl and stir well to blend. Cover and refrigerate until ready to use. (The cheese spread can be made up to 3 days in advance.)

2. Combine 1 cup of the flour, the remaining ½ teaspoon black pepper, and ½ teaspoon of the salt in a shallow baking dish. Whisk together the eggs and buttermilk in a second shallow baking dish. Combine the cornmeal, remaining ½ cup flour, 1 teaspoon salt, and the garlic powder and cayenne on a third shallow dish.

3. Attach a deep-frying thermometer to the side of a dutch oven. Add 2 inches of oil and heat to 350°F over medium heat. (Alternatively, an electric skillet or deep fryer set to 350°F can be used.) Preheat the oven to 175°F.

4. One at a time, dredge the sliced tomatoes on both sides in the seasoned flour, then in the egg mixture, and then in the seasoned cornmeal. Place the coated tomato slices on a baking sheet.

5. Using tongs, gently lower the coated tomatoes one at a time into the hot oil. Fry until golden brown, about 1½ minutes per side. Transfer to a baking sheet lined with paper towels to drain. Fry the remaining tomatoes. Keep the fried tomatoes warm in the oven while frying.

6. Arrange the warm fried green tomatoes on a serving platter and top each one with 1 tablespoon of the Peppadew cheese spread before serving.

Peppadew is the trade name for pickled peppers that have a flavor all their own. Look for them at World Market, Whole Foods, and gourmet groceries. The bright red color and perfect blend of sweet and tart give a special touch to traditional pimento cheese. This recipe makes extra for sandwiches or with crackers for a snack.

THE BLUES ALONG THE RIVER

It's hard to imagine food along the Lower Mississippi without hearing a bit of the blues with every bite. Just as each city (such as St. Louis, Memphis, and New Orleans) has its own style of cooking, it also has its own style of blues.

How the blues got its name and where this style of American music first began is open to argument and conjecture. Most evidence directs the origin to African Americans working in the Missis-

sippi Delta at the beginning of the twentieth century. Starting with homemade guitars and songs from the heart, legend has it that Robert Johnson knelt down at the crossroads of Highways 61 and 49 and made a deal with the devil to let him play and sing the blues like nobody else. The Delta Blues Museum in Clarksdale (deltabluesmuseum.org), about ninety minutes from Memphis, hosts exhibits and festivals and is definitely worth a visit.

As the century unfolded so did the blues. Somewhere around 1917, St. Louis made its mark on the music by bringing the guitar and piano together for a new take. Around 1945, Memphis added a dirtied-up electric sound as done by Willie Johnson, Sonny Boy Williamson, and the unforgettable Howlin' Wolf.

Since then, the music and the food that go along with it have innovated, evolved, and made their way into more and more people's hearts and souls. As contemporary New Orleans bluesman Tab Benoit sings, "The blues is here to stay." Indeed it is.

1. Place the whole cornhusks in a large bowl. Add enough hot water to cover the husks and weight with a plate to keep submerged. Soak the husks until pliable, 2 to 3 hours.

2. In the bowl of a stand mixer fitted with a paddle attachment, whip the lard and salt on high speed until fluffy, about 2 minutes. Add the cornmeal and beat at low speed until well mixed. Add 1 cup of the broth and mix until well combined. Add some of the remaining broth, 1 tablespoon at a time, mixing until a light but not runny batter is formed.

3. Combine the catfish, lime zest, chilies, and 6 ounces of the salsa and the green onions in a bowl. Reserve the remaining 6 ounces of salsa. Stir well to combine. Cut two dozen 10-inch lengths of butcher's twine and prepare a large steamer by lining it with broken cornhusks.

4. Drain the corn husks. To make the tamales, lay one cornhusk flat on a work surface, narrow end facing you. Pat dry and flatten with a kitchen towel. Spread about ¼ cup of the cornmeal batter onto the husk to form a 4-inch square, leaving a ¾- to 1-inch border on all sides. Spread about 2 tablespoons of the catfish mixture down the center of the batter. As though wrapping a package, fold both sides of the husk toward the center to enclose the filling. Bring the bottom and top sides over the filling, overlapping as much as possible to tightly enclose the filling. Wrap the middle of the tamale with a piece of butcher's twine, and then twist the twine up and over to form a tight bundle. Knot the twine. Lay the tamale on a large plate and repeat with the remaining ingredients.

5. Stand the tamales in a steamer insert set 2 inches over a pot of gently boiling water. Cover with a layer of the small or broken husks. Cover with a tight-fitting lid and steam, replenishing the water as needed so the pot does not go dry, until the tamales are cooked through, 1 to 2 hours. After 1 hour, test the tamales for doneness by attempting to unwrap one. The husk should pull away easily from the dough, and the dough should be firm. If not, the continue cooking the tamales, testing them again in the same manner after 15 minutes and up to 1 hour.

MAKES 2 DOZEN

24 dried whole cornhusks, plus a few broken husks to line the steamer insert

1 cup lard

2 teaspoons kosher salt

2 cups yellow cornmeal

1½ cups low-sodium chicken broth or vegetable broth

2 cups (about ¾ pound) smoked catfish or smoked trout (see Source Guide, page 316), in ½-inch dice

1 teaspoon finely grated lime zest

1 (4-ounce) can diced green chilies, drained

1 (12-ounce) jar Mrs. Renfro's Jalapeño Green Salsa (see Source Guide, page 316)

¼ cup chopped green onions, white bottoms and green tops

MAKES 2 DOZEN

1 (15.25-ounce) Pillsbury white
 cake mix

1 cup all-purpose flour

1 cup sugar

½ teaspoon table salt

4 large egg whites

1 cup sour cream

2 tablespoons vegetable oil

1 teaspoon pure almond extract

1 teaspoon pure vanilla extract

1 recipe Seven-Minute Icing

1. Preheat the oven to 325°F. Line two 12-cup muffin tins with paper liners.

2. Whisk together the white cake mix, flour, sugar, and salt in a bowl.

3. Combine 1⅓ cups water and the remaining ingredients (except the icing) in the bowl of a stand mixer fitted with a paddle attachment. Beat on medium speed until well blended, 1 to 2 minutes. Add the dry ingredients to the wet ingredients and beat on medium speed for 2 minutes.

4. Divide the batter evenly among the muffin cups. Bake on the middle rack of the oven until a toothpick inserted into the centers comes out clean, about 18 minutes. Remove from the oven and let cool in the pan for 5 minutes. Gently remove cupcakes onto a wire rack to cool completely before icing. The cupcakes should be completely cool before frosting.

The cupcakes can be made and frozen for up to 2 weeks ahead in a deep, airtight container. Make sure the lid does not touch the frosting. Let cupcakes come to room temperature before serving.

Seven-Minute Icing

MAKES 4 CUPS ICING

2 cups sugar

3 large egg whites

3 tablespoons light corn syrup

1 teaspoon pure vanilla extract

1 (7-ounce) bag sweetened coconut
 flakes

1. Combine the sugar, egg whites, corn syrup, 3 tablespoons water, and the vanilla in a stainless steel bowl. Place the bowl over a pot of barely simmering water, making sure that the water does not touch the bottom of the bowl. Beat the mixture with a handheld electric mixer on high speed until the frosting forms peaks when the beaters are raise, at least 7 minutes and up to 10 or 11 minutes.

2. Remove the icing from the heat. Immediately frost the cooled cupcakes with the warm icing and sprinkle with the coconut before the icing dries.

JEFFERSON COLLEGE DINNER (FOR 4)

Creole Corn and Crab Bisque

Roasted Cornish Hens with Mushroom Dressing

Brussels Sprouts with Bacon and Creole Mustard

Buttermilk Chess Pie

Before Jefferson Davis became the president of the Confederate States of America (1861–65), he was a US senator from Mississippi. Davis's home was his family's plantation, Rosemont, built in Woodville in 1810. Long before he entered politics, Davis attended Jefferson College in Natchez, where his social life included many dinner dances with the young women of the Elizabeth Academy on the nearby Natchez Trace.

It may have been at those evenings that he developed a taste for a favorite dish—corn and crab bisque—and for chess pie. Most corn and crab bisques have a cream base, but on the Natchez section of the River, they have traditionally been thickened Creole style with a dark roux and made with a tomato base. For this menu, I stuff Cornish game hens with a buttery mushroom-sage dressing and serve them with caramelized brussels sprouts, smoked bacon, and Creole mustard. Chess pie, although a southern classic for nearly two hundred years, comes in many varieties. Sweetened buttermilk makes this the best version of this dessert. I believe Jefferson Davis would approve.

Creole Corn and Crab Bisque

MAKES 2 QUARTS

1 small yellow onion, peeled and quartered

1 small green bell pepper, quartered and seeded

2 cups fresh corn kernels (if using frozen, thaw and drain excess liquid), divided

2 green onions, sliced crosswise into thirds

2 tablespoons minced garlic

2 tablespoons minced fresh basil leaves

3 tablespoons unsalted butter

4 cups Shellfish Stock (page 314)

2 cups tomato puree

½ cup Dark Roux (page 311)

½ lemon, seeded

2 teaspoons Cajun Seasoning (page 311)

1 pound lump crabmeat, picked over for shells and cartilage

2 tablespoons chopped green onions, green tops only, for garnish

1. Place the onions, bell peppers, 1 cup of the corn kernels, the green onions, garlic, and basil in a food processor. Pulse until the mixture is pureed, about 30 seconds.

2. Melt the butter in a large pot over medium-high heat. When the butter is just beginning to brown, add the pureed vegetables and cook, stirring, until the vegetables are soft, 2 to 3 minutes. Add the stock, tomato puree, and roux. Cook, stirring, until the roux is absorbed into the liquid, about 5 minutes.

3. Add the lemon (do not squeeze) and Cajun seasoning. Bring to a boil, then reduce the heat and simmer, uncovered, for 30 minutes, stirring occasionally to make sure it does not stick to the bottom of the pot. Soups made with a roux in them will often stick if not stirred well.

4. Remove the lemon half. Stir in the remaining 1 cup corn kernels and the crabmeat. Return to a simmer and cook, stirring occasionally, for 15 minutes. Remove from the heat and ladle into soup bowls. Garnish with the chopped green onions and serve.

You can make a larger batch by doubling the recipe, and then freeze half of the bisque for up to 3 months.

2 (1¼ to 1½ pounds each) Cornish game hens

1 tablespoon extra virgin olive oil

1 teaspoon kosher salt

1 teaspoon freshly ground black pepper

1 lemon, quartered

8 sprigs fresh rosemary

6 garlic cloves, peeled

½ cup low-sodium chicken broth

½ cup dry white wine

1 recipe Mushroom Dressing (page 231)

1. Preheat the oven to 450°F.

2. Rub the skins of the hens with the olive oil and season on all sides with the salt and pepper. Place a lemon quarter and a sprig of the rosemary in the cavity of each hen. Squeeze the juice of the remaining 2 lemon quarters over the birds and place one in each cavity. Place the hens in a roasting pan, breast side up. Surround with the garlic cloves and 2 sprigs of the rosemary. Roast for 25 minutes.

3. Whisk together the chicken broth and wine in a bowl. Pour the wine mixture over the hens. Reduce the oven temperature to 350°F and baste with the pan juices every 5 minutes. Roast until an instant-read thermometer inserted into the thickest part of the thigh reads 155°F. Transfer the hens to a cutting board and tent with aluminum foil to keep warm.

4. Place the roasting pan over 2 burners on top of the stove set to medium heat. Bring the pan juices to a boil and cook, scraping up any browned bits on the bottom of the pan, until reduced by half in volume, 2 to 3 minutes. Add any accumulated juices from the birds to the pan juices.

5. Using a heavy knife or poultry shears, cut the hens in half lengthwise along the backbone and through the breast. Discard the lemon quarters and rosemary sprigs inside the cavities. Arrange one half bird on each of four plates, accompanied by a generous spoonful of mushroom dressing.. Spoon half of the pan gravy and garlic around the hens. Serve the remaining gravy over the mushroom dressing. Garnish each plate with one of the remaining rosemary sprigs before serving.

Mushroom Dressing

1. If you have one oven, you can bake this dressing when you turn the oven down to 350°F to finish baking your Cornish hens. Grease a 9 × 13-inch baking dish with 1 tablespoon of the butter.

2. Melt the remaining 3 tablespoons butter in a skillet over medium heat. Add the shallot and green onions and cook, stirring, until soft, 2 minutes. Add the mushrooms and cook until the mushrooms are tender and have given off their liquid, about 4 minutes. Add the salt, pepper, and sage and stir to combine. Add the bread cubes, tossing well to combine.

3. Transfer the bread mixture to the prepared baking dish. Bake until crusty brown on top, about 40 minutes. Serve hot with the Cornish hens and pan gravy.

4 tablespoons salted butter, divided

1 shallot, minced

½ cup diced green onions, white bottoms and green tops

6 ounces button mushrooms, stems trimmed and sliced

1 teaspoon kosher salt

½ teaspoon freshly ground black pepper

1 teaspoon dry rubbed sage

3 cups cubed white or French bread

Brussels Sprouts with Bacon and Creole Mustard

2 thick slices smoked bacon, diced

12 ounces brussels sprouts, bottoms trimmed and cut in half

2 tablespoons dry white wine

1 tablespoon Creole or other whole grain mustard

1. Cook the bacon in a skillet over medium-high heat, stirring frequently, until just browned and cooked through but not crisp, about 4 minutes. Add the brussels sprouts, cut sides down, and cook, stirring to prevent them from sticking, until golden brown, about 5 minutes.

2. Add the wine, 2 tablespoons water, and the mustard and cook, stirring, until the liquid evaporates and the brussels sprouts are fork tender but not falling apart, about 4 minutes.

Creole mustard is a spicy whole grain mustard with a touch of horseradish in it.

THE NATCHEZ TRACE

The Natchez Trace was originally a walking trail. Once the flat-boatmen delivered their goods to Natchez, New Orleans, and other towns along the River, they demolished their boats, sold the wood, and walked back to their homes in Pennsylvania, Ohio, and Kentucky. Regardless of where these boatmen came from, they were collectively known as "Kaintucks." Swamps, rivers, and mountains as well as outlaws made for difficult and dangerous travel along the Trace, While you can still walk sections of the Trace, most people drive the stunning 444-mile Natchez Trace Parkway from Natchez, Mississippi to Nashville, Tennessee. Along the Trace, you can still visit two-thousand-year-year old burial mounds built by Native Americans and visit other points of historical interest.

1. On a lightly floured surface, roll out the dough into a 12-inch circle, about ⅛ -inch thick. Transfer to a 9-inch pie pan. Crimp the edges of the crust in a decorative pattern and refrigerate while assembling the filling.

2. Preheat the oven to 325°F.

3. Combine the butter and 3 tablespoons flour in a bowl. Stir to combine with a heavy wooden spoon. Add the buttermilk and stir to blend. In separate bowl, slightly beat the eggs. Add the sugar and whisk to combine. Add the buttermilk mixture and the zest, and whisk to combine.

4. Pour the filling into the prepared pie shell. Bake until the custard is an even golden brown on top and the filling is set, 50 to 55 minutes. Let cool on a wire rack for 1 hour before serving.

½ recipe Sweet Pie Dough (page 315)

½ cup (1 stick) salted butter, melted and cooled

3 tablespoons all-purpose flour

1½ cups buttermilk

3 large eggs

1 cup sugar

1 teaspoon finely grated lemon zest

KING'S TAVERN LUNCH (FOR 2)

Lettuce Hearts with Shaved Pears, Roasted Pecans, and Preserved Lemon Vinaigrette

Flatbread with Smoked Bacon, Greens, and Mozzarella

Black Bottom Ice Cream Pie

King's Tavern, circa 1789, is believed to be the oldest standing building in the Natchez Territory. From the 1790s to the 1830s, the tavern was a secure rest stop and gathering place for flatboat river travelers and for people traveling by foot or horseback on the Natchez Trace. A Mr. Richard King built King's Tavern using flatboat timbers that were hewn to size and put together with wooden pegs. King owned and operated the tavern for thirty-four years until he sold it in 1823, at which point the building became a private home. After nearly 150 years, in 1970, the house became a tavern once again, but it fell into disrepair and was vacated in 2012, remaining empty for more than a year.

My husband Doug and I were so charmed by the building and its historical significance that we purchased it. Now restored, King's Tavern is once again a gathering spot for the people of Natchez as well as for visitors who can enjoy wood-fired flatbreads topped with local ingredients and handcrafted liquors and beers. Doug and our son Jean-Luc, now part–time rum distillers in a building adjacent to the tavern, make Charboneau Rum from sugarcane grown in the region that was once the original Natchez Territory.

When I was creating the menu for King's Tavern, I wanted the food to have some traditional touches with modern influences. A wood-fired oven was installed to bake tavern flatbread, but the recipe here has been adapted for the home oven. The secret to my dough is that I add a touch of local sugarcane syrup for a hint of sweetness. Steen's Cane Syrup from Louisiana is available throughout the United States. My favorite pizza topping is collard greens and smoked bacon with some locally produced mozzarella melted on top. Also popular is a salad of chilled lettuce hearts, shaved pears, and roasted pecans dressed with preserved lemon vinaigrette. All King's Tavern desserts are ice cream based. In this menu, black bottom ice cream fills a gingersnap crust and is finished off with a bourbon whipped cream cheese topping. The pie serves six people, but it will keep well in the freezer. It never goes to waste.

Lettuce Hearts with Shaved Pears, Roasted Pecans, and Preserved Lemon Vinaigrette

1 teaspoon salted butter

2 tablespoons pecans

2 cups mixed lettuce hearts

1 ripe Bartlett red or green pear, cored and thinly sliced

2 tablespoons Preserved Lemon Vinaigrette (page 313)

1. Melt the butter in a skillet over medium heat. Add the pecan pieces and cook until lightly brown, 1 minute. Do not overcook or they will become bitter. Transfer the pecans to a plate.

2. Arrange the lettuce hearts on salad plates. Top with the sliced pears. Drizzle the preserved lemon vinaigrette on the salads and garnish with toasted pecans.

THE GHOST OF KING'S TAVERN

In the 1960s, when workers were expanding the fireplace at King's Tavern, they tore out the chimney wall and discovered the skeletal remains of a woman as well as a jeweled Spanish dagger. The dagger was assumed to have been the instrument of her demise, and the woman was thought to have been Richard King's mistress, Madeline. When his wife found out about the affair, legend has it, she had Madeline killed and bricked her remains into the fireplace in the main dining room. There were also two male skeletons found under the floor by the fireplace. Who they were is anyone's guess. Madeline's ghost still inhabits the tavern, according to those who have seen her roaming the premises.

1. To make the dough, put the flour, salt, and yeast in the bowl of a stand mixer fitted with a paddle attachment. Blend on low speed for 15 seconds. Place 6 tablespoons water in a microwave-safe measuring cup. Microwave on high to 110°F, 5 to 10 seconds. Add the cane syrup and stir to combine. With the machine on low speed, slowly add the warm water mixture to the dry ingredients. Mix to make a sticky dough, about 45 seconds. Do not overmix the dough.

2. Place 1 teaspoon of the oil in a bowl. Add the dough, turning to coat on all sides with the oil. Cover with plastic wrap and set aside at room temperature until doubled in size, 1 to 1½ hours. Punch the dough down and turn in the bowl. Cover and refrigerate for 12 hours.

3. Remove the dough from the refrigerator and let it come to room temperature while covered, about 1 hour. Lightly grease a baking sheet with 1 teaspoon of the oil. Place the dough on the baking sheet, turning it over on itself several times. Stretch the dough into a large rectangle, 12 × 15 inches. Let the dough sit uncovered on the baking sheet at room temperature while preparing the remaining ingredients.

4. Preheat the oven to 450°F. Set the oven rack to its highest position.

5. Cook the bacon in a skillet over medium-high heat, stirring frequently, until just browned and cooked through but not crisp, about 4 minutes. Using a slotted spoon, transfer to paper towels to drain, reserving the bacon grease in the skillet. Add the collard greens to the skillet and cook over medium-high heat, stirring, until slightly wilted, about 2 minutes. Drizzle the remaining 1 teaspoon oil on the dough. Season the top of the dough evenly with the salt and red pepper. Arrange the greens, bacon, and mozzarella over the dough.

6. Bake until the dough is browned around the edges and the underside is browned and crisp, 12 to 14 minutes. Remove the flatbread to a cutting board. Cut into 12 squares and serve immediately.

1 cup 00 Italian pizza flour or all-purpose flour

1 teaspoon kosher salt

¼ teaspoon active dry yeast

1 teaspoon cane syrup, such as Steen's Pure Cane Syrup (see Source Guide, page 316)

3 teaspoons extra virgin olive oil, divided

4 thick slices smoked bacon, diced

2 cups (6 ounces) collard greens, tough stems removed, rinsed well and drained, cut into 2-inch pieces

¼ teaspoon kosher salt

¼ teaspoon red pepper flakes

3 ounces fresh mozzarella, sliced crosswise into 6 pieces

The dough is best when made and refrigerated the day before it is baked.

SERVES 6

1 cup (about 15) gingersnap cookies

2 tablespoons salted butter, melted

*1 pint good-quality dark chocolate
ice cream, softened*

*8 ounces cream cheese, at room
temperature*

2 tablespoons bourbon

1½ cups confectioners' sugar

*4 ounces good-quality dark
chocolate, chilled*

1. Preheat the oven to 350°F.

2. Place the cookies in a food processor and process to crumbs. Add the butter and pulse to make a dough. Press the gingersnap mixture evenly across the bottom and up the sides of a 9-inch Pyrex pie plate. Place another pie plate on top to press the piecrust into place; this will make it more uniform. Bake until set, about 8 minutes. Let cool completely on a wire rack.

3. Spread the ice cream over the crust. Place in the freezer until the ice cream is hardened.

4. Place the cream cheese in a bowl and beat with a handheld mixer until smooth, about 2 minutes. Add the bourbon and beat for 1 minute. Slowly add the confectioners' sugar 3 to 4 tablespoons at a time, beating well after each addition. Beat until the frosting mixture is smooth, 2 to 3 minutes.

5. To make chocolate shavings, scrape a vegetable peeler across the edge of the chocolate.

6. Remove the pie from the freezer. Spread the frosting over the ice cream and cover the top with chocolate shavings. Return the pie to the freezer for at least 1 hour or overnight. Remove the pie from the freezer and let it sit at room temperature for 5 minutes before slicing and serving.

KING'S TAVERN
(BLEDSOE HOUSE)

Oldest building in Natchez. Standing before 1789. Operated as a tavern, stage stop, and a mail station at end of Natchez Trace. Now owned and restored by the Pilgrimage Garden Club of Natchez.

MISSISSIPPI DEPARTMENT OF ARCHIVES AND HISTORY   1974

POST RIDERS

Before the establishment of the US Postal Service in 1780, people who lived along the Natchez Trace relied on hundreds of privately paid post riders to deliver mail and other communications. It took at least two weeks for these independent post riders to cover the distance between Nashville and Natchez on horseback. When the US Postal Service was inaugurated, it served two thousand miles of post roads with seventy-five post offices, but just twenty-six government post riders. The independent post riders were allowed to continue to deliver letters, papers, and packages on their respective routes. Post riding was a dangerous but lucrative profession. In 1838 Congress passed a law making all railroads in the United States official post roads, which allowed the railroads to transport mail. Post riders were limited to working in postal districts that were not on railway routes.

BREAKFAST FOR SUPPER AT TWIN OAKS
(FOR 12)

Champagne Cocktails

Soft Scrambled Eggs

Regina's Butter Biscuits with Orange Marmalade Butter

Pan-Fried Peppered Quail with Bacon

Shrimp in Smoked Tomato Cream Sauce with Rosemary Grits

Pears Poached in Port with Creole Cream Cheese and Pecans

Throughout the South, breakfast foods are often served for supper. This tradition may have been born of lean times, when grits, game, and eggs were the only things available to eat, morning, noon, and night. My family and friends often sit down to breakfast for supper on Sunday nights. It's a more elaborate meal than those served in previous generations, but with the same local ingredients—quail, pecans, Gulf shrimp, and so on. Quail, and of course bacon, have long been served as breakfast meats on this part of the River. Anyone who comes to Twin Oaks knows there will be plenty of my biscuits on the table. Follow the instructions carefully—the technique is different from most biscuit recipes—and you'll be rewarded with

tender, flaky biscuits. Whether I stick with the basics or enhance the menu with pan-fried quail and with shrimp in smoked tomatoes to top the grits, it is a hit.

I enjoy every room in my home; my dining room is one of the most used and appreciated rooms in the house. Before we get to the dining room, I greet my guests with a classic cocktail, whether a perfect martini, a Sazerac, or a classic champagne cocktail. The conversation continues as we gather around the dining table. Flowers are a must, whether hydrangeas from my summer garden or rosemary and camellias in the winter—when you set a pretty table even a meal of biscuits and grits seems elegant.

Champagne Cocktails

12 sugar cubes

Angostura orange bitters or
  Bittermens grapefruit bitters

2 (750-ml) bottles Champagne or
  other sparkling wine

12 orange peel twists, for garnish

Put 2 drops of bitters on each sugar cube. Put a sugar cube in the bottom of each of twelve champagne flutes. Fill each flute with Champagne, garnish each with an orange twist, and serve.

1. Put the eggs, cream, salt, and pepper in a blender. Blend until smooth.

2. Slowly melt the butter in a nonstick skillet on low heat. Do not let the butter brown; it should be foamy. Pour the egg mixture into the skillet. Using a rubber spatula, scrape the eggs from the sides and bottom of the pan as they cook and fat curds form. The cooked eggs should be slightly wet, not dry. Serve hot.

1 dozen large eggs

¼ cup heavy cream

½ teaspoon kosher salt

½ teaspoon freshly ground black pepper

2 tablespoons salted butter

Regina's Butter Biscuits with Orange Marmalade Butter

MAKES 2 DOZEN

4 cups all-purpose flour

¼ cup baking powder

¼ cup sugar

½ cup (1 stick) salted butter, chilled and cut into 2-inch cubes

1½ cups (3 sticks) salted margarine, chilled and cut into 2-inch cubes

1¾ cups buttermilk, chilled

I prefer Calumet baking powder and Land O Lakes salted butter and salted margarine. Also note that freezing the biscuits before they're baked is essential—it adds to the flakiness, and they can be made ahead and kept for up to 2 months in the freezer.

1. Put the flour, baking powder, and sugar in the bowl of a stand mixer. Turn the machine on low and blend the dry ingredients for 15 seconds.

2. Add the butter and margarine cubes and the buttermilk to the flour mixture before turning on the mixer. Turn the mixer on medium and count to ten. This goes very quickly; the key is to not overmix the dough. There will be large chunks (the size of quarters) of butter and margarine in the dough. That's just how it should be. Don't mix it any more. Once the dough is rolled and folded, it will become smooth.

3. Scrape the dough from the bowl onto a generously floured work surface and shape into a rectangle about 2 inches thick. Fold the dough into thirds and, with a rolling pin, roll the dough out to a 2-inch thickness. Fold it again into thirds, give the dough a one-quarter turn, and roll it out again to a 2-inch thickness. Continue folding, turning, and rolling the dough until it is smooth and the dough has yellow ribbons of butter and margarine. This is a sign that the biscuits will be flaky.

4. Roll the dough to 1½-inch thickness. Using a 2-inch biscuit cutter, cut the dough into rounds. When rerolling the dough, gently stack it to retain the layers. Do not overwork the dough.

5. Place the biscuits on a baking sheet and freeze. Once frozen, transfer the biscuits to plastic bags. The unbaked biscuits can be frozen for 2 months.

6. To bake, preheat the oven to 350°F. Place however many frozen biscuits you want to serve in the cups of muffin tins. Let thaw in the refrigerator for 20 minutes. Bake until golden brown, 23 to 25 minutes. Serve right out of the oven—biscuits are best freshly baked. Baking them in muffin tins is key, as it helps the biscuits keep their shape and get the perfect crispness on the bottom.

Orange Marmalade Butter

1. Put the butter and marmalade in a mini food processor and pulse to combine. (Alternatively, whisk together the butter and marmalade in a bowl.) Using a rubber spatula, transfer the butter to a decorative serving bowl.

2. Serve the butter with hot biscuits or other breakfast pastries.

The butter also can be spread onto a sheet of plastic wrap, shaped into a log, wrapped, and frozen. Bring to room temperature before serving, either on a butter dish or cut into thin slices.

½ cup (1 stick) salted butter, at room temperature

3 tablespoons sweet orange marmalade

Pan-Fried Peppered Quail with Bacon

1. Preheat the oven to 350°F. Line a baking sheet with aluminum foil.

2. Combine the pepper, garlic powder, and salt in a small bowl. Pat the quail dry and season them on all sides with half of the pepper mixture. Combine the remainder of the pepper mixture with the flour in a shallow baking dish. Dredge the quail in the seasoned flour and transfer to the prepared baking sheet.

3. Lay the bacon in a cast-iron or other large, heavy skillet. Cook the bacon over medium heat until the fat is rendered and the bacon is almost done but not crisp, 6 to 8 minutes. Remove from the heat, reserving the grease in the pan. Drain the bacon on paper towels.

4. Return the bacon grease to medium heat. Add the quail in batches and cook until browned, about 4 minutes on each side. Remove the browned quail to the baking sheet and top each one with two of the halved slices of bacon to form an × over the breast.

5. Bake the quail for about 20 minutes or until an instant-read thermometer registers 155°F. Remove from the oven and let the quail rest for 5 minutes before cutting in half. Arrange quail halves on a serving platter, each topped with a half slice of bacon, and serve hot.

2 teaspoons cracked black pepper

1 teaspoon garlic powder

1 teaspoon kosher salt

6 semi-boneless quail, breastbones removed (see Source Guide, page 316)

½ cup all-purpose flour

6 thick slices smoked bacon, cut in half crosswise

MAKES 2¼ CUPS

1 cup heavy cream

1 cup half-and-half

3 tablespoons unsalted butter

2 tablespoons all-purpose flour

3 dozen (about 2 pounds) large shrimp, peeled and deveined (best purchased locally—if not available to you, see Source Guide, page 316)

2 teaspoons freshly ground black pepper

1 teaspoon kosher salt

2 tablespoons extra virgin olive oil

1 teaspoon minced garlic

1 teaspoon fresh thyme leaves

1 sprig fresh rosemary

12 Oven-Smoked Tomatoes quarters (page 313)

1 recipe Cream Sauce (above)

1 recipe Rosemary Grits (page 251)

Cream Sauce

1. Put the cream and half-and-half in a microwave-proof 2-cup measuring cup. Heat on high until warm, about 100°F, 45 seconds to 1 minute.

2. Melt the butter in a saucepan over low heat. Slowly add the flour and cook, stirring constantly with a wooden spoon to make a light roux, 2 to 3 minutes. Stir in the warm cream mixture and bring to a boil. Lower the heat and simmer, stirring, until the sauce is thick, 4 to 5 minutes.

3. Remove from heat and cover to keep warm, stirring occasionally, until ready to finish the sauce with the shrimp and smoked tomatoes.

Shrimp with Smoked Tomatoes

1. Season the shrimp on both sides with the pepper and salt.

2. Heat the olive oil in a dutch oven over medium-high heat. Add the shrimp, garlic, thyme, and rosemary and cook, stirring constantly, until the shrimp are pink and firm, 4 to 5 minutes.

3. Reduce the heat to medium. Add the cream sauce and stir well to combine. Add 6 of the smoked tomato quarters without over-stirring, cook until the sauce is warmed through, then remove from the heat.

4. To garnish, place the remaining 6 tomato quarters in a small skillet. Gently cook over low heat until just heated through. Remove from the heat.

5. Spoon the shrimp and sauce onto a serving platter and arrange the warmed tomato quarters on the side. Serve hot.

Rosemary Grits

1. Bring 6 cups of water and the 2 teaspoons of salt to a simmer in a large pot over medium heat. Slowly stir in the grits, reduce the heat, and, still stirring, add heavy cream. Reduce the heat to low and cook, stirring occasionally, until the grits are thick and creamy and no longer retain a bite, about 30 minutes for stone-ground grits and 5 to 15 minutes for other types. Add ¼ cup additional cream or water as needed to achieve a creamy texture, and continue cooking for 5 to 10 minutes until the liquid is reduced and the desired texture is reached.

2. Add the cream cheese, 2 rosemary sprigs, and the garlic and stir well to incorporate the cream cheese. Cook, stirring, over low heat until the grits are fragrant from the rosemary, 3 to 5 minutes.

3. Discard the rosemary sprigs. Pour the grits into a serving dish, garnish with the remaining 6 fresh rosemary sprigs, and serve hot with the Shrimp in Smoked Tomato Cream Sauce.

2 teaspoons kosher salt

2 cups grits, stone-ground if possible (see Source Guide, page 316)

1 cup heavy cream

4 ounces cream cheese at room temperature

8 sprigs rosemary

1 teaspoon minced garlic

Old-fashioned or quick-style grits will require less cooking time, ranging from 5 to 15 minutes. If you use this type of grind rather than stone-ground, refer to the manufacturer's package instructions and adjust your time accordingly. The same goes for the proportion of cooking liquid to grits.

Pears Poached in Port with Creole Cream Cheese and Pecans

6 Bartlett pears, peeled, halved
   lengthwise, and cored

3 cups ruby port

8 ounces Creole cream cheese (see
   Source Guide, page 316) or
   mascarpone, at room temperature

½ cup confectioners' sugar

¼ teaspoon ground cinnamon

¼ cup coarsely chopped pecans,
   toasted (page 311)

1. Arrange the pear halves cut side down in a skillet. Add the port. Cook over medium heat until the pears can be easily pierced with a fork, 13 to 15 minutes. Transfer the pears, cut side up, to a shallow serving dish.

2. Put the cream cheese, sugar, and cinnamon in a bowl and whip with a handheld mixer until fluffy. Fold in the pecans.

3. Fill the center of each pear with the whipped cheese mixture and serve.

Creole cream cheese is a type of mild farmer's cheese, so named for its New Orleans origins. Made from a mixture of buttermilk and skim milk, it has a tart, slightly sweet flavor.

BRIDESMAIDS' LUNCHEON (FOR 4)

Meyer Lemon–Rosemary Spritzers

Demitasses of Chilled Cucumber Soup with Fried Green Tomato Croutons

Cast-Iron Chicken with Arugula Salad

Pear Bavarians with Raspberries in Orange Sauce

There have been weddings along the River for hundreds of years, whether they were "tying the knot" or "jumping the broom." We southerners love an event, so weddings are right up our alley. The cocktail parties and showers that go along with a southern wedding are enjoyed by many, but one of the most inspired parties and always a favorite memory of the bride is the last luncheon before the wedding—the bridesmaids' luncheon. Today's weddings often reach a dozen bridesmaids, so this menu is easily multiplied.

Like my home of Twin Oaks, a home known for hospitality and entertaining is the Burn. Owners Bridget and Glenn Green are always gracious about opening their home to visitors and to the community. I created this menu for my friend Bridget, who seems to often take on the task of the classic bridesmaids' luncheon for friends' weddings. It features a not-so-strong starter: a white wine spritzer with lemon-rosemary syrup. The first course is a light chilled soup of cucumbers served with a side of tart, crisp green tomato croutons. The thin cast-iron chicken topped with arugula is not too heavy, yet satisfying enough for a luncheon or a long day ahead for a bride. And to finish off, the pear custard offers three dimensions of taste with pears, raspberries, and orange.

½ cup sugar

Juice and zest of 1 Meyer lemon or regular lemon

4 sprigs rosemary

1 (750-ml) bottle dry white wine

1 cup soda water, chilled

1. Put the sugar, ½ cup water, the lemon juice and zest, and 2 rosemary sprigs in a saucepan over medium heat. Simmer until the sugar is dissolved and the syrup is reduced by half, about 10 minutes. Remove from the heat and let cool to room temperature. Strain the syrup into a glass serving pitcher. Discard the sediment.

2. Stir in the white wine and the remaining 2 rosemary sprigs. Cover and refrigerate until well chilled.

3. At serving time, stir in the soda water and pour into wine glasses or goblets.

This can be made 1 day in advance through step 2.

WEDDING LORE

Lore has it that it was customary along the Natchez Trace and the Mississippi, when a preacher was not available for a ceremony, that a couple would tie their hands together to symbolize their acknowledgement that they were bound to go down the same path for life. This is where "tying the knot" came from. Another custom along the River, "jumping the broom," is not so much lore as history, as it came from the West African country of Ghana with the arrival of slaves. In their homeland of Ghana the broom held spiritual significance, such as sweeping away wrongs; more significantly, as part of a wedding ceremony, it symbolized the commitment of the wife to keep the house in order.

1. Put the cucumber, 1 cup buttermilk, lemon juice, salt, garlic, dill, and mint in a blender. Puree until smooth, about 2 minutes. Add the cream and blend for 10 seconds.

2. Transfer the soup to a bowl, cover, and chill until ready to serve.

3. To serve, divide the soup into demitasse cups and garnish with the green tomato croutons. I put them on the side of the cup for a nicer presentation.

1 cucumber, peeled, halved, and seeded

1 cup buttermilk

1 tablespoon fresh lemon juice

½ teaspoon kosher salt

¼ teaspoon Roasted Garlic (page 314)

¼ teaspoon dried dill weed

4 mint leaves

¼ cup heavy cream

1 batch Fried Green Tomato Croutons (below)

Fried Green Tomato Croutons

1. To make the croutons, heat 2 inches of oil in a cast-iron skillet to 350°F.

2. Put the flour on a plate and the buttermilk in a shallow bowl. Combine the cornmeal, salt, and pepper on another plate.

3. In batches, dredge the green tomato cubes first in flour, then dip them into the buttermilk, and finally roll them in the seasoned cornmeal. Using tongs or a skimmer, gently lower the battered cubes into the hot oil. Fry until golden brown, about 2 minutes. Using a slotted spoon, remove the fried croutons to paper towels to drain. Repeat with the remaining ingredients.

Vegetable oil, for frying

1 green tomato, seeded and cut into ½-inch cubes

½ cup all-purpose flour

½ cup buttermilk

½ cup cornmeal

½ teaspoon salt

½ teaspoon freshly ground black pepper

2 tablespoons olive oil

4 (5-ounce) boneless, skinless chicken breasts, pounded to ½-inch thickness

4 cups arugula

3 tablespoons Mustard-Lemon Vinaigrette (page 312)

2 teaspoons capers, drained

1. Heat the oil in a large cast-iron skillet over medium-high heat. Add the chicken breasts and cook until brown and cooked through, 3 minutes on each side. Place one chicken breast on each of four plates.

2. Place the arugula in a bowl and toss with the vinaigrette. Divide the tossed greens among the chicken breasts and garnish each with ½ teaspoon capers before serving.

1 (¼-ounce) envelope (1 tablespoon)
   unflavored gelatin

1 cup heavy cream

1¼ cups sugar, divided

1 teaspoon finely grated orange zest,
   divided

1 cup pureed pear, from canned
   pear halves

1 teaspoon pure vanilla extract

¼ cup fresh orange juice

1 cup fresh raspberries, for garnish

1. Combine 1 tablespoon cool water and the gelatin in a small bowl and stir to blend. Let stand until the gelatin softens, about 5 minutes.

2. Combine the cream, ¾ cup of the sugar, and ½ teaspoon orange zest in a saucepan and bring to a simmer over medium heat. Remove from the heat, add the gelatin, and stir to dissolve. Stir in the pear puree and vanilla and divide among four custard cups. Cover and refrigerate overnight.

3. To make the orange sauce, combine the orange juice, the remaining ½ cup sugar, and the remaining ½ teaspoon orange zest in a saucepan over low heat. Cook until thick and syrupy but still a pourable consistency, about 5 or 6 minutes or until liquid is reduced by half. Remove from the heat and let cool slightly. (If the syrup crystalizes or hardens as it cools, add 1 tablespoon water and microwave in a ramekin on high until crystals are gone, 20 seconds to 1 minute.)

4. Unmold each custard onto a dessert plate, surround with ¼ cup raspberries, and drizzle the orange sauce over the custard.

The custards keep well for up to 3 days.

COCKTAIL PARTY AT LONGWOOD (FOR 8)

Orange-Mint Juleps

Ham with Pineapple-Jalapeño Jam

Sweet Potato Biscuits

Broiled Oysters with Pepper Marinade

Catfish en Croute with Artichoke and Peppadew Ragout

Among the many antebellum homes in Natchez, Longwood remains the most fascinating and most visited. The original design of the octagonal house called for six floors and thirty-two rooms. It took a little over a year to finish the exterior structure. But by mid-1861, with the Civil War raging, the northern artisans who had been brought in to carve interior marble and woodwork had fled, leaving rafters and unfinished brick walls. In 1862 the slaves at Longwood finished the eight basement rooms. The owner, Dr. Haller Nutt, a cotton plantation owner in Louisiana and Mississippi who didn't support secession from the United States, looked to the Union to protect his assets. As a result, he was ostracized by local members of the Confederacy, and eventually Union troops burned his cotton fields and his original home. He died in 1864, leaving his wife Julia to raise their eight children—in the unfinished house. Four generations followed, all living in the only finished part of this home, the first floor. The house remains as it was to this day, owned and preserved by the Natchez Pilgrimage Garden Club. Thousands of yearly visitors, destination weddings, donations, and fund-raisers help maintain this American treasure.

I created this menu for just such an annual cocktail party fund-raiser. Orange-mint juleps offer a refreshing twist on a classic southern cocktail. Flaky sweet potato biscuits are filled with baked ham glazed with pineapple-jalapeño jam for the perfect bite. My father was well known in Natchez for his broiled peppered oysters. And artichoke hearts and tart Peppadews are a perfect duo for catfish en croute.

Orange-Mint Juleps

*2 cups fresh mint leaves, plus
    8 sprigs for garnish*

1½ cups sugar

1 orange, quartered

1 quart bourbon

1. To make the orange-mint syrup, put the 2 cups of mint leaves, the sugar, one orange quarter (rind and all), and 2 cups water into a blender. Process until the mint leaves and orange are pureed, about 2 minutes. Pour the mixture into a saucepan and cook over medium heat until the sugar dissolves, about 3 minutes.

2. Pour the mixture into a pitcher and refrigerate overnight. Strain the syrup into a clean pitcher and add the bourbon. Discard the sediment.

3. To make the juleps, cut the remaining orange quarters into three wedges each. Fill eight julep cups or old-fashioned glasses with crushed ice. Divide the bourbon-syrup mixture among the cups and garnish each with an orange wedge and a mint sprig.

1. Combine the pineapple, sugar, and vinegar in a saucepan over medium heat. Cook until thick, stirring frequently, about 15 minutes. Add the jalapeños, stir, and pour into a bowl to cool. Refrigerate until well chilled, at least 2 hours.

2. Preheat the oven to 350°F.

3. Place the ham in a roasting pan and brush with 1 cup of the pineapple-jalapeño jam. Bake uncovered for 1 hour.

4. Place the ham on a serving platter with the remaining jam in a decorative serving bowl. You may serve the sweet potato biscuits on the side, or you may split the biscuits and place a slice of ham and a teaspoon of pineapple jam inside each biscuit for easier serving.

1 (14-ounce) can crushed pineapple, drained

1 cup sugar

1 tablespoon apple cider vinegar

2 tablespoons minced pickled jalapeños

1 (4-pound) bone-in spiral-sliced ham

MAKES 24

3 cups all-purpose flour

3 tablespoons baking powder

3 tablespoons sugar

½ cup (1 stick) salted butter, chilled and cut into 2-inch cubes

1 cup (2 sticks) salted margarine, chilled and cut into 2-inch cubes

1 small sweet potato, baked, peeled, mashed, and chilled (to measure 1 cup)

1¼ cups buttermilk, chilled

Although these use the same technique as my butter biscuits, they are a softer-sweeter biscuit because of the sweet potato.

1. Put the flour, baking powder, and sugar in the bowl of a stand mixer fitted with the paddle attachment. Blend the dry ingredients on low for 15 seconds.

2. Add the butter, margarine, mashed sweet potato, and buttermilk to the bowl. Turn the mixer on medium speed and count to ten. There should be visible chunks of margarine and butter in the dough.

3. Generously flour a work surface. Roll the dough into a rectangle about 2 inches thick, fold into thirds, and roll again. Turn the dough one-quarter turn and roll out again to a 2-inch thickness. Fold into thirds again and repeat the process for a total of four to five times until the dough is smooth. The dough should have a yellow ribbon effect where the butter and margarine are rolled out. This is a good sign that the biscuits will be flaky.

4. Roll the dough one last time to a 1½-inch thickness. Using a 2-inch floured biscuit cutter, cut the dough into rounds. When rerolling the dough, gently stack it to retain the layers. Do not overwork the dough.

5. Arrange the biscuits on a baking sheet and freeze. The biscuits are best if first frozen. Once frozen, transfer into a zippered plastic bag. (Unbaked biscuits can be frozen for 2 months.)

6. When ready to bake, preheat the oven to 350° F. Place the frozen biscuits in the cups of 2 muffin tins; these biscuits are best if not baked on a baking sheet. Let the biscuits thaw in the tins in the refrigerator for 20 minutes. Bake until the tops of the biscuits are golden, 23 to 25 minutes. Turn the biscuits out onto a wire rack and serve warm.

1. Preheat the broiler.

2. Combine the butter, olive oil, Worcestershire sauce, basil, pepper, and garlic in a saucepan over low heat. Simmer for 15 minutes, stirring occasionally.

3. Arrange the shucked oysters on the half shell on a large baking sheet. Spoon about 2 teaspoons of the sauce over the top of each oyster. Broil until the edges of the oysters curl and the sauce sizzles, about 1 minute. Serve hot.

½ cup (1 stick) salted butter

2 tablespoons extra virgin olive oil

¼ cup Worcestershire sauce

1 tablespoon fresh minced basil leaves

1 tablespoon cracked black pepper

2 teaspoons minced garlic

2 dozen oysters, shucked and on the half shell

4 (4-ounce) fillets of catfish, or other firm white fish such as cod

1 tablespoon plus 1 teaspoon Cajun Seasoning (page 311)

3 tablespoons extra virgin olive oil

1 cup canned artichoke hearts, drained and quartered

½ cup diced Peppadew peppers (see Source Guide, page 316), or other roasted mild peppers, such as cherry peppers or red bell peppers

1 package frozen puff pastry (2 sheets), thawed in the refrigerator

1 egg whisked with 1 tablespoon water, for an egg wash

1. Preheat the oven to 350°F. Line a large baking sheet with a piece of parchment paper.

2. Cut the catfish pieces in half crosswise. Season them with 1 tablespoon of the Cajun Seasoning.

3. Put 1 tablespoon of the olive oil in a skillet and heat over medium heat. When the oil is hot, add the catfish to the skillet in batches to prevent overcrowding. Cook until golden brown on both sides, about 30 seconds per side. Transfer the catfish to a plate to cool. Use 1 tablespoon of oil in each batch.

4. Combine the artichoke hearts, Peppadew peppers, and 1 teaspoon of the Cajun Seasoning in a bowl.

5. On a lightly floured surface, one at a time roll each sheet of puff pastry to measure 10 × 10 inches. Cut each sheet into four 5-x 5-inch squares. Place four of the pastry squares on the baking sheet.

6. Put one piece of the catfish on each of the four puff pastry squares on the baking sheet, and top with 2 tablespoons of the artichoke-pepper filling. Fold the pastry one end over the other to enclose the filling and form a triangle. Press the edges together with a fork to seal. Place the remaining four pastry squares on the baking sheet and repeat with the filling. Brush on egg wash, then rearrange the pastry triangles so there is at least a 1-inch space between them. Bake until the pastry is risen and golden brown, about 20 minutes. Serve hot.

SUGARCANE SYRUP PARTY (FOR 8)

Rum Punch

Braised Mustard Greens with Fennel, Smoked Tomatoes, and Cracklings

Pork Roast with Fall Vegetables in Cane Syrup Glaze

Sweet Potato Salad with Mustard Dressing

Pecan Pralines

When I moved back to Natchez, my friend Judge David Bramlette invited me to an annual event in Woodville, Mississippi: a full day of making cane syrup followed by a huge celebration. We went from the "press" (the crushing of the sugarcane to release its liquid) to the "strike" (the precise moment when the cooked liquid is removed from the fire so it turns into syrup) to the roasting of wild hogs.

Cane syrup making requires equal parts science and art and a little help from nature. The rains have to cooperate and be abundant enough, or the cane will not produce enough liquid to turn into syrup. Even if all goes well, you're lucky to get one gallon of syrup after pressing eight to ten gallons of sugarcane juice. If not properly cooked, the syrup will turn to sugar, or, even worse, within two weeks the jar tops may pop off! Judge Bramlette says it best: "You can use thermometers, hydrometers, motors, or mules, but when it comes down to it, a good syrup maker just knows."

Sugarcane is also at the heart of rum, so this meal begins with a rum punch. The combination of pork, turnips, and potatoes with cane syrup is hands down my favorite pork roast recipe. I give this warm salad of braised mustard greens a lift with fennel and smoked tomatoes, and topped with salty pork cracklings. Sweet potatoes, which are grown in the Woodville area, are perfect in a chilled potato salad. A homemade praline is the ideal sweet finish to a big meal.

¼ cup confectioners' sugar

1 cup canned pineapple juice

½ cup fresh orange juice

¼ cup fresh lime juice

8 dashes Angostura bitters

2 cups Myers's or other dark rum

1 lime, sliced into 8 thin rounds, for garnish

1. Place the sugar in a pitcher. Add ¼ cup water and stir to dissolve. Add the pineapple, orange, and lime juices, bitters, and rum. Stir well.

2. Fill eight rocks glasses with crushed ice. Pour the punch into the glasses and garnish each with a slice of lime before serving.

1. Heat the olive oil in a skillet over medium heat. Add the garlic and cook, stirring, until fragrant and just soft, 30 seconds. Add the fennel and cook, stirring, until soft, 2 to 3 minutes. Add the greens, salt, and pepper and cook, stirring, until wilted, about 2 minutes. Add ¼ cup water and cook uncovered, stirring, until tender, 5 minutes. Add the tomato quarters and cook, stirring, just until warm, 2 minutes.

2. Transfer the vegetables into a casserole dish. Spread the chopped cracklings in a layer over the top of the greens and serve.

3 tablespoons extra virgin olive oil

3 garlic cloves, thinly sliced

1 fennel bulb, stalks trimmed, tough inner core removed, cut crosswise into ⅛-inch thick slices

2 bunches (about 14 ounces total) mustard greens, rinsed well and chopped

1 teaspoon kosher salt

1 teaspoon freshly ground black pepper

16 quarters Oven-Smoked Tomatoes (page 313)

1 cup pork cracklings (see Source Guide, page 316), chopped in food processor

Pork Roast with Fall Vegetables in Cane Syrup Glaze

1 (3½-pound) boneless pork loin
  roast

3 tablespoons McCormick Grill
  Mates Montreal Steak Seasoning,
  divided

1½ cups pure cane syrup, such as
  Steen's Pure Cane Syrup (see
  Source Guide, page 316)

1 tablespoon minced garlic

4 medium turnips, peeled and
  quartered

8 small red potatoes

8 medium carrots

1. Preheat the oven to 450°F.

2. Season the pork roast on all sides with 2 tablespoons of the seasoning blend. Place the roast, fat side up, in a large roasting pan. Roast until well browned on top, 12 to 15 minutes. Remove the roast and reduce the oven temperature to 325°F.

3. Pour 1 cup of the cane syrup over the pork loin and top with minced garlic. Add 1 cup water to the bottom of the roasting pan. Arrange the vegetables around the pork roast. Drizzle the remaining ½ cup cane syrup and sprinkle the remaining 1 tablespoon seasoning over the vegetables.

4. Roast until an instant-read thermometer inserted into the thickest part of the meat registers 155°F and the vegetables are tender, about 45 minutes. Transfer the roast to a cutting board and tent with foil to rest for 10 minutes. Transfer the vegetables to a holding dish.

5. Transfer the pan drippings to a saucepan, skimming off the top layer of fat. Bring the liquid to a simmer over medium heat and cook until reduced by about one-third, about 10 minutes. (For thicker gravy, make a slurry by combining 1 tablespoon cornstarch and 3 tablespoons water in a small bowl. Stir to dissolve and add to the simmering gravy. Cook, stirring, until thick, about 2 minutes.)

6. Carve the pork into ½-inch slices and arrange on a platter surrounded by the vegetables. Pour a portion of the gravy over the meat and serve the remainder in a gravy boat.

4 medium sweet potatoes, peeled and cut into 2-inch cubes

1 medium red onion, quartered and thinly sliced

3 tablespoons packed light brown sugar

2 tablespoons Dijon mustard

2 tablespoons extra virgin olive oil

1. Place the sweet potatoes in a saucepan, cover with water by 2 inches, and bring to a boil. Cook until the potatoes can easily be pierced with a fork but are not falling apart, about 4 minutes. Drain in a colander and refresh under cold running water.

2. Combine the potatoes and onions in a bowl.

3. In a separate bowl, whisk together the sugar, mustard, and olive oil until the sugar dissolves. Pour the dressing over the sweet potatoes and onions and toss well to evenly coat. Serve at room temperature or chilled.

This can be made 1 day in advance and kept refrigerated until ready to serve.

JOHN JAMES AUDUBON

John James Audubon is known for his detailed paintings of American birds. One of his earliest journals is *The Mississippi River Journal.* He made his first entry on October 12, 1820, on a voyage that was supposed to take him from Kentucky to New Orleans. With little money for his travels, he debarked from the riverboat Éclat in Natchez, where he found his connection to my family when he worked as a tutor to the daughter of Spanish businessman Joseph Quegles. Audubon taught French, art, and music to fourteen-year-old Melania Francisca Catarina Quegles, my great-great-great-great-grandmother. During his sojourn he painted his only known landscape of Natchez. In these lean financial times, Audubon painted some thirty-two birds in 1822 while in residence in St. Francisville, Louisiana, before making his way down the River to New Orleans.

Pecan Pralines

1. Line a baking sheet with waxed paper.

2. Clip a candy thermometer to the side of a heavy-bottomed pot. Melt the butter in the pot over medium heat. Add the sugar, baking soda, and buttermilk, stirring with a heavy wooden spoon until the sugar is just dissolved. (The reaction of the baking soda and buttermilk will cause the mixture to bubble up, so stir just enough to keep it from boiling over. As the mixture continues to cook, the foaming will stop as the praline mixture caramelizes.) Boil the mixture until it reaches the soft-ball stage, or 240°F on the candy thermometer. Continue cooking, keeping an eye on the thermometer, until it reaches 250°F. Remove the pot from the heat. Add the pecans and stir until the mixture cools slightly and thickens enough to be spooned into place.

3. Using two teaspoons (one to push the praline mixture off the other spoon), drop the mixture by the teaspoonful onto the prepared baking sheet. Let the pralines cool completely at room temperature before removing them from the waxed paper, usually 2 hours. A finished praline should be able to be broken in half but is still creamy and not sugary.

4. Store in airtight container.

MAKES 2 DOZEN

½ cup (1 stick) salted butter

1 pound sugar

½ teaspoon baking soda

1 cup buttermilk

1 cup pecan halves

My cooking teachers insisted that only a stainless steel spoon would do when working with sugar. Well, they must not have made pralines, because if I don't use a wooden spoon, they don't come out as well. Always use a wooden spoon; some things cannot be scientifically explained. Also, be very careful when working with hot sugar.

RÉVEILLON DINNER (FOR 8)

Sazerac Cocktails

Tomato Aspic with Fried Oysters and Creole Sauce

Réveillon Gumbo

Daube Glacé with Horseradish Sauce

Almond Tart

Réveillon, a nineteenth-century Creole celebration, translates into "awakening." The first réveillon, held following midnight mass on Christmas Eve, consisted of an elaborate meal. The celebration went on until the early morning when it was time to open gifts. The second réveillon came on New Year's Eve, and was just as festive.

I learned about réveillon from my great-aunt Nan Marie Trosclair Caldwell, who shared her recipes and memories with me. She told me stories about Christmas Eve at the house she grew up in, which we always referred to as "the big house." She remembered eating daube glacé, a seasoned, jelled beef, as one of many dishes served on Christmas Eve. Many years later I was surprised when my French friend Arlette Romand told me she enjoyed the same dishes at Christmas in Provence where she grew up.

A typical réveillon menu had daube glacé or veal grillades, egg dishes, breads, and puddings, and would often include turtle soup and oysters.

Naturally there was an abundance of wines, cordials, and other fortified drinks. Like many other Creole traditions on the River, the réveillon dinner slowly disappeared. In recent years some New Orleans restaurants have revived it to attract more visitors to the city during the holiday season. The beauty of the réveillon is that it is all about "awakening" the senses with food and celebrating all the joy that Christmas and the New Year bring.

It doesn't matter what's on your menu as long as it is plentiful, flavorful, and brings your family together. Making a good Sazerac cocktail is an art; I walk you through the steps. Fried oysters accompany tomato aspic. There is also a rich gumbo of chicken, sausage, and shrimp with the addition of black-eyed peas and greens for good luck. Although the daube glacé is an aspic as well, it complements this festive late-night menu. And many of these dishes can be made ahead, so you can enjoy your holiday. The almond tart is so easy, you will find it on your table all year long.

MAKES 4 COCKTAILS

8 sugar cubes

8 dashes Peychaud's bitters

12 ounces rye or American whiskey

2 ounces Herbsaint, Pernod, or Absinthe

4 orange twists, orange slices for garnish

1. Chill four old-fashioned glasses by filling them with ice and letting them sit while preparing the cocktails.

2. Muddle the sugar cubes and bitters together in a cocktail shaker. Add the rye, fill with ice, and shake until chilled.

3. Discard the ice in the chilled glasses. Pour the Herbsaint into one glass and swirl to coat the inside of the glass. Pour the Herbsaint from the first glass into a second glass and swirl to coat. Continue the process with the remaining 2 glasses. Pour any remaining Herbsaint from the fourth glass into the cocktail shaker and shake to combine.

4. Strain the rye mixture into the prepared glasses. Garnish each with an orange twist and slice (lemon is traditional, but I enjoy the combination of orange and whiskey). Serve.

Traditionalists insist that the lemon twist should be squeezed over the cocktail to release its essences but not dropped into the glass itself. I like how the lemon garnish looks in the glass, so I drop it in. Since a cocktail shaker can make only four drinks at a time, you'll need to make two batches to serve eight people.

Tomato Aspic with Fried Oysters and Creole Sauce

Tomato Aspic

Vegetable oil spray

1 (¼-ounce) envelope (1 tablespoon) powdered gelatin

3 cups V-8 juice

2 tablespoons finely chopped celery

2 tablespoons minced green onions, green tops only

1 teaspoon Worcestershire sauce

1 teaspoon Tabasco or other hot pepper sauce

Creole Sauce

½ cup mayonnaise

¼ cup Creole or other whole grain mustard

3 tablespoons ketchup

Fried Oysters

Vegetable oil, for frying

2 cups cornmeal

1 tablespoon Cajun Seasoning (page 311)

2 dozen oysters (see Source Guide, page 316), shucked and drained

1. Lightly spray eight 6-ounce ramekins or molds with vegetable oil spray.

2. To make the aspic, combine 1 tablespoon cool water and the gelatin in a small bowl and stir to blend. Let stand until the gelatin softens, about 5 minutes.

3. Place the V-8 juice in a saucepan and bring to a simmer over medium heat. Remove from the heat, add the gelatin, and stir to dissolve. Remove from the heat and stir in the celery, green onions, Worcestershire sauce, and Tabasco.

4. Divide the aspic among the prepared molds. Cover with plastic wrap and refrigerate until firm, at least 6 hours and up to 24 hours.

5. To make the sauce, whisk together the mayonnaise, mustard, and ketchup in a bowl. Cover and refrigerate until ready to serve.

6. To fry the oysters, clip a deep-frying thermometer to the side of a large cast-iron skillet or dutch oven. Half fill the pot with oil, and heat over medium-high heat to 350°F. (Alternatively, an electric skillet or deep fryer set to 350°F can be used.) Line a dish with paper towels. While the oil is heating, whisk the cornmeal and Cajun Seasoning in a shallow baking dish. Dredge the oysters in the cornmeal, a few at a time, to coat evenly. Shake to remove any excess coating. Using tongs or a skimmer, gently lower the oysters in batches of 4 or 5 into the hot oil. Deep-fry the oysters until golden brown, turning once, about 2 minutes. Transfer to the paper towels to drain.

7. To serve, run the bottoms of the aspic molds under warm water and turn them out onto salad plates. Arrange the fried oysters around the aspics, and serve the sauce in a bowl on the side.

1. Place the andouille in a dutch oven over medium heat. Cook, stirring occasionally, until the sausage is browned on all sides, 4 to 5 minutes. Add the onions, celery, and bell peppers and cook, stirring, for 2 minutes. Add the garlic and Cajun seasoning and cook, stirring, for 1 minute. Add the roux and stir until well blended.

2. Stir in the okra, the diced tomatoes and their liquid, 1 quart water, and the chicken broth and bring to a boil. Reduce the heat to medium-low. Simmer, stirring occasionally, for 1 hour

3. Add the chicken, black-eyed peas, and greens and cook for 15 minutes. Add the shrimp and cook for 5 minutes. Taste and adjust the seasoning and the consistency. If the gumbo is too thick, stir in equal amounts of chicken broth and water to obtain the desired consistency. Ladle the gumbo into bowls, garnish with the green onions, and serve.

½ pound andouille or other spicy smoked sausage, diced

1 cup diced onion

1 cup diced celery

½ cup diced green bell pepper

1 teaspoon minced garlic

1 tablespoon Cajun Seasoning (page 311)

¼ cup Dark Roux (page 311)

1 cup canned sliced okra, drained and rinsed, or frozen

1 cup canned diced tomatoes and their liquid

1 quart low-sodium chicken broth

½ pound boneless, skinless chicken breasts, diced

1 cup canned black-eyed peas, drained and rinsed

1 cup chopped greens, such as collards, mustards, or spinach, rinsed well and drained

1 pound large shrimp, peeled and deveined

¼ cup minced green onions, green tops only, for garnish

Daube Glacé with Horseradish Sauce

1. Lightly spray a 9 x 5 × 3-inch loaf pan with vegetable oil spray. Preheat the oven to 375°F.

2. Heat a cast-iron skillet over medium heat. Season the beef on both sides with the salt and garlic powder. Heat the olive oil. Add the beef and cook, turning, until evenly browned on all sides. Place the skillet in the oven and cook the beef 20 minutes. Transfer the beef to a cutting board and let rest for 20 minutes. Cut the beef into ¼-inch-thick slices, then into ¼-inch strips, and then into ¼-inch dice.

3. Combine the carrots, green onions, and beef broth in a saucepan and bring to a boil. Remove from the heat.

4. Pour the gelatin over 1 tablespoon water in a small bowl and stir to blend. Let stand until the gelatin softens, about 5 minutes. Add the gelatin and 2 teaspoons of the horseradish to the broth mixture and stir to dissolve the gelatin. Add the chopped beef to the pan and stir to combine. Transfer to the prepared loaf pan and cover with plastic wrap. Refrigerate for at least 6 hours and up to 24 hours.

5. To serve, run a thin-bladed knife under warm water and run the knife around the inside of the pan to loosen the daube. Place the top of a serving platter over the daube, invert, and turn out onto the platter.

6. To make the horseradish sauce, whisk together the remaining 1 tablespoon horseradish, the sour cream, and mayonnaise in a small decorative bowl. Slice the daube and serve with crusty French bread and the sauce on the side.

Vegetable oil spray

1½ pounds beef filet mignon

2 teaspoons kosher salt

1 teaspoon garlic powder

1 tablespoon extra virgin olive oil

1 carrot, peeled and minced

¼ cup minced green onions, green tops only

2 cups low-sodium beef broth

1 (¼-ounce) envelope (1 tablespoon) powdered gelatin

2 teaspoons plus 1 tablespoon prepared horseradish

¼ cup sour cream

2 tablespoons mayonnaise

Daube glacé is usually made with a lesser cut of beef and the knuckles and gelatinous parts. By using filet of beef, the recipe is less work and has better flavor.

Almond Tart

Vegetable oil spray

5 large egg whites

½ cup plus ⅓ cup sugar

1 teaspoon pure almond extract

⅔ cup almond flour

½ cup cake flour

1 cup (2 sticks) salted butter, melted

1 cup sliced almonds

½ teaspoon ground cinnamon

Confectioners' sugar, for garnish

1. Preheat the oven to 350°F. Spray a 9-inch tart pan with a removable bottom with vegetable spray oil.

2. Place the egg whites, ½ cup of the sugar, and the almond extract in a large bowl. Whisk or beat with a handheld mixer until the mixture is thick and airy, about 2 minutes.

3. Using a rubber spatula, whisk, or mixer on low speed, beat the almond and cake flours into the egg white mixture until just combined. Add the melted butter and blend well. Pour the batter into the prepared tart pan.

4. Combine the almonds, remaining ⅓ cup sugar, and cinnamon in a bowl. Sprinkle the almonds evenly over the top of the batter.

5. Bake until the tart is golden brown and a toothpick inserted into the center comes out clean, about 30 minutes. Let cool for ½ hour on a wire rack before removing outer ring, then continue to cool for another ½ hour before slicing. Dust the top with confectioners' sugar before serving.

This tart is easily mixed together by hand.

ST. JOSEPH'S DAY CELEBRATION (FOR 8)

Satsuma-cello

Muffaletto Salad

Red Bean and Artichoke Salad

Eggplant with Wild Rice and Sausage

Miss Angie's Italian Cream Cake

Every March nineteenth, those New Orleans residents whose families emigrated from Sicily celebrate St. Joseph, the patron saint of workers and of the Italian island. In addition to parades and plenty of food, the feast day is also known for the elaborate altars created by businesses and families. The owners of Montalbano's Muffaletto shop in the French Quarter set the standard with an extravagant altar that brought visitors in. It was displayed every year until the store closed in the 1960s. Today altars with flowers, foods, wine, candles, and figurines are still set up in people's homes to give thanks, pray for someone who is ill or has recovered, and offer gratitude.

An aperitif of the Italian liqueur limoncello and local satsuma oranges is a festive start to the celebration. The Italian bean salad in this menu has marinated artichokes and New Orleans's cherished red beans and crisp red onions. Instead of the traditional muffaletto sandwich, offer up a salad that consists of the traditional meats and cheeses with the marinated olive salad as a topping on crisp lettuce. Baked stuffed eggplant with fennel sausage can be made ahead and even frozen in advance. Some classics should not be altered, however. A family friend, Miss Angie, made the first and best Italian cream cake I have ever had; here is the recipe.

Satsuma-cello

1 cup fresh satsuma or navel
  orange juice

¼ cup sugar

8 ounces vodka

1. Combine the orange juice and sugar in a saucepan over medium heat. Simmer until thick and syrupy, about 5 to 6 minutes. Remove from the heat and let cool to room temperature.

2. Once the syrup is cool, stir in the vodka. Pour into a glass jar and refrigerate until well chilled, at least 2 hours and up to 24 hours. Serve chilled in sherry glasses.

Muffaletto Salad

½ cup pitted green olives with
  pimentos

½ cup pitted canned black olives

½ cup extra virgin olive oil

¼ cup red wine vinegar

2 tablespoons capers, drained

1 teaspoon minced garlic

1 teaspoon paprika

2 romaine hearts, cut into 1-inch
  pieces

4 ounces ham, thinly sliced and cut
  into ½-inch strips

4 ounces hard salami, thinly sliced
  and cut into ½-inch strips

4 ounces Swiss cheese, thinly sliced
  and cut into ½-inch strips

4 ounces Provolone, thinly sliced
  and cut into ½-inch strips

1. Place the green and black olives, olive oil, vinegar, capers, garlic, and paprika in a food processor. Pulse to chop the olives coarsely and blend the other ingredients, about 1 minute.

2. Arrange the lettuce on a serving platter and top with the meats and cheeses. Pour the olive mixture over the salad and serve.

1. Whisk together the olive oil, vinegar, shallots, sugar, and salt in a bowl.

2. Combine the red beans, artichoke hearts, and onions in a serving bowl. Add the dressing and toss to coat. Cover and refrigerate for at least 3 hours before serving.

½ cup extra virgin olive oil

¼ cup red wine vinegar

1 shallot, minced

1 teaspoon sugar

½ teaspoon kosher salt

2 (15.5-ounce) cans red kidney beans, rinsed and drained

2 cups quartered artichoke hearts, rinsed and drained

2 cups thinly sliced red onions

The salad can be made 1 day ahead.

Eggplant with Wild Rice and Sausage

1. Combine 1 cup water, the rice, and salt in a saucepan. Bring to a boil, lower the heat to a simmer, and cook, uncovered, until the rice is tender, 45 to 60 minutes. Drain the rice in a colander and then return it to the saucepan. Cover and let steam, off the heat, for 10 minutes.

2. Preheat the oven to 350°F. Lightly oil a baking sheet.

3. Place the eggplants, cut side down, on the baking sheet. Roast until tender, about 30 minutes. Remove the eggplants from the oven, but leave the oven on.

4. Let the eggplants cool on the baking sheet. When cool enough to handle, using a tablespoon, scoop the inside flesh from the eggplants, leaving the skin and ¼ inch of the flesh intact to hold the filling. Reserve the eggplant flesh.

5. Melt the butter in a large saucepan over medium heat. Add the onion, celery, green onions, bell peppers, basil, garlic, and oregano and cook, stirring, until the vegetables are soft, 5 to 6 minutes. Add the reserved eggplant flesh and wild rice, mix well, and cook for 1 minute more. Transfer the mixture to a large bowl.

6. Place the sausage in the same saucepan and return to medium heat. Cook, stirring, until the sausage is cooked through and the fat is rendered, 5 to 7 minutes. Remove the sausage with a slotted spoon to the bowl with the eggplant mixture. Discard the fat remaining in the pan.

7. Divide the eggplant-sausage mixture among the 8 eggplant shells. Place the stuffed eggplants, stuffing mixture up, on a baking sheet. Bake until heated through and browned on top, 15 to 18 minutes.

¼ cup wild rice

½ teaspoon kosher salt

4 medium eggplants, cut in half lengthwise

½ cup (1 stick) salted butter

1 cup diced white onions

1 cup diced celery

1 cup diced green onions, white bottoms and green tops

½ cup diced green bell peppers

2 teaspoons minced fresh basil leaves

2 teaspoons minced garlic

1 teaspoon minced fresh oregano leaves

1½ pounds Italian pork sausage, removed from casings

I prefer Italian pork sausage with fennel. Sausage has enough salt and pepper, so there's usually no need to add more to this dish.

MAKES 1 (9-INCH) CAKE

Vegetable oil spray

2 tablespoons plus 3 cups sifted cake flour

2 teaspoons baking soda

¼ teaspoon ground cinnamon

¾ cup (1½ sticks) salted butter

3 cups sugar

5 large eggs, separated

1½ teaspoons pure vanilla extract

1 cup extra virgin olive oil

1 cup buttermilk

¾ cup sweetened coconut flakes

¾ cup finely chopped pecans, toasted (page 311)

1. Preheat the oven to 350°F. Spray three 9-inch round cake pans with the vegetable oil spray. Lightly flour the insides of the pans with 2 tablespoons of the flour and shake out the excess.

2. Whisk together the remaining 3 cups flour, baking soda, and cinnamon in a bowl.

3. In the bowl of a stand mixer fitted with a paddle attachment, cream together the butter and sugar on medium speed until light and fluffy, 3 to 4 minutes. Add the egg yolks one at a time, beating until each is incorporated and scraping down the sides of the bowl as needed. Add the vanilla and beat until combined, 30 seconds. Add the olive oil and beat until combined, 30 seconds.

4. Add the dry ingredients to the wet ingredients one-third at a time, alternating with the buttermilk, to make a smooth batter. Fold in the coconut and pecans by hand.

5. In a clean bowl with clean beaters, beat the egg whites to stiff peaks. Using a rubber spatula, gently fold the egg whites into the batter, being careful not to deflate the egg whites. Evenly divide the batter among the three prepared pans.

6. Bake the cakes on the middle rack of the oven until a tester inserted into the center of each cake comes out clean, about 35 minutes. Cool the cakes on a wire rack in their pans for 10 minutes. Turn out the cakes onto the wire rack to cool completely before icing. (The cake layers can be cooked one day in advance before assembling the cake. Wrap the individual layers tightly in plastic wrap and refrigerate until ready to use.)

7. To make the icing, in a clean bowl with clean beaters, beat the butter on high speed until light yellow and fluffy, 2 minutes. Add the cream cheese and buttermilk and beat until smooth, about 4 minutes. Add the rum and beat on medium speed until well incorporated, 1 minute. Slowly add the confectioners' sugar with the machine on low, and beat until well blended, 1 to 2 minutes.

8. To assemble the cake, place one layer upside down in the center of a cake plate or large circular platter. Spread icing over the top of the first layer, repeating with each layer. Frost the sides and smooth the top with the remaining icing. Use the coconut and chopped pecans to decorate the top and sides. Serve immediately, or refrigerate until ready to serve.

The assembled cake can be refrigerated, uncovered, for 1 day.

Frosting

1 cup (2 sticks) salted butter, at room temperature

12 ounces cream cheese, at room temperature

1 teaspoon buttermilk

1 tablespoon dark rum

4 cups confectioners' sugar

¼ cup sweetened coconut flakes

¼ cup finely chopped pecans, toasted (page 311)

BEAUVOIR

In 1877 Jefferson Davis, former US senator and president of the Confederate States of America, was looking for a quiet retreat to work on his books and papers. While he was visiting Biloxi on the Mississippi Gulf Coast, a Mrs. Dorsey, a family friend, encouraged Davis to stay at her home, Beauvoir, in one of the two pavilions in front of the main house. After two years he fell in love with the property, and Mrs. Dorsey agreed to sell it to him. Six months after Davis made the first of six payments, she died, leaving him the house and the rest of her wealth. Davis lived at Beauvoir until he died in 1889. In August 2005, Hurricane Katrina devastated most of the house and all of the surrounding buildings. After years of hard work and philanthropic gifts, the main house and library have been restored. www.beauvoir.org

GULF SEAFOOD DINNER (FOR 4)

Citrus Daiquiris

Mirliton-Orange Salad

Fried Soft-Shell Crabs with Lump Crabmeat

Spicy Vegetable Boil

Frozen Lime Soufflés

Venice is the southernmost community on the Mississippi River that is accessible by car. As it marks the end of the Great River Road, Venice is often referred to as "the end of the world." But for me, it's the beginning of all the things I love about this area. Louisiana's Plaquemines Parish, where the Mississippi River meets the Gulf of Mexico, is a region of natural wonders, with its many tributaries and other waterways, as well as bountiful fishing and hunting. Many people believe that the best citrus fruit in the country comes from here. Testament to that is the yearly Orange Festival held in the town of Buras every December. While local oranges are celebrated, the festival offers contests: seafood eating, shrimp peeling and de-heading, oyster shucking, catfish skinning, and duck calling.

This is also where I had my first glimmer of what I wanted to do in life and where I learned the importance of using fresh, local, quality ingredients. I can thank my father, J. P. Trosclair, for that lesson. We once took a road trip to pick up some oysters and satsuma oranges in Plaquemines Parish. My father, whose cooking was legendary in Natchez, had a culinary road map to the best bakers, butchers, farmers, and fishermen in South Louisiana. We brought back sacks of slightly dented, locally grown oranges. When I asked him why they weren't perfectly round and bright grocery-store orange in color, he answered, "This is what real food looks like, Regina. Food is not grown with letters stamped on it."

To honor my father and his impeccable taste, we start with satsuma daiquiris, followed by a light salad of mirlitons (chayote) and fresh oranges with lime vinaigrette. Pear-shaped mirlitons grow on vines and are less watery and firmer than cucumbers. They are popular throughout the South and the Caribbean. (My father cooked them with a crab stuffing.) I deep-fry soft-shell crabs and top them with softened onions and lump crabmeat and some lemon and fresh basil. Spicy shrimp boil mix adds flavor to a platter of colorful artichokes, potatoes, and carrots. Refreshing lime soufflés can be made in advance and frozen to enjoy at the end of this meal.

Citrus Daiquiris

¼ cup fresh lemon juice

¼ cup fresh lime juice (or Satsuma
 juice)

¼ cup Simple Syrup (page 314)

1 cup white rum

4 lime twists, for garnish

1. Pour the lemon and lime juices and the simple syrup into a pitcher. Add the rum and stir well.

2. Fill a cocktail shaker with ice and add the rum mixture. Shake well and pour into four martini glasses. Garnish the rim of each glass with a lime twist and serve.

 ## Mirliton-Orange Salad

2 mirlitons (chayotes)

1 cup fresh navel orange segments

½ red onion, thinly sliced

2 tablespoons extra virgin olive oil

1 teaspoon fresh lime juice

1 teaspoon fresh lemon juice

1 teaspoon sugar

¼ teaspoon kosher salt

1. Bring 1 quart of salted water to a boil. Add the mirlitons and cook until they are tender and can easily be pierced with a fork, 25 to 30 minutes. Drain in a colander. When cool enough to handle, peel the mirlitons and slice in half lengthwise. Using a spoon, remove the seeds and tough inner hull and discard. Slice the mirlitons ¼ inch thick.

2. Combine the sliced mirlitons, orange segments, and onions in a bowl.

3. To make the dressing, combine the olive oil, lime and lemon juices, sugar, and salt in a bowl and whisk to combine. Pour the dressing over the mirliton mixture and toss to coat evenly. Cover and chill before serving, at least 2 hours and up to 24 hours.

1. Clip a candy or deep-frying thermometer to the side of a dutch oven. Add oil to a depth of 3 inches and heat to 350°F over medium heat. Preheat the oven to 175°F. Line a baking sheet with paper towels.

2. Whisk together the flour and 2 teaspoons Cajun Seasoning in a shallow baking dish. To make an egg wash, whisk together the egg and buttermilk in a separate baking dish.

3. Season the crabs lightly on all sides using ½ teaspoon of the Cajun Seasoning for each crab. One at a time, lightly dredge the crabs first in the seasoned flour and then in the egg wash. Dredge again in the flour to coat evenly on all sides, shaking to remove any excess coating. Lower the crabs slowly, one at a time, into the hot oil and fry until golden brown, turning once, about 2 minutes per side. Drain on the paper towels and place in the oven to stay warm while frying the remaining crabs.

4. Melt the butter in a skillet over low heat. Add the onions and cook, stirring, until soft but not colored, 6 minutes. Add the lemon juice and basil, and cook, stirring, until fragrant, 40 seconds to 1 minute. Add the crabmeat, gently stir to incorporate, and cook until just warmed through, being careful not to break up the lumps, 1 to 2 minutes. Remove from the heat. Remove the crabs from the oven and place one on each of four plates. Spoon the crabmeat sauce over the crabs and serve immediately.

Vegetable oil, for frying

1 cup all-purpose flour

4 teaspoons Cajun Seasoning (page 311), divided

1 large egg

½ cup buttermilk

4 large soft-shell crabs (see Source Guide, page 316), cleaned

3 tablespoons salted butter

1 small white onion, halved and thinly sliced

2 tablespoons fresh lemon juice

1 tablespoon thinly sliced fresh basil leaves

1 pound lump crabmeat (see Source Guide, page 316), picked over for shells and cartilage

2 lemons, cut in half

2 tablespoons Zatarain's Crawfish, Shrimp & Crab Boil in a bag (see Source Guide, page 316)

2 artichokes, stems trimmed

8 small red potatoes

4 whole carrots

4 ears of corn

Don't remove any of the vegetables from the pot while the others are cooking, and they all come out perfectly at the same time.

1. Fill a stockpot with 3 quarts water, the lemons, and crab boil. Add the artichokes and bring to a boil. Boil the artichokes for 10 minutes. Add the potatoes and boil for 5 minutes. Add the carrots and corn and boil for 5 minutes.

2. Remove the pot from the heat and let the vegetables sit for 5 minutes to absorb more flavor. Drain in a colander. When the artichokes are cool enough to handle, press the leaves gently back so the inner choke and prickly leaves are revealed. Pull out the cone of undeveloped white leaves and gently scrape out the fuzzy choke with a teaspoon so as not to damage the heart. Discard the fuzzy choke and prickly leaves. Cut each artichoke in half and arrange on a platter with the other vegetables. Serve warm.

1. Lightly spray four 6-ounce ramekins or molds with vegetable oil spray.

2. Clip a candy thermometer to the side of a heavy-bottomed saucepan over medium heat. Add 1 cup of the sugar and ¼ cup water and cook over medium heat until the syrup reaches the soft ball stage and the thermometer registers 235°F, about 12 minutes. Remove the saucepan from the heat, stir, and let cool for 15 minutes.

3. In the bowl of a stand mixer fitted with the whisk attachment, beat the egg whites to soft peaks. With the machine running on medium speed, slowly add the sugar syrup a tablespoon at a time and beat to stiff and glossy peaks, 5 to 6 minutes, being careful not to overbeat.

4. In a clean bowl, beat the egg yolks and the remaining 1 tablespoon sugar with a handheld or stand mixer until pale yellow, about 3 minutes. Add the lime juice, heavy cream, and lime zest and beat until smooth, 1 minute. Using a rubber spatula, fold the egg whites into the egg yolk mixture until no streaks remain. Pour the mixture into the ramekins, cover, and freeze at least 12 hours and up to 2 weeks.

5. To serve, let the soufflés sit at room temperature for 5 to 10 minutes so that they are still frozen but not too hard.

Vegetable oil spray

1 cup plus 1 tablespoon sugar

3 large eggs, separated

¼ cup fresh lime juice

¼ cup heavy cream

1 tablespoon finely grated lime zest

BLESSING OF THE FLEET LUNCH (FOR 4)

Blackberry-Rum Fizzes

Shrimp-Stuffed Sesame Rice Balls

Trout Tacos with Salsa Verde

Spicy Basil Chicken Wings

Mango-Kiwi Rice Puddings

The Blessing of the Fleet marks the beginning of the shrimping season in the Gulf. Each May, Catholic priests bless a procession of thousands of boats in Gulf towns to ensure a safe and prosperous fishing season. As with other traditions on the River, it wouldn't be an event unless there was food—and plenty of it. This menu starts with a blender of rum fizzes with blackberry syrup. The influences of the Vietnamese of the Gulf region add a welcomed freshness to Mississippi River cuisine. Spicy marinated shrimp stuffed in rice balls with toasted sesame seeds are a favorite, whether you serve them warm or chilled. Chicken wings with a sticky, spicy basil sauce are a fresh take on the traditional wings with a vinegar-based hot sauce. A departure from the Asian influences, the soft tacos are an easy-to-prepare complement to this meal. I prefer spotted sea trout, which is well managed and abundant in Louisiana and Florida waters, making it a Best Choice from Seafood Watch, the Monterey Bay Aquarium's sustainable seafood program. For a celebratory finish, rice pudding sweetened with coconut milk or an almond-flavored cream is delicious by itself and even better topped with rum-soaked diced mango and kiwi.

Blackberry-Rum Fizzes

1 cup frozen blackberries

¼ cup Simple Syrup (page 314)

2 tablespoon fresh lemon juice

1 cup white rum

4 liquid (pasteurized) egg whites (about ½ cup), or 4 large egg whites

1. Combine the blackberries and simple syrup in a blender and puree on high speed. Pour the blackberry puree through a fine mesh strainer into a clean container, pressing with the back of a spoon to extract as much juice as possible. Discard the sediment.

2. Rinse the blender to remove any seeds. Return the blackberry syrup to the blender, add the lemon juice, rum, and egg whites and mix on high speed until frothy, 1 to 2 minutes. Add 2 cups of ice and pulse to break up ice. Pour into martini glasses and serve as preferred, on ice, or strained and straight up.

 ## Shrimp-Stuffed Sesame Rice Balls

¾ cup diced green onions, white bottoms and green tops

2 tablespoons sesame oil

1 teaspoon Sriracha

1 dozen large shrimp (about ½ pound), peeled and deveined

1 tablespoon chopped fresh cilantro leaves

1 teaspoon chopped fresh basil leaves

1 teaspoon chopped fresh mint leaves

1½ cups cooked Sticky Rice (page 315), at room temperature

2 tablespoons toasted sesame seeds (page 311)

1. Combine the green onions, sesame oil, and Sriracha in a large skillet and cook over medium heat for 30 seconds. Add the shrimp and cook for 1 minute, turning once. Stir in the cilantro, basil, and mint and cook, stirring occasionally, until the shrimp are pink and firm, 2 to 3 minutes.

2. Remove the pan from the heat and let the shrimp sit until cool enough to handle. Discard any sauce remaining in the pan.

3. Place a piece of waxed or parchment paper on a work surface. Divide the cooled sticky rice into twelve equal portions of 2 tablespoons each. Place one cooled shrimp in the center of each rice portion and gently press the rice around the shrimp to completely enclose and form a ball.

4. Roll the shrimp in toasted sesame seeds. Serve at room temperature or chilled.

1. Preheat the oven to 175°F. Wrap the tortillas in aluminum foil and place in the oven to warm while preparing the fish. Line a baking sheet with paper towels.

2. Pour the milk into a shallow baking dish. Cut the fish into eight strips, place them in the milk, and let them soak, turning once, for 15 minutes. In a separate shallow baking dish, whisk together the corn flour and Cajun seasoning. Dredge the fish strips on both sides in the seasoned masa, shaking to remove any excess.

3. Meanwhile, heat the vegetable oil in a skillet over medium-high heat.

4. Add the fish strips to the skillet in batches and cook, turning once, until golden brown, about 2 minutes on each side. Place the cooked fish on the paper towels to drain. Remove the tortillas from the oven.

5. Fill each tortilla with two pieces of the cooked fish, 2 tablespoons cabbage, the cilantro, and salsa to taste. Serve additional salsa on the side.

4 (6-inch) corn tortillas

½ cup milk

12 ounces trout fillets, or other firm white fish such catfish, flounder, or walleye

½ cup corn flour or masa harina

1 teaspoon Cajun Seasoning (page 311)

3 tablespoons vegetable oil

½ cup shredded cabbage

1 tablespoon chopped fresh cilantro leaves

½ cup Mrs. Renfro's Jalapeño Green Salsa (see Source Guide, page 316)

¼ cup packed dark brown sugar

2 tablespoons minced fresh basil, divided

1 tablespoon fresh lime juice

1 tablespoon sesame oil

1 tablespoon soy sauce

¼ teaspoon Vietnamese fish sauce

¼ teaspoon crushed red pepper

8 chicken drumettes (or 4 whole wings split into 4 drumettes and 4 wing portions)

1. Combine the brown sugar, 1 tablespoon of the basil, the lime juice, sesame oil, soy sauce, fish sauce, and red pepper in a shallow baking dish and whisk to combine. Add the wings to the sauce, turning to coat on all sides. Cover with aluminum foil and let marinate in the refrigerator for at least 2 hours but not longer than 8 hours.

2. Preheat the oven to 400°F.

3. Place the baking dish in the oven and roast the wings, covered with the aluminum foil, for 15 minutes. Remove the foil, stir the wings with a long-handled spoon, and roast for 15 minutes, turning after 8 minutes. Transfer the hot wings to a serving platter. Pour the remaining pan juices over the wings and garnish with the remaining 1 tablespoon basil. Serve hot or at room temperature.

1. Position the rack in the center of the oven and preheat the oven to 325°F. Lightly spray four 6-ounce ramekins or molds with vegetable oil spray and place in a medium roasting pan.

2. Combine the cooked rice, coconut milk, and eggs in a bowl. Stir in the brown sugar, vanilla, and salt. Divide the mixture among the four ramekins, filling each about three-quarters full.

3. Add enough hot water to the roasting pan to come halfway up the sides of the ramekins. Bake until the puddings are set and lightly browned on top, yet still jiggle slightly when shaken, about 35 minutes. Remove the ramekins from the water bath and cool on a wire rack. Refrigerate until well chilled, at least 4 hours or overnight.

4. Combine the mangos and kiwis in a bowl. Add the rum and stir to coat the fruit evenly. Cover and refrigerate until ready to serve. Spoon the fruit over the custards and serve.

Vegetable oil spray

1 cup cooked Sticky Rice (page 315)

1 (12-ounce) can sweetened coconut milk, or 1½ cups heavy cream mixed with 2 teaspoons pure almond extract

2 large eggs, lightly beaten

¾ cup packed light brown sugar

1 teaspoon pure vanilla extract

¼ teaspoon kosher salt

1 mango, peeled, seeded, and diced

2 kiwis, peeled and diced

2 tablespoons Myers's or other dark rum

Techniques

Bacon, Diced and Pan-Fried

Cook the bacon over medium-high heat, stirring frequently, until browned and crisp, about 5 minutes. Using a slotted spoon, transfer to paper towels to drain, reserving the bacon grease for use in the recipe or another purpose.

Place the bacon in a cold skillet; it will cook more evenly.

Bacon, Oven-Cooked

Line a baking sheet with aluminum foil. Arrange the bacon on the foil in a single layer. Put the baking sheet in the oven and turn on the oven to 400°F. Bake until the bacon is browned and crisp and the fat is rendered, 10 to 15 minutes. Remove from the oven and drain on paper towels.

This method is best when a recipe calls for a large amount of bacon.

Deep-Frying

Follow these tips to guarantee that your deep-fried foods will be crisp every time:

- Fish, shellfish, or chicken should be marinated in seasoned liquid for at least 1 and up to 24 hours for better flavor.

- Chicken is best marinated in seasoned water, whereas fish and shellfish do well with milk or buttermilk.

- Canola and other vegetables oils are my preferred frying oils, because they have a high smoking point.

I avoid peanut oil because so many people have nut allergies.

- If possible, use an electric deep fryer with a built-in thermometer and keep the oil's temperature at a constant 350°F. Keep an eye on your thermometer as you add food to the fryer.

- Adding too many pieces of food at once will cause the oil temperature to drop and the food to become oily rather than crisp.

- If you don't have a deep fryer, clip a deep-frying thermometer to the side of a heavy, deep pot. Add oil to the pot (enough oil to "deep fry" or submerge what you are frying under oil). Slowly heat the oil to 350°F.

- Drain fried food on paper towels or brown paper bags.

- Place fried food on a foil-lined sheet pan and keep warm, uncovered, in a 175°F oven while frying the remaining pieces.

Hard-Boiled Eggs

1. For best results, remove eggs from refrigerator and let sit out for 2 hours.

2. Place in pan of cool water, leaving space so that they do not knock against each other and crack when the water boils.

3. Place pan over medium heat and bring to a boil. Once water is boiling, turn heat down to a simmer and cook for 6 minutes.

4. Remove pan from heat and run cool water over eggs until they are cool to the touch. Add a few ice cubes and let stand for 10 minutes.

5. To peel, gently crack the egg and, under running water, begin at the rounded end. The water will help with the removal of the shell.

Toasting Nuts or Seeds

Heat a skillet over medium heat. Once the pan is hot, add the nuts in a single layer. Stir frequently with a wooden spoon or spatula, until the nuts release their aromas. Watch them carefully, as nuts can go from toasted to burnt in seconds. As soon as the nuts are toasted, transfer them to a bowl or plate; the hot pan would continue to cook them. Once toasted, use as directed within two days.

Basics

Cajun Seasoning
MAKES ABOUT 1¾ CUPS

1 cup fine sea salt

¼ cup ground cayenne pepper

2 tablespoons ground white pepper

2 tablespoons ground black pepper

2 tablespoons sweet paprika

2 tablespoons onion powder

2 tablespoons garlic powder

Place all the ingredients in a food processor and blend for 1 minute. Transfer to a container with a tight fitting lid. Store at room temperature for up to 6 months.

Dark Roux
MAKES 1½ CUPS

½ cup vegetable oil

1 cup all-purpose flour

1. Heat the oil in a cast-iron skillet over medium heat until just smoking. Whisk in the flour, 1 tablespoon at a time, and cook, whisking constantly, until the mixture becomes smooth and thick.

2. Continue to cook, constantly stirring with a heavy wooden spoon and reaching all over the bottom of the pan, until the roux smells nutty and darkens to a rich, brown color, 18 to 25 minutes.

3. Transfer the roux to a metal bowl, where it will continue to cook but not burn. It will become a chocolate brown color, which I find to be the perfect roux.

Roux will keep refrigerated in a plastic container or glass jar with a tight fitting lid for up to 2 months.

Hollandaise (*Herbsaint or Absinthe*)

Using the blender method to make a hollandaise is much easier and quicker than making it over a double boiler and whisking by hand. If you cannot find Herbsaint, Pernod is an acceptable substitute.

MAKES 1 CUP

½ cup (1 stick) unsalted butter

4 large egg yolks

1 tablespoon fresh lemon juice

¼ teaspoon kosher salt

¼ teaspoon ground white pepper

2 tablespoons Herbsaint or Absinthe (Pernod is a good substitute)

1. Melt the butter in a saucepan and cook over low heat until foamy. Remove from the heat and let stand for 5 minutes. Clarify the butter by skimming the foam from the top and discarding the milk solids on the bottom of the pan. Heat clarified butter on low in microwave to register 120°F on instant read thermometer.

2. Place the egg yolks, lemon juice, salt, and white pepper in a blender and process until smooth, 30 seconds. With the motor on low, very slowly add about 1 tablespoon of the clarified butter and process until well blended, about 15 seconds. With the machine running, slowly add the remaining butter in a thin stream.

3. Once all butter has been added, blend until thickened, 45 seconds to 1 minute. Add the Herbsaint in a thin stream and process until incorporated. Adjust the seasoning to taste and serve immediately.

Homemade Bread Crumbs

MAKES ABOUT 1 CUP

2 slices sourdough or white bread

1. Preheat the oven to 200°F.

2. Place the bread directly on an oven rack and toast until hard and golden brown, about 30 minutes. Remove the toast and cool on a wire rack.

3. Over a bowl, crumble the toast with your hands into fine crumbs. Store in an airtight container until ready to use.

The bread crumbs will keep in an airtight container at room temperature for 1 month.

Mustard-Lemon Vinaigrette

This is my go-to vinaigrette, and I always keep a jar of it in my refrigerator. I suggest you double the amount, as you'll find it goes on a variety of salads.

MAKES ½ CUP

Finely grated zest and juice of 2 lemons

1 teaspoon minced fresh tarragon leaves, optional

1 medium shallot, roughly chopped

1 tablespoon apple cider vinegar

3 tablespoons Dijon mustard

1 tablespoon sugar

1 cup vegetable oil

1. Combine the lemon zest, tarragon, and juice, shallot, and vinegar in a blender. Blend until the shallot is pureed. Add the Dijon mustard and sugar and blend to combine.

2. With the motor running, slowly add the oil in a thin stream, processing until the oil is incorporated and the mixture is the consistency of mayonnaise.

3. Pour the dressing into a covered container and refrigerate.

The dressing will keep refrigerated in an airtight container for up to 2 weeks. Stir well before using.

Oven-Smoked Tomatoes

Smoked tomatoes are great in pasta sauces, winter salads, or soups. Make a big batch when tomatoes are in season and freeze them in plastic bags for future use.

MAKES 24 QUARTERS

6 plum tomatoes, quartered

¼ cup extra virgin olive oil

2 tablespoons liquid hickory smoke

1 teaspoon Tabasco

2 teaspoons freshly ground black pepper

1 teaspoon kosher salt

1. Preheat the oven to 250°F. Line a baking sheet with aluminum foil or parchment paper. Arrange the tomato quarters on the baking sheet in a single layer.

2. Whisk together the olive oil, liquid hickory smoke, and Tabasco in a bowl. Evenly drizzle the mixture over the tomatoes. Sprinkle with the pepper and salt. Bake until the tomatoes are shriveled but still moist, about 90 minutes.

3. Transfer the tomatoes to a bowl, reserving any juices on the baking sheet to flavor a recipe.

Preserved Lemon Vinaigrette

This salad dressing keeps for up to 2 weeks in the refrigerator. It is good on any green salad, such as the Lettuce Hearts with Shaved Pears, Roasted Pecans, and Preserved Lemon Vinaigrette (page 236), and I even have used it for chicken salad.

Preserved Lemons

6 medium lemons

¼ cup kosher salt

1. Using a small serrated knife, score the lemons lengthwise, ½ inch apart, from top to bottom, cutting into the peel but not into the flesh.

2. Place the lemons in a pot. Add the salt and enough water to cover by 3 inches. Bring the water to a boil, lower the heat, and simmer uncovered until the lemons are soft but not falling apart, about 45 minutes. Remove from the heat and allow to cool in the cooking liquid.

3. Transfer the lemons to a 1-quart Mason jar and add enough cooking water to cover by ½ inch. Let cool completely to room temperature. When cool, close tightly and refrigerate.

These preserved lemons will keep for 2 months in the refrigerator.

Vinaigrette
MAKES 1 CUP

¼ preserved lemon

½ small shallot, peeled and halved

1 teaspoon apple cider vinegar

1 tablespoon Dijon mustard

1 teaspoon sugar

1 cup vegetable oil

1. Place the preserved lemon quarter, shallot, and vinegar in a blender. Blend on medium speed until completely pureed. Add the Dijon mustard and sugar. Blend until well combined.

2. Slowly add the oil in a thin stream with the motor running and blend until the dressing is smooth and emulsified.

3. Store in glass dressing bottle or an airtight container.

The dressing will keep refrigerated for 2 weeks.

Roasted Garlic

MAKES 2 TABLESPOONS

1 head garlic, top third cut off
1 teaspoon extra virgin olive oil
Pinch of kosher salt
Pinch of ground white pepper

1. Preheat the oven to 325°F.

2. Place the garlic in a small baking dish, drizzle the top with the oil, and season with salt and pepper. Turn cut side down and roast until the cloves are soft and golden brown, about 1 hour.

3. Remove from the oven and let sit until cool enough to handle. Squeeze the garlic head gently to release the flesh.

4. Store in airtight container or ziplock bag.

The garlic will keep refrigerated for up to 3 days.

Shellfish Stock

Gumbo crabs are found in the frozen food sections of many groceries in the South. If you can't find gumbo crabs, use shrimp shells instead.

MAKES 1 QUART

1 medium white onion, diced
2 teaspoons vegetable oil
1 quart water
12 ounces cleaned gumbo crabs, or 12 ounces shrimp shells (from 3 pounds shrimp)
1 teaspoon pickling spice
¼ teaspoon red pepper flakes
2 teaspoons kosher salt

Put the onions and oil in a saucepan over medium heat. Cook until the onion is soft but not brown. Add 1 quart water, the gumbo crabs or shrimp shells, pickling spice, red pepper, and salt. Simmer for 30 minutes. Strain the stock through a fine mesh strainer. Use immediately or cool completely before refrigerating.

Simple Syrup

Simple syrup is used as a sweetener for cocktails and nonalcoholic drinks such as sweet tea and lemonade. You can make any amount of syrup using the basic ratio here.

Many variations on simple syrup are found throughout this book for use in cocktails and desserts. Among these are the syrup infused with satsuma (or orange) juice on page 292 and the slightly sweeter one used to make the Blackberry-Orange Sorbet on page 168. I encourage you to experiment with different flavors and adapt your simple syrup to suit your tastes.

MAKES ABOUT 1 CUP

1 cup granuated sugar

1 cup water

Combine the sugar and water in a small saucepan. Bring to a boil, lower the heat, stir, and simmer until the sugar is dissolved, about 5 minutes. Remove from the heat and let cool to room temperature.

The syrup will keep in an airtight container for up to 2 weeks.

Sticky Rice

The ratio I use for sticky rice is 1 part rice to 1½ parts water—for example, for 4 servings, 1 cup rice to 1½ cups water; for 8 servings, 2 cups rice to 3 cups water.

1. Bring water and rice to a boil and cook for 2 minutes. Lower the heat, cover, and simmer undisturbed until all of the liquid has been absorbed, about 20 minutes.

2. Remove the pan from the heat. Fluff the rice with a fork, cover, and let sit for 10 minutes before serving.

Sweet Pie Dough

This is a failsafe recipe for sweet pie dough. It is used in the Blueberry Pie with Lemon Drop Candy Dust (page 71) and the Cinnamon Crisps for the Deconstructed Apple Strudel (page 79).

MAKES 2 PIECRUSTS, ROLLED TO 11 INCHES

2½ cups all-purpose flour

¾ cup cold butter-flavored shortening, cut into ½-inch pieces

2 tablespoons cold salted butter, cut into ½-inch pieces

1 tablespoon sugar

1. Place all the ingredients in a food processor and pulse until the shortening and butter pieces are the size of nickels, about 6 or 7 times. With the machine running, add ¼ cup ice water and pulse to form a smooth ball, adding up to 3 tablespoons additional water as needed, and being careful not to overmix.

2. Divide the dough into two balls. Wrap each piece in plastic wrap and let rest, refrigerated, for at least 30 minutes and up to 24 hours before using.

Sweetened Whipped Cream

Whipped cream should be soft, light, and billowy. I also believe it should not be too sweet. You will get the best results if you make this in a chilled stainless steel bowl with chilled beaters.

MAKES 2 CUPS

1 cup heavy whipping cream

1 tablespoon sugar

Put the heavy cream and sugar into a chilled bowl. Let sit for 3 minutes to let the sugar begin to dissolve. Using a hand mixer on medium speed, whip until soft peaks form, 1½ to 2 minutes.

Source Guide

Andouille sausage and other Louisiana sausages
www.cajunsausage.com

Smoked country bacon
Benton's Smoky Mountain Country Hams & Bacon
(423) 442-5003
bentonscountryham.com

Coffee concentrate
Cool Brew® Fresh Coffee Concentrate—
Original, 1 Liter
www.amazon.com

Corn flour
Bob's Red Mill
www.bobsredmill.com

Creole cream cheese
Mauthe's Progress Milk Barn
2033 Joe Tucker Road
McComb, MS 39648
(601) 542-3471
mauthefarms@yahoo.com
mauthefarms.blogspot.com

Fresh Louisiana seafood (including live crawfish and crabs, fresh oysters, shrimp, and catfish, and Cajun sausage)
Kyle LeBlanc Crawfish Farms
(985) 226-6444
www.klcrawfishfarms.com

Louisiana pantry items and fresh seafood (including Steen's Pure Cane Syrup, pork cracklings, live and boiled crawfish, fresh oysters, fresh soft-shelled crabs, and Zatarain's Crawfish, Shrimp & Crab Boil Dry Seasoning)

(888) 272-9347
www.cajungrocer.com

Jalapeño Green Salsa
www.renfrofoods.com

Lychee juice
www.asianfoodgrocer.com

Pecans, walnuts, dried figs
www.nuts.com

Peppadew peppers
www.peppadew.com

Plantation quail (all natural)
www.plantationquail.net

Seafood watch
Monterey Bay Seafood Watch
A guide to sustainable seafood
www.seafoodwatch.org

Smoked catfish, smoked trout
Valley Fish & Cheese
(608) 326-4719
www.valleyfishmarketpdc.com

Stainless steel reusable oyster tins
sosoystershells.com

Stone-ground cornmeal and grits
(662) 202-6822
www.deltagrind.com

Upper Mississippi River Valley wines
Nine wineries located near the Mississippi River in Minnesota, Wisconsin, and Iowa
www.greatriverroadwinetrail.org

Index

About the Author

Regina Charboneau has launched numerous top restaurants, including Regina's at the Regis and Biscuits & Blues in San Francisco and the recently opened King's Tavern in Natchez. She is the culinary director of the *American Queen,* a luxury paddle-wheel boat that travels the Mississippi, and was a longtime culinary contributor to the *Atlantic.* Charboneau hosts visitors at Twin Oaks Bed and Breakfast, her antebellum home in Natchez, Mississippi, where she also owns the historic King's Tavern. She is the author of *Regina's Table at Twin Oaks.* Visit her at ReginasKitchen.com.

Acknowledgments

I live the belief that you are only as good as the people you surround yourself with. I so wisely (or luckily) chose my husband Doug. I lucked out on fabulous children Jean-Luc, Martin, and Catherine, who make it easy to love them above all else I do. The team behind this book was stellar, a true collaborative effort: shining star Harriet Bell, who helped make my writing readable and was like my personal coach along the way, and my agent, Jonah Straus, who introduced us long ago and guided me to and through this project. Forever thanks to my best friend and mentor P. Allen Smith; Ben Fink; the creative touches during the photo shoot of Joe Tully; the team of Stephen Flowers; and Kate Stanley, who helped in so many ways. Thanks to Mary Norris and her A-team at Lyons Press and to my right hand at Twin Oaks, Janet Tyler. Many thanks to Julia Reed for taking time from her schedule to read this book from cover to cover before it went to print. In addition, thanks always to my friends who come to my house for "Biscuit Love" and bring other good friends into our fabulous circle of friendship—you know who you are.